Jens Lehne

Crisis at the WTO: Is the Blocking of Appointments to the WTO Appellate Body by the United States Legally Justified?

Edited by Daniel Hürlimann and Marc Thommen

Volume 6

Jens Lehne

Crisis at the WTO: Is the Blocking of Appointments to the WTO Appellate Body by the United States Legally Justified?

Author:
Prof. Dr.oec. et lic.iur. Jens Lehne
Winterthur, Switzerland

This work has been published as a monograph in the book series *sui generis*, edited by Daniel Hürlimann and Marc Thommen (ISSN 2569-6629 Print, ISSN 2625-2910 Online).

The German National Library (*Deutsche Nationalbibliothek*) lists this work in the *Deutsche Nationalbibliografie*; detailed bibliographic data is available in the internet via http://dnb.d-nb.de.

DOI:10.24921/2019.94115941

Acknowledgements

I am very grateful to Peter Hettich, professor of public law at the University of St. Gallen, for his careful review of the text, many thoughtful suggestions and inspiring discussions. Furthermore, I want to thank Danielle Adams-Hausheer, translator and editor at the ZHAW School of Management and Law, for her meticulous proofreading of the manuscript. I am also indebted to the editors of the book series *sui generis*, Daniel Hürlimann, assistant professor of business law at the University of St. Gallen, and Marc Thommen, professor of criminal law and criminal procedure at the University of Zurich, for including this book in their series. Moreover, I with to thank the team at Carl Grossmann Verlag for their highly professional and efficient support during the publication process. Most of all, thank you to my family for their patience during the writing of this book.

Jens Lehne

Winterthur, September 2019

Contents

I. Introduction

The dispute settlement system of the World Trade Organization (WTO) has been described by the first Director-General of the WTO, Renato Ruggiero, as *„in many ways the central pillar of the multilateral trading system"*,[1] and it is one of the most active dispute settlement systems in international law. From its inauguration in 1995 until August 2019, WTO member states have filed altogether 586 complaints, which have resulted so far in more than 250 panel reports and about 140 Appellate Body reports.[2]

Compared to its predecessor, the GATT dispute settlement system (1948 – 1994),[3] the WTO dispute settlement system is more effective and more legalized. Under the old system, both the establishment of a dispute settlement panel and, following the panel proceedings, the adoption of the panel report required the consensus of all member states (positive consensus), which gave each member state, including the respondent in the case, the power to block the establishment of a panel or later the adoption of the panel report. This problem of blockage, and, more generally, insufficient enforcement mechanisms within the GATT system developed into a major issue for the United States in the 1980s and early 1990s. The US reacted with the threat of unilateral trade sanctions, which in turn seriously worried its trading partners.[4] The new WTO dispute settlement that emerged from the Uruguay Trade Round (1987 – 1994), embodied in the Understanding on Dispute Settlement (DSU), addressed these concerns. The Dispute Settlement Body (DSB), in which all member states are represented, now establishes panels and adopts their reports unless all members disagree (negative consensus),[5] meaning that the establishment of panels and the adoption of reports have become quasi-automatic. In addition, if a member state does not comply with the recommendations of a report, the complaining party can request the DSB to authorize

---

1 Ruggiero (1997).

2 See https://www.wto.org/english/tratop_e/dispu_e/dispu_e.htm for statistical data on WTO dispute settlement.

3 On GATT dispute settlement, see WTO (2018a) (overview and one-page summaries of all disputes), WTO (2018b) (dispute settlement rules), WTO (2007), pp. 261 – 266, and Hudec (1993) (most comprehensive and detailed account of the development of the GATT dispute settlement system).

4 See, for instance, WTO (2007), pp. 265 – 266; see also infra, fn. 475 and accompanying text

5 Arts. 6.1 (establishment of a panel) and 16.4 (adoption of panel report) of the DSU.

trade sanctions, which are also subject to the negative consensus rule.[6] In return for this more powerful multilateral enforcement mechanism, the US accepted a prohibition of unilateral sanctions.[7] Finally, and most importantly in our context, since panel reports could no longer be blocked, and a number of panel reports had been criticized in the past for the low quality of their legal reasoning, the member states sought another way to deal with legally faulty reports. To that end, they created a standing review body, the Appellate Body, to which a party can appeal for a review of legal interpretations of a panel.[8] The reports of the Appellate Body, like those of the panels, are adopted by the DSB by negative consensus.[9]

Despite its successes, this effective and binding dispute settlement system is today under an existential threat. Since mid-2017 the US has blocked all appointments of new members to the Appellate Body, and it shows no signs of changing this policy. As a consequence, only three of the seven seats on the Appellate Body are currently occupied. If nothing unexpected happens, the number of sitting Appellate Body members will drop to only one in December 2019, when the terms of two of the three sitting members will end.[10] Since three Appellate Body members are required for the disposition of an appeal,[11] this means that from December 2019 onwards the Appellate Body will no longer be able to hear new appeals. In that situation, by filing a notice of appeal a party could suspend dispute settlement proceedings indefinitely. In effect, this would give each party the power to block the adoption of a panel report, thus returning the dispute settlement system to pre-WTO times.

6 Art. 22 of the DSU.

7 Art. 23 of the DSU; see further on this provision supra, fn. 477 and accompanying text.

8 Art. 17 of the DSU; on the reasons for creating the Appellate Body, see Cossy (2015), pp. 302 – 303; Steger (2015), p. 468; and Lacarte-Muró/Castro (2004), p. 45; further on the negotiating history of the Appellate Body, see infra, Section V.A.

9 Art. 17.14 of the DSU.

10 The terms of Appellate Body members Ujal Singh Bhatia and Thomas R. Graham end on 10 December 2019 (see minutes of the DSB meeting of 25 November 2015 [WT/DSB/M/370], paras. 7.3 – 7.4). The only remaining member will then be Zhao Hong, whose term runs until 30 November 2020 (see minutes of the DSB meeting of 23 November 2016 [WT/DSB/M/389], paras. 13.3 – 13.4).

11 Art. 17.1 of the DSU.

Various aspects of this grave crisis of the WTO dispute settlement system have already been discussed in the literature.[12] This study adds three elements. First, it describes, based on a detailed review of the minutes of the DSB meetings since 2017, how a dispute that seemed initially to be about obscure issues of appointment procedure, baffling many observers, turned into the most severe crisis of the WTO dispute settlement system yet. It gives an account of the shifting reasons offered by the US for its blockage, culminating, in August 2018, in broad accusations of judicial overreach and disregard of WTO rules by the Appellate Body. The US alleges that the Appellate Body has been engaging in such overreach, on the one hand, in the area of substantive law, and, on the other hand, concerning six distinct issues of procedure and interpretive approach. Its focus in the DSB, however, has been on the latter, and it has presented to the member states extensive statements on all of these six issues. Second, and foremost, the study analyzes each of the six procedural and interpretative issues raised by the US, and asks, from a legal point of view, whether the Appellate Body has indeed overstepped its mandate with regard to any of these issues, and whether the Appellate Body's jurisprudence on these issues, either individually or as a whole, can justify the blockage of appointments to the Appellate Body. For that purpose, it takes a particularly close look at the statements of the US in the DSB, and the reactions of other WTO members to these statements. Third, it places the detailed analysis of the reasons stated by the US for its blockage in a larger legal and political context in order to gain a better understanding of the motives driving the US.

The structure of the study follows this outline of its main contributions. Chapter II lays the basis by briefly explaining the rules on appointments to the Appellate Body and discussing past experiences with the appointment process. Chapter III chronicles the development of the current crisis, from early 2017 until the summer of 2019.[13] Chapter IV, the central part of the study, contains a detailed analysis of the issues of procedure and interpretative approach that the US has invoked as reasons for its blockage and answers the question whether these reasons can legally justify the blockage. Chapter V

12 See, for instance, Ansong (2019); Bacchus (2018); Bahri (2019); Bhala/Gantz/Keating/Witmer (2019), pp. 257 – 274; Claussen (2018); Creamer (2019); Fabry/Tale (2018); Hillman (2018a); Hoekman/Mavroidis (2019); Kong/Guo (2019); Kuiper (2017); McDougall (2018); Pauwelyn (2019); Payasova/Hufbauer/Schott (2018); Petersmann (2018) and (2019); Raina (2018); Shaffer (2018); Steinberg (2018); and Vidigal (2018) and (2019).

13 For the purposes of this study, events, case law, and publications up to the end of August 2019 were considered.

puts the often narrow and technical legal issues analyzed in Chapter IV in a broader explanatory framework. Chapter VI concludes with a summary of the main results and a few thoughts on whether a better understanding of the legal reasons stated by the US for its blockage might contribute to a resolution of the appointment crisis or otherwise be of practical value.

II. Appointments to the Appellate Body: Legal rules and past controversies

The basic rules on the composition of the Appellate Body and the appointment of its members are stipulated in Arts. 17.1 to 17.3 of the DSU. According to Art. 17.1 of the DSU, the Appellate Body is composed of seven persons, three of whom (a so-called division) serve on any one case. Pursuant to Art. 17.2, „*[t]he DSB shall appoint persons to serve on the Appellate Body for a four-year term, and each person may be reappointed once*", and, moreover, „*[v]acancies shall be filled as the arise.*" Decisions by the DSB on appointments and reappointments have to be made by consensus (Art. 2.4 of the DSU). The expected qualifications of Appellate Body members are prescribed in Art. 17.3 of the DSU, which names three criteria, namely, they have to be, first, „*of recognized authority, with demonstrated expertise in law, international trade and the subject matter of the covered agreements generally*", second, „*unaffiliated with any government*", and, third, „*broadly representative of membership in the WTO.*"

The DSU provides no further details on the appointment process. Based on recommendations for the establishment of the Appellate Body by the Preparatory Committee for the WTO, which were approved by the DSB in early 1995,[14] the following practice emerged:[15] For first-term appointments a selec-

14 Establishment of the Appellate Body, Recommendations by the Preparatory Committee for the WTO approved by the Dispute Settlement Body on 10 February 1995 (WT/DSB/1).

15 See the description of the processes in the DSB on the occasion of the appointment and reappointment decisions: Minutes of the DSB meetings of 1 and 29 November 1995 (WT/DSB/M/9), pp. 1 – 8 (appointment of Bacchus, Beeby, Ehlermann, El-Naggar, Feliciano, Lacarte-Muró, and Matsushita); 25 June 1997 (WT/DSB/M/35), pp. 6 – 7 (reappointment of Ehlermann, Feliciano, and Lacarte-Muró); 27 October and 3 November 1999 (WT/DSB/M/70), pp. 32 – 35 (reappointment of Bacchus and Beeby); 7 April 2000 (WT/DSB/M/78), paras. 70 – 94 (appointment of Abi-Saab and Ganesan); 25 May 2000 (WT/DSB/M/82), paras. 1 – 12 (appointment of Taniguchi); 25 September 2001 (WT/DSB/M/110), paras. 22 – 39 (appointment of Baptista, Lockhart, and Sacerdoti); 7 November 2003 (WT/DSB/M/157), paras. 58 – 71 (appointment of Janow; reappointment of Taniguchi, Abi-Saab, and Ganesan); 31 July 2006 (WT/DSB/M/2018), paras. 1 – 12 (appointment of Unterhalter); 19

tion committee consisting of the Director-General and the chairpersons of the Goods Council, Services Council, TRIPS Council and General Council would be established by the DSB. Member states could submit nominations of candidates, and the selection committee would then interview the candidates, consult with interested member states, and finally submit one candidate to the DSB for decision. If a sitting Appellate Body member was willing to serve for a second term, the chairperson of the DSB would consult with member states, and, if no objection was raised, would propose the sitting member for reappointment to the DSB.

Since 1995, the DSB has appointed altogether 27 persons to the Appellate Body, and reappointed 17 of these for a second term.[16] Although most of these appointments and reappointments proceeded more or less smoothly, there were a number of noteworthy incidents and controversies.[17] The appointment of the first seven Appellate Body members in 1995 took almost a year, mainly because the US and the EU initially each insisted on two Appellate Body members, which was opposed by most of the other member states. Eventually, first the US and then, at the eve of the DSB's appointment decision, the EU gave in and accepted, in the case of the EU only very grudgingly, to have only one member each on the Appellate Body (for the US James Bacchus, and for the EU the German Claus-Dieter Ehlermann).[18] A second controversy occurred in November 2007, when Taiwan blocked the Chinese candidate Yuejiao

and 27 November 2007 (WT/DSB/M/242), paras. 1 – 30 (appointment of Bautista, Hillman, Oshima, and Zhang); 19 June 2009 (WT/DSB/M/270), paras. 82 – 91 (appointment of Ramírez Hernández and Van den Bossche; reappointment of Unterhalter); 18 November 2011 (WT/DSB/M/307), paras. 1 – 14 (appointment of Bhatia and Graham); 24 May 2012 (WT/DSB/M/316), paras. 1 – 14 (appointment of Chang; reappointment of Zhang); 26 March 2013 (WT/DSB/M/330), paras. 4.1 – 4.4 (reappointment of Ramírez Hernández); 25 November 2013 (WT/DSB/M/339), paras. 1.1 – 1.10 (reappointment of Van den Bossche); 26 September 2014 (WT/DSB/M/350), paras. 2.1 – 2.23 (appointment of Servansing); 25 November 2015 (WT/DSB/M/370), paras. 7.1 – 7.17 (reappointment of Bhatia and Graham); and 23 November 2016 (WT/DSB/M/389), paras. 13.1 – 13.27 (appointment of Zhao and Kim).

16 For a list of all Appellate Body members and their terms, see the Appellate Body Annual Report for 2018, March 2019 (WT/AB/29), pp. 148 – 151.

17 On the appointment and reappointment processes since 1995 in general, see Elsig/Pollack (2014) and Appleton (2016).

18 See Steger (2015), pp. 449 – 450, and Elsig/Pollack (2014), p. 403; on the criticism of the first appointment process by the EU and other members, notably India, Brazil, and Switzerland, see minutes of the DSB meeting of 1 and 29 November 1995 (WT/DSB/M/9), pp. 3 – 6.

Zhang, presumably because of the long-running political conflict between China and Taiwan, and only relented after intensive consultations.[19] These first two controversies were about national representation, reflecting the fact that, although Appellate Body members are required to be *„independent and impartial“*[20] and, as mentioned, *„unaffiliated with any government“*,[21] national representation is still considered important by most member states. By contrast, the major appointment conflicts after that did not concern the nationality, but rather the attitude and performance (but not qualification) of the disputed candidates, and it was always the US who had objections.

A first harbinger of what was to come were two incidents that did not cause much stir at the time, but, with hindsight, were telling. As a matter not of law but of political practice, the US is entitled to one seat on the Appellate Body. However, the US was not satisfied with the two US Appellate Body members that followed James Bacchus (1995 – 2003), namely Merit Janow (2003 – 2007) and Jennifer Hillman (2007 – 2011), and refused to support their reappointment, forcing both to declare that they were not available for a second term. This was contrary to the prevailing convention at the time to reappoint Appellate Body members who wished to continue. In both cases, the US believed that, once in office, its candidate had not lent sufficient support to the US, in particular in trade remedy disputes.[22]

The US also became more scrutinizing of reappointments of Appellate Body members nominated by other delegations. When the DSB chairman anno-

19 See Lester (2007); minutes of the DSB meeting of 19 and 27 November 2007 (WT/DSB/M/242), pp. 2 – 4 and 7.

20 Para. 1 of sect. II in conjunction with para. 1 of sect. IV of the Rules of Conduct for the Understanding on Rules and Procedures Governing the Settlement of Disputes (WT/DSB/RC/1), adopted by the DSB on 3 December 1996.

21 Art. 17.3 of the DSU.

22 On Merit Janow, see minutes of the DSB meeting of 22 May 2007 (WT/DSB/M/232), para. 87; Dunoff/Pollack (2017), pp. 267 – 268; and Elsig/Pollack (2014), p. 412 (quoting a former US Trade Representative as saying on Janow: *„We were not happy with US AB members who bend over backwards to show their independence by ruling against the US“*). On Jennifer Hillman, see minutes of the DSB meeting of 21 April 2011 (WT/DSB/M/295), para. 91; Hillman (2017), p. 367 (mentioning *„the United States Trade Representative (USTR)'s apparent expression of hope that a new U.S. AB member ‚will be more willing to boldly defend U.S. interests in Geneva than Hillman‘ and observers noting that ‚USTR perceived outgoing Appellate Body member Jennifer Hillman as not being sufficiently aggressive in issuing dissenting opinions on trade remedy cases‘“*); Blumstein (2017), pp. 11 – 13; Dunoff/Pollack (2017), p. 268; Elsig/Pollack (2014), p. 409; and Hufbauer (2011).

unced in March 2013 that he would start informal consultations on the possible reappointment of the EU Appellate Body member Peter Van den Bossche,[23] whose first term would expire in December 2013, the US demanded interviews with the candidate. Apparently, Van den Bossche refused to be questioned by the US only, and, as a compromise, other members, too, were given the opportunity to talk with Van den Bossche.[24] At the DSB meeting at which Van den Bossche was subsequently reappointed, in November 2013, some members voiced concerns that this more probing process might affect the integrity and independence of the Appellate Body.[25] Again primarily on the initiative of the US, the investigative nature of the reappointment process was taken one step further with the simultaneous reappointments of Ujal Singh Bhatia from India and Thomas R. Graham from the US in November 2015, who were only reappointed after they had been questioned at a meeting open to all interested delegations.[26]

The until then most serious appointment crisis came about when the South African Appellate Body member David Unterhalter, whose second term ended in December 2013, had to be replaced. The selection committee had tacitly

23 See minutes of the DSB meeting of 26 March 2013 (WT/DSB/M/330), para. 4.3.

24 See Bentes (2017), p. 2: „*Then, we had a situation when Peter Van den Bossche was about to be reappointed, the United States requested ... one-on-one interviews with Peter Van den Bossche before deciding whether or not to reappoint him. ... So, Peter Van den Bossche said, well, I'm not going to consult bilaterally with the U.S. about specific cases. And then a decision was made informally that, if there were to be any consultations, it should have been with a broader group of members, not only the United States. So you had the most frequent users of the Appellate Body coming in: Brazil, EU, U.S., China, Korea, Japan, and then consulting with Peter prior to his re-appointment, which finally went through.*"

25 See minutes of the DSB meeting of 25 November 2013 (WT/DSB/M/339), paras. 1.1 – 1.8; for an earlier expression of such concerns, see minutes of the DSB meeting of 25 September 2013 (WT/DSB/M/337), para. 9.3.

26 See minutes of the DSB meeting of 25 November 2015 (WT/DSB/M/370), paras. 7.1 – 7.15; see on the background of that process Sacerdoti (2016), pp. 5 – 6: „*For the first time in this instance some WTO members, principally the US, asked a previous meeting with the two Appellate Body members. This request prompted formal and informal discussions, within the DSB, the Appellate Body and between the chairs of the two bodies on a format and type of questioning that would safeguard on the one hand the independence of the Appellate Body members and the confidentiality of its deliberations, and respond positively to the interest of the WTO members to meet the two judges. At the end a compromise was found in that it was agreed that the encounter, where only questions on general issues concerning the functioning of the Appellate Body could be put to them, would take place at an informal meeting of the DSB.*"

selected James Thuo Gathii from Kenya, a professor of international law at the Loyoloa University Chicago School of Law, who was apparently backed by the vast majority of member states. His appointment was opposed, though, by the US because Gathii had complained in his academic writings about a bias in the WTO in favor of rich and against developing countries.[27] As a consequence, the appointment process, which had been timely launched in May 2013,[28] had to be relaunched a year later, in May 2014,[29] and could only be concluded in September 2014, with the appointment of Shree Baboo Chekitan Servansing from Mauritius,[30] after Unterhalter's seat had been vacant for more than nine months.[31]

Whereas the opposition of the US to Mr. Gathii was only known to insiders at the time, the next controversy, which directly preceded the current crisis, was a different matter. It concerned public accusations leveled by the US against a sitting Appellate Body member, the Korean Seung Wha Chang. Chang's first term expired at the end of May 2016, and he had indicated his willingness to stay on for a second term. Following established practice, the DSB had requested the DSB chairman in January 2016 to carry out consultations on the possible reappointment of Chang.[32] The reappointment decision was scheduled for the DSB meeting of 23 May 2016. At that meeting, however, the US declared that *„it did not support reappointing"* Chang and *„would object to any proposal to reappoint him."*[33] This was the first time that an Appellate Body member seeking reappointment with the support of his or her home country had been blocked by another member state.[34] The US explained that it *„had*

27 See, for instance, Gathii (2006) and (2004).

28 See Appointment/Reappointment of Appellate Body Members, decision adopted by the DSB on 24 May 2013 (WT/DSB/60).

29 See Appellate Body Selection Process, decision adopted by the DSB on 23 May 2013 (WT/DSB/63).

30 See minutes of the DSB meeting of 26 September 2014 (WT/DSB/M/350), paras. 2.1 – 2.23.

31 On the background of this appointment crisis, see Shaffer/Elsig/Puig (2016), p. 271; Howse (2014), pp. 71 – 72; Sacerdoti (2015), p. 5; and Bhala/Gantz/Keating/Simoes (2014), pp. 478 – 479.

32 Appointment/Reappointment of Appellate Body Members, decision adopted by the DSB on 25 January 2016 (WT/DSB/70), item 5.

33 Minutes of the DSB meeting of 23 May 2016 (WT/DSB/M/379), para. 6.2; a few days before the meeting, on 11 May 2016, the US had informed the DSB chairman and the press about its opposition, see idem, para. 6.1.

34 Until that time, out of 23 Appellate Body members who had been eligible for reappointment (up to and including Bhatia and Graham), 17 had been reappointed; four had

reviewed carefully the member's service on the divisions for the various appeals" and „*had concluded that his performance did not reflect the role assigned to the Appellate Body by Members in the DSU*",[35] clarifying that its „*position on this issue was not one based on the results of those appeals in terms of whether a measure was found to be inconsistent or not. ... Instead, the concerns raised were important, systemic issues that went to the adjudicative approach and proper role of the Appellate Body and the dispute settlement system.*"[36] More than 20 members took the floor in that DSB meeting in reaction to the US statement, most of them criticizing the US and warning that refusal to reappoint a member because of dissatisfaction with his or her performance would endanger the independence and impartiality of the Appellate Body. The point was made most forcefully by Chang's home country, Korea, which stated that „*this opposition was, to put it bluntly, an attempt to use reappointment as a tool to rein in Appellate Body members for decisions they made on the bench. Its message was loud and clear: ‚If Appellate Body members made decisions that did not conform to US perspectives, they were not going to be reappointed'.*"[37] In an unprecedented step, all current Appellate Body members except Chang, and, separately, all living former Appellate Body members wrote letters warning of the dangers posed by the US action to the Appellate Body as an institution.[38] Nevertheless, the US would not budge, and therefore a selection process for Chang's replacement had to be started, which led, half a year after the end of Chang's term, to the appointment of the Korean Hyun Chong Kim in November 2016.[39]

---

not sought a second term for personal reasons (El-Naggar, Matsushita, Bautista and Oshima) and, as mentioned, the two US Appellate Body members Janow and Hillman had been forced by the US to forego reappointment.

35 Minutes of the DSB meeting of 23 May 2016 (WT/DSB/M/379), para. 6.2.

36 Minutes of the DSB meeting of 23 May 2016 (WT/DSB/M/379), para. 6.9.

37 Minutes of the DSB meeting of 23 May 2016 (WT/DSB/M/379), para. 6.12; other particularly critical members were, for instance, the EU (para. 6.14), Mexico (para. 6.15), Brazil (paras. 6.16 – 6.19), Switzerland (para. 6.22) and Chinese Taipei (para. 6.25); more understanding (although not necessarily support) for the US decision was expressed by Argentina (paras. 6.30 – 6.31), Australia (para. 6.33), Japan (para. 6.35), and Canada (paras. 6.41 – 6.42).

38 Communications to the DSB from current Appellate Body members, dated 18 May 2016, and from former Appellate Body members, dated 31 May 2016, both reprinted in the Appellate Body Annual Report for 2016, March 2017 (WT/AB/27), pp. 102 – 104.

39 See minutes of the DSB meeting of 23 November 2016 (WT/DSB/M/393), paras. 13.1 – 13.27. Together with the first term of Chang, the second term of Appellate Body member Yuejiao Zhang had also ended in May 2016, and a process for the selection of a successor

to Zhang had been started at the same time as the process for the reappointment of Chang. As a reaction to the blocking of Chang by the US, Korea had blocked the selection of a successor to Zhang (see Sacerdoti [2017], p. 8), and the two processes were finally concluded at the same time, with the appointment of Zhao Hong together with Kim. Consequently, not one, but two seats had been vacant from the end of May until the end of November 2016.

III. Chronology of the crisis

A. February to July 2017: Apparent conflict about appointment procedure

The current crisis started in early 2017 with the upcoming endings of the second terms of the Appellate Body members Ricardo Ramírez Hernández of Mexico, whose term expired on 30 June 2017, and Peter van den Bossche of Belgium (nominated by the EU), whose term expired about five months later, on 11 December 2017. The seat of Ramírez Hernández was informally considered to be the South American seat (his predecessors being Luiz Olavo Baptista from Brazil and Julio Lacarte-Muró from Uruguay) and that of Van den Bossche the EU seat (which had previously been held by Giorgio Sacerdoti from Italy and Claus-Dieter Ehlermann from Germany), and therefore initially some assumed (wrongly, as it turned out) that a conflict between the South American states and the EU was driving the conflict.

In the DSB meeting of 16 December 2016, the chairman of the DSB drew attention to the ending of the terms of Ramírez Hernández and Van den Bossche in 2017, and proposed to carry out one selection process for both positions, with a view to completing the process by the end of June 2017, given that members would be busy in the second half of 2017 with the preparations for the Ministerial Conference in December 2017.[40] He announced that he would submit a formal proposal with further details at the beginning of 2017. At the next DSB meeting, on 25 January 2017, the chairman outlined not one, but two approaches for the appointment process.[41] In addition to a single appointment process, to be completed by June 2017, he mentioned the possibility of two separate processes, one for each position and each with its own time line, one to be completed by June 2017 and the other by December 2017. He declared that he would consult with members on these approaches.

40 Minutes of the DSB meeting of 16 December 2016 (WT/DSB/M/390), para. 10.1.

41 Minutes of the DSB meeting of 25 January 2017 (WT/DSB/M/391), para. 8.1.

In the subsequent DSB meeting of 20 February 2017, the chairman reported on his consultations.[42] A majority of delegations, including the EU and at least two South American states, Argentina and Peru, supported a single process. By contrast, two delegations (one of them being Guatemala and the other, possibly, Panama)[43] preferred two separate processes. Finally, one delegation (based on later events most likely the US) suggested that one should, for the time being, only start the process for the more urgent replacement of Ramírez Hernández, and that more time should be given to decide on when to start the process of replacing Van den Bossche. However, those in favor of a single selection process were only willing to consent to two separate processes if both processes could be completed before the summer break, which, in effect, meant that not only the process for the replacement of Ramírez Hernández, but also that for the later vacancy caused by the end of the term of Van den Bossche had to be started right away. In summary, there was no consensus to start the appointment process because a number of members, most notably the EU, insisted that the processes for both vacancies had to start simultaneously, while one member, most likely the US, was only willing to agree to start the process for the replacement of Ramírez Hernández, or, in other words, required delaying the process for the replacement of Van den Bossche.

During the following five months, from the DSB meeting of 21 March 2017 to that of 20 July 2017, the dispute about the procedure for filling the two vacancies crystallized into a conflict between the EU, which would not agree to the start of the procedure for replacing Ramírez Hernández without also starting the process for replacing Van den Bossche, and the US, which would only agree to starting the process for the first, but not the second vacancy.[44] This became obvious in the DSB meeting of 22 May 2017, in which the DSB discussed two formal proposals on the appointment proposals, one by the

42 Minutes of the DSB meeting of 20 February 2017 (WT/DSB/M/392), para. 11.1, with subsequent statements by Peru (para. 11.2), the EU (para. 11.3), Brazil (para. 11.4) and Argentina (para. 11.5).

43 See the later statement of Guatemala in the minutes of the DSB meeting of 21 March 2017 (WT/DSB/M/394), para. 9.5, and that of Panama in the minutes of the DSB meeting of 19 June 2017 (WT/DSB/M/398), para. 9.11.

44 See minutes of the DSB meetings of 21 March 2017 (WT/DSB/M/394), paras. 9.1 – 9.15; 19 April 2017 (WT/DSB/M/396), paras. 6.1 – 6.13; 22 May 2017 (WT/DSB/M/397), paras. 10.1 – 10.5 and 11.22; 19 June 2017 (WT/DSB/M/398); paras. 8.1 – 8.6 and 9.1 – 9.33; and 20 July 2017 (WT/DSB/M/399), paras. 4.1 – 4.4 and 5.1 – 5.23.

EU[45] and the other by seven South American states under the leadership of Mexico.[46] The EU proposed that the DSB should start two independent appointment processes for the two vacancies, but that both should start and end at the same time. By contrast, the South American group proposed only the start of one selection process, that for the replacement of Ramírez Hernández, in order to get at least that process going in the absence of a consensus on starting both. The US was the only member which opposed the EU proposal, and in turn the EU was the only one which opposed the South American proposal.[47] As to the other member states which made statements on the issue, while a few expressed a preference for the EU proposal,[48] all would have been willing to go along with either proposal.

At the time, the reasons for the intransigence of both the US and the EU were difficult to understand, and indeed a number of members said, in DSB meetings between March and July 2017, that they would like to know the reasons for the delay.[49] The stated reasons of the US and the EU did not seem able to explain the blockage. The US expressed an explicit position on the appointment process for the first time in the DSB meeting of 22 May 2017. Its representative „*said that, given the ongoing transition in the United States' political leadership and the very recent confirmation of a new US Trade Representative [Robert Lighthizer was confirmed by the US Senate as US Trade Representative on 11 May 2017], the United States was not in a position to support the proposed*

45 Communication of 11 May 2017 from the EU, Appointment of Appellate Body, Proposal by the European Union (WT/DSB/W/597), with later revisions of 8 June 2017 (Rev. 1), 7 July 2017 (Rev. 2), 18 August 2017 (Rev. 3), 19 September 2017 (Rev. 4), and 12 October 2017 (Rev. 5).

46 Communication of 8 May 2017 from Argentina, Brazil, Colombia, Chile, Guatemala, Mexico and Peru, Proposal regarding the Appellate Body selection process (WT/DSB/W/596), with later revisions of 8 June 2017 (Rev. 1), 7 July 2017 (Rev. 2), 18 August 2017 (Rev. 3), 18 September 2017 (Rev. 4), and 12 October 2017 (Rev. 5).

47 Minutes of the DSB meeting of 22 May 2017 (WT/DSB/M/397), paras. 10.3 (statement of the US on the EU proposal) and 11.3 (statement of the EU on the South American proposal).

48 Norway, Hong Kong and Switzerland, see minutes of the DSB meeting of 22 May 2017 (WT/DSB/M/397), paras. 11.9, 11.10 and 11.12.

49 See, for instance, statements in the minutes of the DSB meetings of 21 March 2017 (WT/DSB/M/394), paras. 9.4 (Chile) and 9.13 (India); 19 April 2017 (WT/DSB/M/396), paras. 6.2 (Mexico on behalf of itself and Argentina, Brazil, Colombia, Chile, Guatemala, and Peru) and 6.7 (India); 22 May 2017 (WT/DSB/M/397), paras. 11.5 (India) and 11.14 (Chinese Taipei); 19 June 2017 (WT/DSB/M/398), para. 9.18 (India); and 20 July 2017 (WT/DSB/M/399), paras. 5.11 (Ecuador) and 5.18 (Venezuela).

decision to launch a process to fill a position on the Appellate Body that would only become vacant in December 2017. Nevertheless, the United States was willing to join a consensus for the DSB to take the decision proposed by Argentina, Brazil, Colombia, Chile, Guatemala, Mexico, and Peru."[50] It repeated this position more or less verbatim in the subsequent two DSB meetings of June and July 2017.[51] The mere fact that top officials had only recently entered office did not seem a particularly plausible reason not even to start the appointment process, and the argument became even less plausible with the passage of time.

The EU's position appeared to be, if anything, even less explicable. In the DSB meeting of 20 February 2017, the EU gave two reasons for choosing a single process,[52] namely, first, that it followed past practice because for the appointments of Ramírez Hernández and Van den Bossche in 2009 a single process had also been used,[53] and, second, that a single process was more efficient. It referred to or repeated these reasons in all subsequent DSB meetings between March and July 2017.[54] In the DSB meetings of May, June and July 2017, the EU added that it failed to see why one process should be singled out. While these were perfectly good reasons for starting both processes rather than just one, they do not explain why, in the face of the US opposition to starting both processes, the EU should prefer starting no process at all to starting at least one process.

With hindsight, the US blockage of the Van den Bossche replacement process was just a precursor of its complete blockage of the appointment process from August 2017 onwards. From today's perspective, it might be more surprising that the US at the time consented at least to the launch of the process to replace Ramírez Hernández than that it blocked the process to replace Van den Bossche. As to the motives for the EU's blockage of the process to replace Ramírez Hernández, one can only speculate. Maybe the EU feared or had indications that the US planed to delay the replacement of Van den Bossche

---

50 Minutes of the DSB meeting of 22 May 2017 (WT/DSB/M/397), para. 10.3.

51 See minutes of the DSB meetings of 19 June 2017 (WT/DSB/M/398), para. 8.3, and 20 July 2017 (WT/DSB/M/399), para. 4.3.

52 See minutes of the DSB meeting of 20 February 2017 (WT/DSB/M/392), para. 11.3.

53 See on that appointment process the minutes of the DSB meeting of 22 December 2008 (WT/DSB/M/261), paras. 74 – 77.

54 See minutes of the DSB meetings of 21 March 2017 (WT/DSB/M/394), para. 9.3; 19 April 2017 (WT/DSB/M/396), para. 6.3; 22 May 2017 (WT/DSB/M/397), paras. 10.2 and 11.3; 19 June 2017 (WT/DSB/M/398), paras. 8.2 and 9.3; and 20 July 2017 (WT/DSB/M/399), paras. 4.2 and 5. 3.

for an indefinite period, given the widely diverging views of the EU and the US on the role of the Appellate Body, and that it hoped that by linking the two appointment processes the pressure of the other member states on the US to end its resistance would increase.

B. Since August 2017: US blockage of all appointments

On 1 August 2017, Appellate Body member Hyun Chong Kim unexpectedly tendered his resignation[55] because he had been nominated as, and was shortly afterwards appointed as, Korean trade minister.[56] He resigned with immediate effect, i.e., as of 1 August 2017, despite the fact that Art. 14(2) of the Appellate Body Working Procedures requires that such a resignation should take effect only 90 days after the notification unless the DSB decides otherwise, which would allow a resigning member to finish any appeal he or she might be still serving on within the 90-day period of Art. 17.5 of the DSU. With the term of Ramírez Hernández having ended on 30 June 2017, there were now two vacancies on the Appellate Body, with a third, that of Van den Bossche, to follow only four months later.

In that situation, the US pointed out at the DSB meeting of 31 August 2017 that Kim and Ramírez Hernández were sitting on the division of the pending appeal *EU – Fatty Alcohols (Indonesia)*, and that Ramírez Hernández served on the divisions of two further pending appeals, *EC and certain member States – Large Civil Aircraft (Article 21.5 – US)* and *Indonesia – Import Licensing Regimes.*[57] The participation of Ramírez Hernández in these pending appeals was

55 Communication of 1 August 2017 from Appellate Body member Hyun Chong Kim to the chair of the Appellate Body (WT/DSB/73).

56 See WTO, Appellate Body member Hyun Chong Kim resigns, 1 August 2017 (https://www.wto.org/english/news_e/news17_e/ab_01aug17_e.htm); for further background, see Reuters, South Korea names new trade minister amid U.S. push to amend FTA, 30 July 2017 (https://www.reuters.com/article/us-southkorea-usa-trade-idUSKBN1AF091); Center for Strategic & International Studies, Impact Player: trade Minister Kim Hyun-chong, 4 August 2017 (https://www.csis.org/analysis/impact-player-trade-minister-kim-hyun-chong).

57 See minutes of the DSB meeting of 31 August 2017 (WT/DSB/M/400), paras. 5.3 – 5.5.

based on Rule 15 of the Appellate Body's Working Procedures,[58] which states that „[*a*] *person who ceases to be a Member of the Appellate Body may, with the authorization of the Appellate Body and upon notification to the DSB, complete the disposition of any appeal to which that person was assigned while a Member, and that person shall, for that purpose only, be deemed to continue to be a Member of the Appellate Body.*" The Working Procedures had been drawn up by the Appellate Body, in accordance with Art. 17.9 of the DSU. The US now argued that under Art. 17.2 of the DSU, which gives the DSB the power to appoint Appellate Body members, it was the sole authority of the DSB, and not the Appellate Body, to decide whether someone whose term had expired should continue to serve on appeals. It then stated that it would not consent to the start of any appointment processes before the DSB had not addressed the issue of continued service of former Appellate Body members without DSB authorization.[59]

For the next nine months, from the DSB meeting of 29 September 2017 to that of 28 May 2018, the US invoked the Rule 15 issue as the sole reason for blocking the appointment process.[60] This blockage meant that after the expiration of Van den Bossche's term on 11 December 2017, the number of vacancies on the Appellate Body had risen to three. The US further stoked the conflict by claiming that any Appellate Body report which had been issued by a division on which a former Appellate Body member had served based on Rule 15 was not an Appellate Body report at all, and therefore its adoption was not subject to the negative consensus rule of Art. 17.4 of the DSU, but rather the positive consensus rule of Art. 2.4 of the DSU,[61] thus striking at one of the core inno-

58 See Appellate Body reports *EU – Fatty Alcohols* (*Indonesia*), para. 1.15; *EC and certain member States – Large Civil Aircraft* (*Article 21.5 – US*), para. 1.35; and *Indonesia – Import Licensing Regimes*, para. 1.17.

59 See minutes of the DSB meeting of 31 August 2017 (WT/DSB/M/400), paras. 7.3 and 7.11.

60 See minutes of the DSB meetings of 29 September 2017 (WT/DSB/M/402), paras. 6.2 and 8.6; 23 October 2017 (WT/DSB/M/403), para. 8.6; 22 November 2017 (WT/DSB/M/404), para. 7.6; 22 January 2018 (WT/DSB/M/407), para. 8.7; 28 February 2018 (WT/DSB/M/409), paras. 7.4 – 7.8 and 7.33; 27 March 2018 (WT/DSB/M/410), paras. 9.4 – 9.6; 27 April 2018 (WT/DSB/M/413), para. 9.3; and 28 May 2018 (WT/DSB/M/413), paras. 11.4 – 11.6.

61 See the minutes of the following DSB meetings: 29 September 2017 (WT/DSB/M/402), para. 5.11 concerning *EU – Fatty Alcohols* (*Indonesia*) (Ramírez Hernández serving based on Rule 15; Kim serving after resignation on 1 August 2017); 22 November 2017 (WT/DSB/M/404), paras. 5.6 and 5.7 concerning *Indonesia – Import Licensing Regimes* (Ramírez Hernández serving based on Rule 15); and 28 May 2018 (WT/DSB/M/413), para. 8.4 concerning *EC and certain member States – Large Civil Aircraft* (*Article 21.5 – US*) (Ramírez

vations of the DSU compared to the earlier GATT dispute settlement system, the removal of the power to veto the adoption of dispute settlement reports.

Even assuming, for argument's sake, that the US was right to claim that the Appellate Body did not have the power under the DSU to adopt and apply Rule 15, it was never very plausible that this issue was the only or even the main reason of the US for its open-ended blockage and thus, as the former Appellate Body member Ramírez Hernández put it in his farewell speech of 28 May 2018, the threat to let the Appellate Body *„die through asphyxiation"*.[62] To begin with, even the US did not criticize the substance of Rule 15, but only the fact that it had been adopted by the Appellate Body rather than the DSB. As the US had stated in the August 2017 DSB meeting, in which it had first made the Rule 15 argument, *„it appreciated that the approach of Rule 15 could contribute to efficient completion of appeals. As a party in two pending appeals, the United States said that it would welcome Mr. Ramírez's continued service on the appeals to which he had been assigned as of 30 June 2017."*[63] Moreover, blocking appointments only aggravated the asserted problem, namely that persons were serving on the Appellate Body without authorization of the DSB because with fewer Appellate Body members each Appellate Body member has to work on more appeals, meaning, first, that appeals will take longer, and thus former Appellate Body members working on such appeals based on Rule 15 would have to stay on for longer, and second, that at the end of his or her term

---

Hernández and Van den Bossche serving based on Rule 15) and paras. 10.8, 10.9 and 10.17 concerning *EC – PET (Pakistan)* (Van den Bossche serving based on Rule 15). In the DSB meeting of 22 June 2018, the US added that issuance of an Appellate Body report beyond the 90-day deadline of Art. 17.5 of the DSU would also make such a report subject to the positive consensus rule of Art. 2.4 of the DSU rather than the negative consensus rule of Art. 17.14 of the DSU (minutes [WT/DSB/M/414], para. 5.21; see also infra, fn. 184 and accompanying text). See further the following DSB meetings: 11 January 2019 (WT/DSB/M/424), para. 3.19 concerning *US – Tuna II (Article 21.5 – US)* (report issued beyond the 90-day deadline of Art. 17.5 of the DSU); 11 April 2019 (WT/DSB/M/427), para. 4.4 concerning *US – Large Civil Aircraft (2nd complaint) (Article 21.5 – EU)* (Servansing and Van den Bossche serving based on Rule 15; report issued beyond the deadline of Art. 17.5 of the DSU); and 15 August 2019, statement of the US (https://geneva.usmission.gov/2019/08/16/statements-by-the-united-states-at-the-august-15-2019-dsb-meeting), pp. 27 – 28, concerning *US – Countervailing Measures (China) (Article 21.5 – China)* (Servansing serving based on Rule 15; report issued beyond the 90-day deadline of Art. 17.5 of the DSU).

62 Ramírez Hernández (2019), p. 120.

63 Minutes of the DSB meeting of 31 August 2017 (WT/DSB/M/400), para. 5.5; this view was repeated by the US at the DSB meetings of 29 September 2017 (see minutes [WT/DSB/M/402], para. 6.2) and 23 October 2017 (see minutes [WT/DSB/M/403], para. 8.6).

an Appellate body member is likely to be sitting on more running appeals and thus Rule 15 will apply in more cases.[64] Finally, and most importantly, if only the lack of DSB authorization and not the continued service as such was the problem, this problem could have been easily resolved, either by an ad-hoc authorization by the DSB in each specific instance, or, preferably, by an amendment of the DSU. Such an amendment could have been adopted by the General Council,[65] which meets several times each year.[66] However, the US never made any specific proposals for either an ad-hoc authorization or a DSU amendment,[67] nor did it offer any other suggestion on how the DSB should address the alleged problem. Also, when one member state, Honduras, in July 2018 finally outlined specific ideas on how to address the Rule 15 issue and submitted them to the DSB,[68] the US never engaged with them substantively, basically ignoring them.[69]

With its argument that the Rule 15 issue justified the blocking of any further appointments to the Appellate Body the US stood alone in the DSB. After the DSB meeting of 31 August 2017, the South American states revised their proposal to include not only the replacement of Ramírez Hernández, but, like the EU proposal, also those of Kim and Van den Bossche. Since there were no longer any substantive differences between the EU and the South American proposals, these proposals were replaced in November 2017 by a common

64 Similar arguments were made by Japan, Canada and Australia in the DSB meeting of 31 August 2017 (see minutes [WT/DSB/M/400], paras. 5.11, 7.5 and 7.7) and by China in the DSB meeting of 29 September 2017 (see minutes [WT/DSB/M/402], para. 6.10); see also communication from the Appellate Body of 27 November 2017, Background note on Rule 15 of the Working Procedures for Appellate Body Review (published in the Appellate Body Annual Report 2017 of February 2018 [WT/AB/28], pp. 74 – 75), paras. 6 – 7.

65 Art. X:8 in conjunction with Art. IV:2 of the WTO Agreement.

66 In the relevant time period from August 2017 to May 2018, the General Council met four times, on 26 October and 30 November 2017 as well as 7 March and 8 May 2018.

67 Twice, in the DSB meetings of October and November 2017, the US suggested that the DSB should „*adopt an appropriate decision*“ to enable the continued service of Hernández Ramírez after the expiration of his term (minutes of the DSB meetings of 23 October 2017 [WT/DSB/M/403], para. 8.6, and 22 November 2017 [WT/DSB/M/404], para. 7.6), but it made no concrete proposals and did not repeat this suggestion after November 2017.

68 Communication of 20 July 2018 from Honduras, Fostering a Discussion on the Functioning of the Appellate Body (JOB/DSB/2); the communication was tabled and discussed at the DSB meetings of 20 July 2018 (minutes [WT/DSB/M/415], paras. 8.1 – 8.6) and 26 September 2018 (minutes of meeting [WT/DSB/M/419], paras. 10.1 – 10.28).

69 See minutes of the DSB meetings of 20 July 2018 (WT/DSB/M/415), para. 8.2, and 26 September 2018 (WT/DSB/M/419), paras. 10.18 and 10.25.

proposal for the filling of all three vacancies, submitted by the EU, the seven South American states and 15 other proponents.[70] With further revisions of this common proposal the number of its official proponents grew until June 2018 to 70 member states, including, among others, the EU states, China, Brazil, Russia, India, Canada and Korea.[71] Only the US opposed these proposals. In the DSB meetings between August 2017 and June 2018, in which these proposals were discussed, altogether 40 delegations, some of them on behalf of larger groups, made statements on the appointment crisis, and all called for an immediate start of the appointment process.[72] A significant number explicitly rejected the link made by the US between the Rule 15 issue and the appointment process. While many expressed a willingness to engage in a discussion of the Rule 15 issue, almost no one acknowledged it as a problem in itself, let alone a problem of such magnitude that it could call into question the further existence of the Appellate Body. Finally, various members complained that the US did not make any specific demands or proposals on how to resolve the alleged Rule 15 problem and thus to unblock the appointment process.[73]

To understand the true motives of the US for the blockage of the appointments, one had to rely on US statements made outside the DSB. Focusing on

70 Communication of 9 November 2017 from 25 delegations, Appellate Body Appointments (WT/DSB/W/609).

71 Revision 1 of 11 January 2018, revision 2 of 15 February 2018, revision 3 of 16 April 2018 and revision 4 of 17 May 2018.

72 See minutes of the DSB meetings of 31 August 2017 (WT/DSB/M/400), paras. 5.1 – 5.21 and 7.1 – 7.17; 29 September 2017 (WT/DSB/M/400), paras. 6.1 – 6.11 and 8.1 – 8.29; 23 October 2017 (WT/DSB/M/400), paras. 8.1 – 8.38; 22 November 2017 (WT/DSB/M/400), paras. 7.1 – 7.33; 22 January 2018 (WT/DSB/M/400), paras. 8.1 – 8.25; 28 February 2018 (WT/DSB/M/400), paras. 7.1 – 7.35; 27 March 2018 (WT/DSB/M/400), paras. 9.1 – 9.32; 27 April 2018 (WT/DSB/M/400), paras. 9.1 – 9.33; 28 May 2018 (WT/DSB/M/400), paras. 11.1 – 1.34; and 22 June 2018 (WT/DSB/M/400), paras. 9.1 – 9.29.

73 As to such complaints, see minutes of the DSB meetings of 29 September 2017 (WT/DSB/M/400), paras. 6.3 (Canada), and 6.5 (Dominican Republic); 23 October 2017 (WT/DSB/M/400), paras. 8.22 (China), and 8.23 (Korea); 22 November 2017 (WT/DSB/M/400), paras. 7.17 (Brazil); 22 January 2018 (WT/DSB/M/400), paras. 8.5 (China), 8.10 – 8.11 (Brazil), and 8.23 (EU); 28 February 2018 (WT/DSB/M/400), paras. 7.14 (Brazil), 7.22 (China), 7.26 (Kazakhstan), and 7.35 (chairman); 27 March 2018 (WT/DSB/M/400), paras. 9.15 (Indonesia), 9.17 (China); 27 April 2018 (WT/DSB/M/400), paras. 9.8 (Russia), 9.11 (Thailand), 9.20 (Panama), 9.26 (China), and 9.30 (Guatemala); 28 May 2018 (WT/DSB/M/400), paras. 11.7 (Canada), 11.16 (Russia), 11.19 (Brazil), 11.23 (China), 11.28 (Guatemala), and 11.30 (Turkey); and 22 June 2018 (WT/DSB/M/400), paras. 9.18 (Hong Kong), and 9.23 (China).

official statements, we will briefly look at the statement of United States Trade Representative (USTR) Robert Lighthizer on 11 December 2017 at the 11th biannual Ministerial Conference in Buenos Aires, the President's 2018 Trade Policy Agenda of 1 March 2018, prepared by the Office of the USTR, and, finally, the statement of Deputy USTR Dennis Shea at the General Council meeting of 8 May 2018.

In his brief opening plenary statement on 11 December 2017 at the 11th Ministerial Conference in Buenos Aires, USTR Lighthizer identified four challenges facing the WTO. The first he mentioned was dispute settlement: „*[M]any are concerned that the WTO is losing its essential focus on negotiation and becoming a litigation-centered organization. Too often members seem to believe they can gain concessions through lawsuits that they could never get at the negotiating table. We have to ask ourselves whether this is good for the institution and whether the current litigation structure makes sense.*"[74]

Lighthizer's concern with concessions gained through litigation rather than negotiation, or, in other words, lawmaking by the WTO dispute settlement institutions, was spelt out at some length in the President's 2018 Trade Policy Agenda of March 2018, under the heading „*U.S. Concerns with WTO Dispute Settlement.*"[75] It stated *that „[i]t has been the longstanding position of the United States that panels and the Appellate Body are required to apply the rules of the WTO agreements in a manner that adheres strictly to the text of those agreements, as negotiated and agreed by its Members. Over time, U.S. concerns have increasingly focused on the Appellate Body's disregard for the rules as set by WTO Members. Successive Administrations and the Congress have voiced those concerns, and the United States called for WTO adjudicators to follow their role as laid out in the DSU. But the problem has been growing worse, and not better.*"[76] The Agenda identified „*disregard for the rule as set by WTO Members*" concerning, first, substantive law, and, second, procedural questions and interpretative approaches, i.e., rules governing dispute settlement itself. Concerning substantive law, the Agenda mentioned trade remedies (anti-dumping duties, countervailing duties and safeguards), subsidies and the interpretation

74 WT/MIN(17)/ST/128, p. 1.

75 Office of the United States Trade Representative, The President's 2018 Trade Policy Agenda, March 2018, pp. 22 – 29.

76 The President's 2018 Trade Policy Agenda (supra, fn. 75), p. 24.

of the non-discrimination principle under the TBT Agreement.[77] Procedural questions and interpretative approaches were addressed in more detail. More specifically, six distinct issues were discussed:[78] (1) disregard for the 90-day deadline for appeals (Art. 17.5 of the DSU); (2) continued service by persons who are no longer Appellate Body members (i.e., the Rule 15 issue); (3) issuing advisory opinions on issues not necessary to resolve a dispute; (4) appellate review of facts; (5) appellate review of a member's municipal law;[79] and (6) treatment of Appellate Body reports as precedents.

Finally, at the General Council meeting of 8 May 2018, China had placed the appointment process on the agenda, and urged the US, supported by many other member states, to end its blockage.[80] In response, the representative of the US, Deputy USTR Shea, did not focus narrowly on the Rule 15 issue, but rather echoed the broad allegations made in the 2018 Trade Policy Agenda when he said, for instance, that „*something had gone terribly wrong in the system when those charged with adjudicating the rules were so consistently disregarding those very rules. ... [T]he Appellate Body had not only rewritten Members' agreements to impose new substantive rules they had never negotiated or agreed upon but had also been ignoring or rewriting the rules governing the dispute settlement system – expanding its own capacity to write and impose new rules.*"[81]

The fact that the Rule 15 issue was not the sole or even main reason for the US blockage of the appointment process, contrary to the US statements in the DSB meetings between September 2017 and May 2018, was at long last also acknowledged by the US in the DSB meetings itself, starting with the meetings of 22 June and 20 July 2018, in which the US referred to the Rule 15 issue only as

77 The President's 2018 Trade Policy Agenda (supra, fn. 75), pp. 23 – 24. The following Appellate Body reports were referred to, directly or indirectly: *US – Offset Act (Byrd Amendment)* and *US – Anti-Dumping and Countervailing Duties (China)* (on anti-dumping and countervailing duties); *US – Lamb* and *US – Line Pipe* (on safeguards); *US – FSC* (on subsidies); and *US – Tuna II (Mexico)* and *US – COOL* (on the TBT Agreement).

78 The President's 2018 Trade Policy Agenda (supra, fn. 75), pp. 24 – 29.

79 In the Agenda as well as in subsequent discussions before the DSB the US usually treated appellate review of facts and appellate review of municipal law together. However, although these two issues are related, they present quite different legal questions (see for more details infra, Section IV.B.4), and are therefore counted here as two separate issues.

80 See minutes of the General Council meeting of 8 May 2018 (WT/GC/M/172), paras. 4.1 – 4.86.

81 See minutes of the General Council meeting of 8 May 2018 (WT/GC/M/172), para. 4.90.

an example of its broader *„systemic concerns“*,[82] without, though, explaining what these *„systemic concerns“* were. The explanation followed in the DSB meeting of 27 August 2018. In that meeting, the chair of the DSB had tabled the reappointment of Appellate Body member Shree Baboo Chekitan Servansing, whose first term ended on 30 September 2018, and who had indicated his willingness to serve for a second term.[83] The US opposed his reappointment and referred for its reasons to the President's 2018 Trade Policy Agenda. It summarized the concerns listed in the Agenda, namely that, in the area of substantive law, *„appellate reports have gone far beyond the text setting out WTO rules“*, particular concerning trade remedies, subsidies and the TBT agreement and, on questions of procedure and interpretative approach, the six distinct issues including, but not limited to, Rule 15.[84] From the DSB meeting of 29 October 2018 onwards, the US repeated these broad allegations as reasons for its continued blockage.[85] Moreover, it made extended separate statements, each running to several pages in the minutes of the DSB meetings, on the six procedural and interpretative concerns it had identified in addition to the Rule 15 issue, namely disregard for the 90-day deadline for appeals (DSB meeting of 22 June 2018),[86] appellate review of facts and of municipal law (27 August 2018),[87] issuance of advisory opinions (29 October 2018),[88] and treating Appellate Body reports as precedents (18 December 2018).[89]

Going beyond Rule 15 and adding broader concerns made the discussion more forthright, but did not lessen the support of the other members for an im-

82 See minutes of the DSB meetings of 22 June 2018 (WT/DSB/M/414), para. 9.3, and 20 July 2018 (WT/DSB/M/415), para. 6.3. As a matter of fact, the US had already once before described the Rule 15 issue in the DSB as merely an example of broader (but unspecified) concerns, namely in the DSB meeting of 31 August 2017, when it had first raised that issue (see para. 7.11 of the minutes of that meeting [WT/DSB/M/400]), but, as explained, had afterwards relied on the Rule 15 issue only.

83 See minutes of the DSB meeting of 27 August 2018 (WT/DSB/M/417), par. 12.1.

84 Minutes of the DSB meeting of 27 August 2018 (WT/DSB/M/417), par. 12.2.

85 See minutes of the DSB meetings of 29 October 2018 (WT/DSB/M/420), paras. 20.5 and 20.28; 21 November 2018 (WT/DSB/M/421), para. 21.4; 18 December 2018 (WT/DSB/M/423), para. 9.4; 28 January 2019 (WT/DSB/M/425), para. 7.5; 25 February 2019 (WT/DSB/M/426), paras. 5.6 and 5.25; 26 April 2019 (WT/DSB/M/428), para. 11.3; 28 May 2019 (WT/DSB/M/429), para. 8.3; and 24 June 2019 (WT/DSB/M/430), para. 8.4.

86 Minutes of the DSB meeting of 22 June 2018 (WT/DSB/M/414), paras. 5.2 – 5.22.

87 Minutes of the DSB meeting of 27 August 2018 (WT/DSB/M/417), paras. 4.2 – 4.17.

88 Minutes of the DSB meeting of 29 October 2018 (WT/DSB/M/423), paras. 4.2 – 4.19.

89 Minutes of the DSB meeting of 18 December 2018 (WT/DSB/M/414), paras. 4.2 – 4.25.

mediate launch of the appointment process for the now four vacancies. To the contrary, the number of members formally sponsoring the common proposal to start the appointment process rose from 70 in June 2018,[90] just before the US had begun its broad attack against the Appellate Body, to 116 in its latest revision of August 2019,[91] and not one member joined the US blockage. At the same time, some members developed proposals to address the US concerns with the aim of unblocking the appointment process. Apart from the already mentioned suggestions of Honduras in July 2018 on the Rule 15 issue, the European Commission and Canada each issued papers on WTO reform in September 2018, including reforms of the dispute settlement system.[92] In November 2018, three different proposals addressed to the General Council followed, one from 11 delegations, among them the EU, China, India and Canada, on DSU amendments regarding the US concerns on procedural questions and interpretative approaches,[93] another one from the EU, China and India on DSU amendments aimed at strengthening the Appellate Body,[94] and a final one from Australia and Singapore regarding the initiation of a solution-focused process of discussions on dispute settlement issues.[95] However, at the General Council meeting of 12 December 2018, the US rejected all proposals on DSU amendments outright as insufficient, without engaging with

90 See supra, fn. 71 and accompanying text.

91 WT/DSB/W/609/Rev.13 (communication of 2 August 2019 from 116 delegations on Appellate Body appointments).

92 European Commission, Concept paper on WTO modernisation, 18 September 2018 (see in particular pp. 13 – 17 on *„proposals on dispute settlement“*); communication of 21 September 2018 from Canada, Strengthening and modernizing the WTO: Discussion paper (JOB/GC/201), in particular pp. 3 – 4 on *„Safeguarding and strengthening the dispute settlement system“*.

93 Communication of 23 November 2018 from the EU China, Canada, India, Norway, New Zealand, Switzerland, Australia, South Korea, Iceland, Singapore and Mexico to the General Council (WT/GC/W/752) (with revisions of 7 and 10 December 2018 Costa Rica and Montenegro, respectively, were added as co-sponsors).

94 Communication of 23 November 2018 from the EU, China, and India to the General Council (WT/GC/753) (with revision of 10 December 2018 Costa Rica was added as co-sponsor).

95 Communication of 29 November 2018 from Australia and Singapore to the General Council, Adjudicative bodies: Adding to or diminishing rights or obligations under the WTO Agreement (WT/CG/W/754) (with revisions of 1 and 11 December 2018 first Costa Rica and then Canada and Switzerland were added as co-sponsors).

them substantively, and without offering any alternative proposals, either on substance or on how to proceed with further discussions.[96]

In an attempt to find a way out of the impasse, the chair of the General Council launched an „informal process on Appellate Body matters“ in January 2019 and appointed a facilitator, New Zealand's WTO ambassador David Walker, to coordinate the discussions.[97] Ambassador Walker reported regularly on the results of these discussions to the General Council.[98] As part of this informal process a number of further proposals were tabled by various members on ways to address the concerns of the US and to overcome the blockage.[99] However, none of these efforts moved the US in any way toward giving up its resistance against new appointments. Moreover, apart from repeating its accusations against the Appellate Body and vaguely calling for members „*to engage in a deeper discussion of why the Appellate Body has felt free to depart from what Members agreed to*“,[100] it also continued to refuse to

96 See minutes of the General Council meeting of 12 December 2018 (WT/GC/M/175), paras. 6.159 – 6.172; see further on the response of the US at this meeting infra, Section V.B, fn. 496 and accompanying text.

97 WTO, General Council Chair appoints facilitator to address disagreement on Appellate Body, 18 January 2019 (https://www.wto.org/english/news_e/news19_e/gc_18jan19_e.htm).

98 First report of 28 February 2019 (JOB/GC/2015), discussed at the General Council Meeting of 28 February 2019 (minutes [WT/GC/M/176], paras. 4.1 – 4.151); second report of 7 May 2019 (JOB/GC/217), discussed at the General Council meeting of 7 May 2019 (minutes [WT/GC/M/177], paras. 4.1 – 4.161); and third report of 23 July 2019 (JOB/GC/220), discussed at the General Council meeting of 23 July 2019.

99 Several proposals from Honduras on the 90-day deadline of Art. 17.5 of the DSU (communication of 18 January 2019 [WT/GC/W/758]), Rule 15 (communication of 18 January 2019 [WT/GC/W/759]), alleged judicial activism (communication of 28 January 2019 [WT/GC/W/760]), and precedent (communication of 1 February 2019 [WT/GC/W/761]); communication of 12 February 2019 from Taiwan, Guideline development discussion (WT/GC/W/763) (revised on 5 April 2019); communication of 28 March 2019 from Brazil, Guidelines for the work of the panels and the Appellate Body (WT/GC/W/767) (revised on 25 April 2019); communication of 17 April 2019 from Japan and Australia, Informal process on matters related to the functioning of the Appellate Body (WT/GC/W/768) (revised on 25 April 2019); communication of 25 April 2019 from Thailand, General Council decision on the dispute settlement system of the DSU (WT/GC/W/769); and communication of 25 June 2019 from the African Group, Appellate Body Impasse (WT/GC/W/776).

100 Statement of the US at the General Council meeting of 23 July 2019 (https://geneva.usmission.gov/2019/07/23/statements-delivered-by-ambassador-dennis-shea-wto-general-council-meeting-july-23-2019); almost identical statements were made by the US at the earlier meetings of the General Council of 12 December 2018 (minutes [WT/GC/175], para.

offer any proposals of its own. Therefore, unless something quite unexpected happens, one has to assume that the US will not end its blockage for the time being, which means that in December 2019, when the terms of two of the three remaining Appellate Body members, Ujal Singh Bhatia and Thomas R. Graham, end, the Appellate Body will cease to be able to hear new appeals.

Recognizing this, members have begun to plan for a time without a functioning Appellate Body. For instance, in July 2019 the EU and Canada announced their intention that, in the absence of a functioning Appellate Body, they would, in disputes between them, as a temporary measure, „*resort to arbitration under Article 25 of the DSU as an interim appeal arbitration procedure*", which should „*replicate as closely as possible all substantive and procedural aspects as well as the practice of Appellate Review pursuant to Article 17 of the DSU*".[101] Other members have agreed regarding pending disputes that they will not appeal panel reports if the Appellate Body does not have at least three members at the time of the circulation of such reports.[102]

6.169]), the DSB of 25 February 2019 (WT/DB/M/426), para. 5.25, and the General Council of 7 May 2019 (minutes [WT/GC/M/177], para. 4.156]).

101 Communication of 25 July 2019 from Canada and the EU, Interim appeal arbitration pursuant to Article 25 of the DSU (JOB/DSB/1/Add.11), paras. 1 and 2. On 4 September 2019 the European Commission adopted a decision enabling it to enter into similar agreements with other countries (https://trade.ec.europa.eu/doclib/press/index.cfm?id=2059). For early proposals of using arbitration under Art. 25 of the DSU as a temporary means to sidestep the blocking of appointments, see Anderson et al. (2017) and Hillebrand Pohl (2017) (further developed in Hillebrand Pohl [2019]).

102 Communication of 22 March 2019 from Indonesia and Viet Nam, *Indonesia – Safeguard on Certain Iron or Steel Products*, Understanding between Indonesia and Viet Nam regarding procedures under Articles 21 and 22 of the DSU (WT/DS496/14), para. 7; communication of 11 April 2019 from Indonesia and Chinese Taipei, *Indonesia – Safeguard on Certain Iron or Steel Products*, Understanding between Indonesia and Viet Nam regarding procedures under Articles 21 and 22 of the DSU (WT/DS490/13), para. 7.

IV. Analysis of the reasons stated by the US for the blockage

A. Overview

In the following, we will analyze the six issues the US has presented as the prime examples of judicial overreach by the Appellate Body in the area of procedure and of interpretative approach, namely Rule 15, the 90-day deadline of Art. 17.5 of the DSU, appellate review of facts and of municipal law, advisory opinions and the role of precedent. By contrast, we will not address the corresponding US allegations in the area of substantive law, in particular trade remedies, subsidies, and the TBT Agreement because, first, this would go far beyond the scope of the present study, and, second, the focus of the US in its justification of its blockage in the DSB has been on the procedural and interpretative issues. Whereas the US has put forward in the DSB since the start of the appointment crisis detailed arguments on all six procedural and interpretative points, it has mentioned its substantive law reasons for the blockage only in passing, without providing any details. Further information on US criticism of the Appellate Body on substantive law can be found elsewhere, for instance in DSB meetings in which Appellate Body reports with which the US disagreed were adopted,[103] but not in DSB discussions in the context of the appointment crisis. One can only speculate about why the US chose to stress the procedural and interpretative rather than the substantive law issues. This

103 See for examples the President's 2018 Trade Agenda 2018 (supra, fn. 75), pp. 23 – 24; see for more recent examples statements of the US at the DSB meetings of 10 April 2019, on the Appellate Body report in *US – Tuna II (Mexico) (Article 21.5 – US) / US – Tuna II (Mexico) (Article 21.5 – Mexico II)* (minutes [WT/DSB/M/424], paras. 3.2 – 3.15); and 15 August 2019, on the Appellate Body report in *US – Countervailing Measures (China) (Article 21.5 – China)* (https://geneva.usmission.gov/2019/08/16/statements-by-the-united-states-at-the-august-15-2019-dsb-meeting, pp. 12 – 29).

choice might be puzzling because policy-wise Appellate Body reports flouting WTO rules concerning substantive law would seem to be more important to the US, given the US claim that these *„reports ... restrict the ability of the United States to regulate in the public interest or protect U.S. workers and businesses against unfair trading practices."*[104] A possible reason might be that the Appellate Body's decisions on substantive law that are characterized by the US as overreach are typically cases which the US lost, while the procedural and interpretive issues affect cases across the board, some with the US on the losing and some with the US on the winning side, and some even without US participation. Therefore, it is more difficult to disregard US criticism of these latter type of issues as simply self-interested and result-driven („sore loser").

The purpose of the subsequent analysis is, first, to determine with regard to each of the six issues mentioned above whether the Appellate Body breached WTO law, and in particular the DSU, and, second, to the extent that such breaches can be found, whether any such breach individually or all breaches taken together can justify blocking all appointments to the Appellate Body. As far as the second purpose is concerned, one has to bear in mind that Art. 17.2 of the DSU prescribes that „[*v*]*acancies* [*on the Appellate Body*] *shall be filled as they arise.*" In other words, under the DSU member states have a legal obligation to appoint new Appellate Body members as soon as a position becomes vacant. Moreover, the DSU provides no exemption from this obligation. Consequently, by blocking all appointments to the Appellate Body the US clearly violates the DSU. In addition, this violation does not just cause some procedural inconvenience, but it is already severely hampering the work of the Appellate Body and, if the blockage continues, will soon bring the operation of the Appellate Body, and possibly, by extension, the whole dispute settlement system, to a complete standstill. Although there are no rules on the kinds of DSU breaches that might justify other DSU breaches, in light of the obviousness of the breach of Art. 17.2 of the DSU and the severity of its consequences, only clear and serious breaches on the part of the Appellate Body, and not just debatable interpretations, could possible justify the obstruction by the US.

Since the evaluation of the US criticism turns to a large extent on the interpretation of the DSU and related provisions of other WTO agreements, a few

104 Minutes of the DSB meeting of 27 August 2018 (WT/DSB/M/417), para. 12.2.

introductory remarks on the method of interpreting the WTO agreements[105] will facilitate the task. On this issue, Art. 3.2 of the DSU states that „*[t]he dispute settlement system of the WTO ... serves ... to clarify the existing provisions of those agreements in accordance with customary rules of interpretation of public international law.*" Regarding the meaning of these „*customary rules of interpretation of public international law*", the Appellate Body explained in its very first report, in the case *US – Gasoline*, that the general rule of interpretation of Art. 31(1) of the Vienna Convention on the Law of Treaties (VCLT) „*has attained the status of a rule of customary or general international law. As such, it forms part of the ‚customary rules of interpretation of public international law' which the Appellate Body has been directed, by Article 3(2) of the DSU, to apply*" when it interprets the WTO agreements.[106] It later extended this reasoning to all provisions of the VCLT on interpretation, that is, Arts. 31 to 33.[107] The general rule of interpretation of Art. 31(1) of the VCLT prescribes that „*[a] treaty shall be interpreted in good faith in accordance with the ordinary meaning to be given to the terms of the treaty in their context and in the light of its object and purpose.*" As one of the founding Appellate Body members, Claus-Dieter Ehlermann, observed, „*[a]mong these three criteria [of Art. 31(1) of the VCLT], the Appellate Body has certainly attached the greatest weight to the first, i.e., ‚the ordinary meaning of the terms of the treaty'. ... The second criterion, i.e., ‚context' has less weight than the first, but is certainly more often used and relied upon than the third, i.e., ‚object and purpose'.*"[108] This „*highly textual approach*"[109] is a distinctive feature of the Appellate Body[110] compared with other international tribunals.[111] It has been criticized by some as too forma-

105 See in general on the method applied by the Appellate Body to the interpretation of the WTO agreements the in-depth study Van Damme (2009).

106 *US – Gasoline*, p. 16.

107 See the following Appellate Body reports: *Japan – Alcoholic Beverages II*, p. 104 (extension to the whole of Art. 31 and to Art. 32 of the VCLT); *United States – Softwood Lumber IV*, para. 59 (extension to Art. 33(3) of the VCLT); *Chile – Price Band System*, para. 271 (application of Art. 33(4) of the VCLT).

108 Ehlermann (2002), pp. 615 – 616.

109 Former Appellate Body member Ganesan (2015), p. 535.

110 There are, however, some who note a trend away from textualism in the more recent jurisprudence of the Appellate Body; see, e.g., Rubini (2017), p. 311 (criticizing the change), and Sadurski (2015), pp. 415 – 417 (welcoming the change).

111 See Pauwelyn/Elsig (2013), pp. 449 – 459, for a comparison of the interpretative styles and methods of different international tribunals, including the Appellate Body.

listic,[112] but has been consistently defended by former and current Appellate Body members.[113]

For the purposes of the present analysis it is noteworthy that on a basic level there is considerable agreement between the US and the Appellate Body on the interpretative approach. The US accepts that the interpretation of the WTO agreements is governed by Arts. 31 to 33 of the VCLT,[114] which it most recently confirmed in a DSB meeting of December 2018.[115] Moreover, like the Appellate Body, the US puts particular emphasis on the text as the foremost interpretive element. For example, when it first announced its blocking of all appointments to the Appellate Body in August 2018, the US invoked *„concerns that appellate reports have gone far beyond the text setting out WTO rules in varied areas“*.[116] And more recently, in May 2019, the US argued in a General Council meeting, after a brief summary of its overreach allegations, *„that the Appellate Body had been acting contrary to the unambiguous text of the DSU.“*[117] So the disagreement is less about the basic criteria which should guide the interpretation of WTO law, but more about the application of these criteria.

112 See, e.g., Bond/Trachtman (2016); Davies (2015), pp. 546 – 547; Magnuson (2010), pp. 124 – 129; Irwin/Weiler (2008), pp. 94 – 95; Diamond (2008); Bhala/Gantz (2006), p. 285; Horn/ Weiler (2005), pp. 251 – 253; Picciotto (2005); and Steinberg (2004), p. 261.

113 See Bhatia (2018), p. 126; Bacchus (2005), pp. 503 – 507, and (2015), pp. 515 – 516; Ganesan (2015), p. 518, 533 – 537; Matsuhita (2012), pp. 526 – 529.

114 Even though the US has not ratified the VCLT (see for the state of ratification of the VCLT the United Nations Treaty Collection, https://treaties.un.org/Pages/Home.aspx), and for that reason had also opposed referring to the VCLT in the DSU; see Kuijper (2018), fn. 20: *„A direct reference to Arts. 31 and 32 could not be agreed during the Uruguay Round, as France and the US among others had not (and have not) ratified the 1969 Vienna Convention.“*

115 See minutes of the DSB meeting of 18 December 2018 (WT/DSB/M/423), statement of the US, para. 4.5: *„And for purposes of understanding the ‚existing provisions‘ of the covered agreements – namely, their text – the DSU directed WTO adjudicators to apply ‚customary rules of interpretation of public international law‘, reflected in Articles 31 to 33 of the Vienna Convention on the Law of Treaties.“*

116 Minutes of the DSB meeting of 27 August 2018 (WT/DSB/M/417), para. 12.2.

117 Minutes of the General Council meeting of 7 May 2019 (WT/GC/M/177), para. 4.154.

B. Issues of procedure and interpretive approach

1. Rule 15 of the Working Procedures of Appellate Review

As already mentioned above, Rule 15 of the Working Procedures of Appellate Review provides that „[*a*] *person who ceases to be a Member of the Appellate Body may, with the authorization of the Appellate Body and upon notification to the DSB, complete the disposition of any appeal to which that person was assigned while a Member, and that person shall, for that purpose only, be deemed to continue to be a Member of the Appellate Body.*“ The Working Procedures, including its Rule 15, are based on Art. 17.9 of the DSU, which states that „[*w*]*orking procedures shall be drawn up by the Appellate Body in consultation with the Chairman of the DSB and the Director-General, and communicated to the Members for their information.*“ The first version of these Working Procedures, which contained Rule 15 in its present form, were drawn up by the first seven Appellate Body members at the beginning of 1996 and, after consultations with the chairman of the DSB, the Director-General and various members, entered into effect and were communicated to the members on 15 February 1996.[118] Transition rules similar to Rule 15 are followed by other international adjudicatory bodies,[119] including the International Court of Justice,[120] the International Tribunal for the Law of the Sea,[121] and the European

118 On the process of drawing up the Working Procedures, see Steger (2015), pp. 450 – 451, and Ehlermann (2015), pp. 489 – 491; on the reactions of members, see the minutes of the DSB meeting of 21 February 1996 (WT/DSB/M/11), pp. 9 – 13.

119 Rule 15 might very well have been inspired by the corresponding rules for the International Court of Justice (ICJ) and the European Court of Human Rights (ECtHR), set out below (fn. 120 and 122), since the first draft of the Working Procedures had been based on an analysis of the procedural rules of other international tribunals, which included the ICJ and the ECtHR; see Steger (2015), p. 451, fn. 13, and infra, fn. 411 and accompanying text.

120 See Art. 13(3) of the Statute of the International Court of Justice: „*The members of the Court shall continue to discharge their duties until their places have been filled. Though replaced, they shall finish any cases which they may have begun.*“ According to Art. 92 of the Charter of the United Nations, the Statute forms an integral part of the Charter.

121 See Art. 5(3) of the Statute of the International Tribunal for the Law of the Sea: „*The members of the Tribunal shall continue to discharge their duties until their places have been filled. Though replaced, they shall finish any proceedings which they may have begun before the date of their replacement.*“ The Statute is annexed to the United Nations Conventions

Court of Human Rights.[122] Before the appointment crisis of 2017, Rule 15 had been applied eleven times in altogether nine appeals,[123] without any objections either by the parties to these appellate proceedings or by member states in the DSB meetings at which the corresponding reports had been adopted. Not at least due to vacancies caused by the appointment crisis, Rule 15 was more frequently applied from 2017 onward, e.g., three times to Ramírez Hernández[124] and five times to Van den Bossche.[125]

The US claims that Rule 15 violates Art. 17.2 of the DSU, according to which *„[t]he DSB shall appoint persons to serve on the Appellate Body for a four-year term, and each person may be reappointed once."* It argues that since Art. 17.2 of the DSU gives the DSB the power to appoint and reappoint Appellate Body members, it is also the DSB who has the *„responsibility to decide whether a person whose term of appointment had expired, should continue serving, as if a member of the Appellate Body"*,[126] and, conversely, that *„the Appellate Body simply did not have the authority to deem someone who was not an Appellate Body member to be a member"*.[127] To arguments by other members that the Working Procedures are based on the DSU, namely Art. 17.9 of the DSU, and that the Rule represents long-standing practice, the US replied that *„[n]either the Appellate Body's authority to draw up its Working Procedures nor ‚practice' could amend the DSU."*[128]

---

on the Law of the Sea (UNCLOS), and forms an integral part of the Convention (Art. 318 of the UNCLOS).

122 See Art. 23(3) of the European Convention on Human Rights: *„The judges shall hold office until replaced. They shall, however, continue to deal with such cases as they already have under consideration."*

123 See https://www.wto.org/english/tratop_e/dispu_e/ab_members_descrp_e.htm: *US – Lead and Bismuth II* (Appellate Body members El-Naggar and Matsushita); *US – Section 211 Appropriations Act* (Ehlermann and Lacarto-Muro); *US – FSC (Article 21.5 – EC)* (Feliciano); *US – Line Pipe* (Lacarte-Muro); *US – Shrimp (Thailand) / US – Customs Bond Directive* (Ganesan); *US – Continued Suspension / Canada – Continued Suspension* (Abi-Saab); *Colombia – Textiles* (Zhang); *India – Solar Cells* (Chang); *EU – Biodiesel (Argentina)* (Zhang).

124 Supra, fn. 58.

125 Appellate Body reports, *EC and certain member States – Large Civil Aircraft (Article 21.5 – US)*, para. 1.35; *EC – PET (Pakistan)*, para. 1.19; *Indonesia – Iron or Steel Products*, para. 1.11; *Brazil – Taxation (Japan)*, para. 1.22; and *US – Large Civil Aircraft (2nd Complaint) (Article 21.5 – EU)*, para. 1.46.

126 Minutes of the DSB meeting of 31 August 2017 (WT/DSB/M/400), para. 5.5.

127 Minutes of the DSB meeting of 22 January 2018 (WT/DSB/M/407), para. 8.7.

128 Minutes of the DSB meeting of 28 February 2018 (WT/DSB/M/409), para. 7.5.

On 24 November 2017, the same day it authorized the continued service of Van den Bossche after the expiry of his term in an unprecedented number of five appeals,[129] the Appellate Body issued a Background Note on Rule 15.[130] In that Note, the Appellate Body explained, among other things, the adoption of the Rule as part of the Working Procedures in 1996, the unchallenged practice of the Rule until the US objections in 2017, the fact that other international adjudicatory bodies follow similar rules, and some of the policy reasons behind the Rule. The US discussed and criticized this Note at some length in the DSB meetings of 28 February and 27 March 2018.[131] It complained, inter alia, that the Note had not addressed how the Rule related to the DSB's appointment power in Art. 17.2 of the DSU, that it had failed to mention that one member state, India, had criticized Rule 15 as a breach of Art. 17.2 of the DSU in the DSB meeting of February 1996 in which the Working Procedures had been discussed right after its adoption, and that transition rules similar to Rule 15 of other international tribunals were explicitly provided for in the international treaties which had created these tribunals,[132] whereas the founding treaty of the Appellate Body, the DSU, contained no such rule.

How are the US arguments to be evaluated? The US relies heavily, if not exclusively, on the wording of Art. 17.2 of the DSU, believing, apparently, that this wording leaves no room for any other interpretation than that it prohibits Rule 15. And, indeed, reading Art. 17.2 of the DSU as prohibiting a practice like that of Rule 15 seems at least plausible and, if only the wording of this provision is considered, might even be the best interpretation of this provision. However, it has to be acknowledged at the same time that the wording of Art. 17.2 of the DSU does not explicitly address or answer the question whether a transition rule like Rule 15 is permissible. Art. 17.2 of the DSU states that the DSB should appoint (or reappoint) persons to serve on the Appellate Body for a four-year term, which obviously implies that no one else can appoint Appellate Body members. Rule 15 of the Working Procedures, though, does not purport to give the Appellate Body the power to appoint Appellate Body members. Rather, it authorizes the Appellate Body to assign to a former Appellate Body member a

---

129 Supra, fn. 125.

130 Communication of 24 November 2017 from the Appellate Body, Background Note on Rule 15 of the Working Procedures for Appellate Body Review (JOB/AB/3), published in the Appellate Body Annual Report 2017 (WT/AB/28), pp. 74 – 75.

131 See minutes of the DSB meetings of 28 February 2018 (WT/DSB/M/409), paras. 7.6 – 7.8, and 27 March 2018 (WT/DSB/M/410), paras. 9.4 – 9.5.

132 See supra, fn. 120-122.

limited task of an Appellate Body member, namely completing the work on an appeal that he or she was assigned during his or her term, and to do so for a very limited time, that is, usually less than 90 days, given the 90-day deadline of Art. 17.5 of the DSU for appellate proceedings. From other tasks of an Appellate Body member, such as taking part in the exchange of views on appeals to which he or she was not assigned, that former member is excluded. Moreover, as China has pointed out in the DSB,[133] the wording of Rule 15 itself recognizes that such a person has ceased to be an Appellate Body member, and is, for the limited purpose of completing the appeal, merely deemed to be a member. The obvious counterargument to this reading is that even though Rule 15 does not explicitly speak of appointing, and only allows a very limited extension of the work an Appellate Body member, the Appellate Body's authorization under Rule 15 is, for this limited extension, still functionally equivalent to an appointment decision.

Interpretation of a provision does not end with its wording, though. As noted above, Art. 31(1) of the VCLA requires a treaty to be interpreted in good faith in accordance with the ordinary meaning to be given to its terms in their context and in the light of its object and purpose. An important part of the context of Art. 17.2 of the DSU is the whole of Art. 17 of the DSU. The first noteworthy point in this respect is that Art. 17 of the DSU is the only article within the DSU that deals in any detail with the Appellate Body. In other words, on the level of the WTO treaties there is only a relative skeletal regulation of the Appellate Body. This contrasts markedly with other international tribunals, like the International Court of Justice, whose statute is an integral part of the Charter of the United Nations[134] and runs to 70 articles, and the Court of Justice of the European Union, whose statute is an integral part of the founding treaties of the EU[135] and contains 64 articles. The second point to note is that according to Art. 17.9 of the DSU the necessary procedural details which are lacking in the DSU are to be added not by the WTO membership, but by the Appellate Body itself, through the adoption of working procedures. Approval of the working procedures by the members had been considered during the drafting of the

133 Minutes of the DSB meetings of 22 January 2018 (WT/DSB/M/407), para. 8.4, and 28 February 2018 (WT/DSB/M/409), para. 7.21.

134 Art. 92 of the Charter of the United Nations.

135 The Statute of the Court of Justice of the European Union is annexed as Protocol No. 3 to the Treaties, i.e. the Treaty on the European Union (TEU) and the Treaty on the Functioning of the European Union (TFEU). Pursuant to Art. 51 of the TEU the Protocols to the Treaties form an integral part thereof.

DSU, but then consciously rejected.[136] Accordingly, the Appellate Body has been given wide discretion to regulate its own procedures, a fact that Claus-Dieter Ehlermann, one of the first seven Appellate Body members, described as *„simply stunning“*, particularly compared with the EU system, and which he ascribed to the potential difficulties to get any working procedures approved by the membership following the traditional consensus principle.[137] In light of the skeletal regulation of the Appellate Body and the wide discretion given to the Appellate Body to fill in the necessary procedural details, Rule 15 does not seem to be a transgression of this wide discretion: First, as the mentioned examples of other international tribunal demonstrate, it is not an unusual rule. Second, as even the US acknowledges, it is not an unreasonable rule.[138] And, third, it is very unlikely that the drafters of the appointment rule of Art. 17.2 of the DSU had wanted to implicitly prohibit a transitional rule like Rule 15, or had even thought about transition rules when they drafted this rule. We will return to the last point, the intentions of the drafters, below.

Another relevant part of Art. 17 of the DSU is the last sentence of Art. 17.1 of the DSU, which reads: *„Persons serving on the Appellate Body shall serve in rotation. Such rotation shall be determined in the working procedures of the Appellate Body.“* This provision was proffered by China in the DSB as an argument in favor of the compliance of Rule 15 with the DSU, stating that *„Rule 15 clearly guaranteed the rotation, which was required by the DSU, and should, thus, form part of the Working Procedures for Appellate Review.“*[139] Rotation is the only aspect which the DSU explicitly requires to be included in the Working Procedures, i.e., it was obviously important to the drafters.[140] However, in

136 See Draft Text on Dispute Settlement of 21 September 1990 (MTN.GNG/NG13/W/45), p. 3: *„Working procedures shall be drafted by the appellate body [and approved by the Council].“* Texts in brackets in such draft documents indicate that there is not yet consensus on the issue. In the final text of the DSU the proposed approval by the Council was removed.

137 Ehlermann (2002), pp. 610 – 611.

138 See supra, fn. 63 and accompanying text.

139 Minutes of the DSB meeting of 22 January 2018 (WT/DSB/M/407), para. 84; see also minutes of the DSB meeting of 28 February 2018 (WT/DSB/M/409), para. 7.21.

140 In line with this emphasis on rotation in the DSU, when the then chair of the Appellate Body, Julio Lacarte-Muró, submitted the Working Procedures after its adoption in February 1996 to the chairman of the DSU, he named *„the need for rotation in the establishment of divisions along with the advantages of collegiality“* as the second of the main concerns which the Appellate Body had in mind when drafting the Working Procedures (Letter of 7 February 1996 of Appellate Body Chairman to the Dispute Settlement Body Chairman, fourth paragraph, https://www.wto.org/english/news_e/pres96_e/ab2.htm).

response to this argument by China, the US said that it *„failed to see how this rotation had any relevance to the question raised by Rule 15"*.[141] And, indeed, on first sight the relationship between rotation and Rule 15 is not self-evident. On closer inspection, though, there is such a nexus. According to Art. 6(2) of the Working Procedures rotation serves to ensure *„random selection, unpredictability and opportunity for all Members to serve regardless of their national origin."* Without a transitional rule like Rule 15, the objectives of random selection and unpredictability[142] would have been endangered during times of transition of the Appellate Body's membership. That is most obvious from the viewpoint of 1995, when the first seven Appellate Body members were appointed. Whereas the normal term of an Appellate Body member is four years, the second sentence of Art. 17.2 of the DSU stipulates that the terms of three of the seven persons appointed immediately after the entry into force of the WTO Agreement are to expire at the end of two years, to be determined by lot. This had the effect that not all seven Appellate Body members would be up for reappointment or replacement at the same time, but that only the terms of groups of three of four members would end simultaneously, thus ensuring a certain continuity within the Appellate Body's membership. However, in the absence of a transition rule like Rule 15, this would also have meant that if a party appealed a report less than 90 days before the end of the final terms of a three- or four-member group, the Appellate Body would, in effect, only have a choice between four or three members. In other words, in such a situation a party would know for certain (in case of four retirements) or almost for certain (in case of three retirements) who would sit on the division deciding its appeal. Rule 15 avoids this by allowing the Appellate Body to choose from all of

141 Minutes of the DSB meeting of 28 February 2018 (WT/DSB/M/409), para. 7.33.

142 On how the Appellate Body ensures random selection and unpredictability, see Steger (2015), p. 456 – 457: *„In order to ensure that the selection process would meet all these requirements and be completely secret and unpredictable, an Appellate Body member devised a mathematical formula that allowed the members to select a certain number of divisions at once. These meetings were held in secret, with only the Appellate Body members in the room, and each of them only drew specific numbers, telling him or her what appeals he or she would be on, not by case name (because it was not predictable whether or not an appeal would be filed) but by the order in which the appeals were filed. Each Appellate Body member only knew his or her own numbers, he or she did not know anyone else's, and the Secretariat was not given any information. When an appeal was filed, the three members who were on that appeal would contact the Director of the Secretariat to advise him or her that they were on that division. They only drew so many numbers at one time, because mathematically if too many were drawn, the sequence would become predictable."*

its seven members, even if the terms of some of these members will run out during the appeal. The fact that rotation was the cause of the application of Rule 15 was in at least two instances explicitly mentioned by the Appellate Body.[143]

In the above, we have already briefly surmised about the intentions of the drafters of the DSU regarding Rule 15. One way to shed light on the intent of the drafters is to look at the parties' practice under their agreement. According to Art. 31(3)(b) of the VCLT, „*[t]here shall be taken into account, together with the context, … any subsequent practice in the application of the treaty which establishes the agreement of the parties regarding its interpretation.*"[144] Therefore, although the US is right in arguing that subsequent practice cannot amend the DSU, it can nevertheless be relevant for determining what it means in the first place. The fact that, as stated above, before the first objection of the US in August 2017, Rule 15 had been applied eleven times in the previous more than 20 years without any objection from any member state indicates that the member states did not believe that Rule 15 violates the DSU. However, what about the fact that, as pointed out by the US, one member state, India, had objected to Rule 15 at the time the Working Procedures had been adopted in 1996, arguing, like the US does today, that Rule 15 is in breach of Art. 17.2 of the DSU? India made this criticism in the DSB meeting of 21 February 1996,[145] at which the Working Procedures, which had entered into force a few days earlier, were discussed by the members, following an earlier informal discussion among members on 1 February 1996. At the meeting of 21 February, seven members made statements on the Working Procedures, including the US.[146] Apart from India none of them commented on Rule 15. So, even though India's intervention had made the membership aware of a potential conflict between Rule 15 and Art. 17.2 of the DSU, none of the other members had expressed support for India's view. So, if anything, this is an indication that in 1996, shortly after the conclusion of the WTO agreements and the DSU, with memories of the drafting still fresh, the membership at large did not see a

143 Appellate Body reports, *US – Shrimp (Thailand) / US – Customs Bond Directive*, para. 16 (application of Rule 15 to Ganesan) and *US – Continued Suspension / Canada – Continued Suspension*, para. 27 (application of Rule 15 to Abi-Saab).

144 On the interpretation of Art. 31(3)(b) of the VCLT, see Gardener (2008), pp. 225 – 249.

145 See minutes of the DSB meeting of 21 February 1996 (WT/DSB/M/11), pp. 11 – 12.

146 See minutes of the DSB meeting of 21 February 1996 (WT/DSB/M/11), pp. 9 – 13.

problem with Rule 15, which is confirmed by its subsequent unchallenged practice until the objection of the US in August 2017.

Even if the unchallenged application of Rule 15 is not considered sufficient for purposes of Art. 31(3)(b) of the VCLT, it is still relevant for another element of interpretation under the VCLT, namely the requirement that, according to Art. 31(1) of the VCLT, a treaty has to be interpreted in good faith. Given that neither the US nor any other member ever challenged the application of Rule 15 until August 2017, and that, as the account of the development of the appointment crisis has shown, invoking Rule 15 for almost a year as the sole reason for blocking the appointments was only a pretext,[147] the US interpretation of Art. 17.2 of the DSU as clearly prohibiting Rule 15 can hardly be called an interpretation in good faith.

In conclusion, although one can plausibly argue that, when read in isolation, the wording of the Art. 17.2 of the DSU prohibits a transition rule like Rule 15, an interpretation of Art. 17.2 in its context – in particular the brevity of the procedural rules on the Appellate Body in the DSU, the powers given to the Appellate Body in Art. 17.9 of the DSU to add the procedural details through the adoption of working procedures, and the requirement in Art. 17.1 of the DSU to include rules in the working procedures that ensure rotation – and in light of the intention of the parties as revealed by their unchallenged practice of Rule 15 until August 2017, leads to the opposite conclusion. The US arguments to the contrary further suffer from a lack of good faith. In any event, even if one should reach a different conclusion when weighing these different elements of interpretation and find a breach of Art. 17.2 of the DSU, such a breach would certainly not be a clear or egregious one that could justify bringing down the Appellate Body by blocking all appointments.

2. 90-day deadline of Art. 17.5 of the DSU

Art. 17.5 of the DSU provides that „*[a]s a general rule, the [appellate] proceedings shall not exceed 60 days from the date a party to the dispute formally notifies its decision to appeal to the date the Appellate Body circulates its report. ... When the Appellate Body considers that it cannot provide its report within 60 days, it shall inform the DSB in writing of the reasons for the delay together with*

147 See supra, fn. 82 and accompanying text.

an estimate of the period within which it will submit its report. In no case shall the proceedings exceed 90 days."

From the very beginning, the Appellate Body almost never met the 60-day deadline considered by Art. 17.5 of the DSU to be the general rule.[148] However, until and including 2010 the Appellate Body complied with the 90-day deadline in the large majority of appeals. Out of 95 reports circulated between the beginning of 1996 and the end of 2010, only nine were circulated outside the 90-day deadline.[149] Put differently, in this period the Appellate Body complied with Art. 17.5 of the DSU in more than 90 % of the cases, with an average delay of about 35 days in the nine cases outside the 90-day deadline. With regard to each of the nine delayed reports, with the exception of the very first one, the Appellate Body sought and received the agreement of the parties to the extension of time for circulating the report, and mentioned that agreement both in the communication to the DSB required by Art. 17.5 of the DSU and in the report itself.[150] Moreover, in the case *US – Upland Cotton* in 2004 and in the next four appeals with delayed reports, the parties to the

148 Since its first report in 1996, the Appellate Body has circulated only four reports within 60 days, namely *Japan – Alcoholic Beverages II* (appeal notified on 8 August 1996, report circulated on 4 October 1996), *US – Wool Shirts* (24 February to 25 April 1997), *Brazil – Aircraft* (*Article 21.5 – Canada*) and *Canada – Aircraft* (*Article 21.5 – Brazil*) (the latter two both 22 May to 21 July 2000).

149 In the following nine cases the 90-day deadline was not met (in chronological order; with the time from notification of the appeal to the circulation of the report in brackets): *EC – Hormones* (114 days), *US – Lead and Bismuth II* (104 days), *EC – Asbestos* (140 days), *Thailand – H-Beams* (140 days), *US – Upland Cotton* (136 days), *EC – Export Subsidies on Sugar* (105 days), *Mexico – Anti-Dumping Measures on Rice* (132 days), *US – Upland Cotton* (*Article 21.5 – Brazil*) (111 days), and *US – Continued Suspension / Canada – Continued Suspension* (140 days).

150 See *EC – Hormones* (communications WT/DS26/11 and WT/DS48/9 of 10 December 1997), *US – Lead and Bismuth II* (communication WT/DS138/6 of 27 March 2000; Appellate Body report, para. 8), *EC – Asbestos* (communication WT/DS135/10 of 20 December 2000; Appellate Body report, para. 8), *Thailand – H-Beams* (communication WT/DS122/5 of 20 December 2000; Appellate Body report, para. 7), *US – Upland Cotton* (communication WT/DS267/18 of 20 December 2004; Appellate Body report, para. 8), *EC – Export Subsidies on Sugar* (communication WT/DS265/26, WT/DS266/26 and WT/DS283/7 of 24 January 2005; Appellate Body report, para. 7), *Mexico – Anti-Dumping Measures on Rice* (communication WT/DS295/7 of 14 September 2005; Appellate Body report, para. 7), *US – Upland Cotton* (*Article 21.5 – Brazil*) (communication WT/DS267/35 of 25 April 2008; Appellate Body report, para. 14), *US – Continued Suspension / Canada – Continued Suspension* (communication WT/DS320/14 and WT/DS321/14 of 24 July 2008; Appellate Body reports, para. 29).

dispute confirmed that they would deem the report issued outside the 90-day deadline nevertheless to be an Appellate Body report circulated pursuant to Art. 17.5 of the DSU (so-called „deeming letters").[151]

The situation changed markedly from 2011 onwards, concerning the number and length of delays as well as the way in which the Appellate Body dealt with those delays. In 2011, five out of six reports were delayed, and looking at the whole period from 2011 to the end of 2018 only six out of 42 reports observed the 90-day deadline.[152] Since May 2015, all reports have been delayed, usually by a large margin. The average delay for late reports increased from about 55 days in 2011 to 300 days in 2018.[153] As to the way in which the Appellate Body handled these delays, even if the Appellate Body had consulted with the parties about the delay or had received their agreement, it no longer mentioned these consultations or any agreement in either its communication to the DSB or its reports. Moreover, for the first time in the case *US – Tyres*, circulated in September 2011, and subsequently with increasing frequency, it no longer even consulted the parties on the delays or sought their agreement, but rather determined the date of circulation on its own. The fact that the Appellate Body changed its practice around the same time as the number of delays started to increase substantially is probably no coincidence. One can assume that as delays became more and more unavoidable, the Appellate Body concluded that it would no longer be meaningful to ask for the consent of the parties because in the absence of consent the delay would occur anyway.

Reasons for the increasing delays in the WTO dispute settlement system[154] were discussed by the Appellate Body in a communication of May 2013,[155] in

151 See references in fn. 150.

152 The reports in the period from 2011 to 2018 that were circulated within 90 days are (date of circulation in brackets) *Philippines – Distilled Spirits* (21 December 2011), *US – Clove Cigarettes* (4 April 2012), *China – GOES* (18 October 2012), *Canada – Renewable Energy / Canada – Feed-in Tariff Program* (6 May 2013), *US – Countervailing and Anti-Dumping Measures (China)* (7 July 2014) and *US – Shrimp II (Vietnam)* (7 April 2015).

153 Calculations by the author based on data available on the WTO website.

154 See Raghu Ram (2018) for a detailed statistical analysis of delays in the WTO dispute settlement system (pp. 310 – 338), and a discussion of their reasons (pp. 343 – 363).

155 Communication of 30 May 2013 from the Appellate Body, The Workload of the Appellate Body (JOB/AB/1), published in the Appellate Body Annual Report for 2013, March 2014 (WT/AB/20), pp. 32 – 40. In the appellate proceedings in the case *US – Cool (Article 21.5 – Canada and Mexico)*, the Appellate Body in a letter of 2 March 2015 to the parties referred

two presentations by Director-General Roberto Azevêdo before the DSB in September 2014[156] and October 2015,[157] and in a speech by the US-appointed Appellate Body member Thomas R. Graham, then chairman of the Appellate Body, in November 2016,[158] all of which focus on the increasing workload. Updates on some of the figures put forward at the time can be found in regular WTO publications[159] and on the WTO website.[160] As far as the Appellate body is concerned, one has to look not only at the appellate level itself, but also at the panel level because increases at the panel level lead to increases at the appellate level, given that, on average, about two thirds of all panel reports are appealed.[161]

In order to determine workload, the obvious starting point is the number of cases. If one looks, for instance, at the overall number of active cases at any given time, one sees a surge of cases at the start of the system, with a rise from two cases in 1995 to 27 in 1999, then a period between roughly 2000 and 2012 where the numbers oscillate around 20 (with a high of 27 in 2005 and a low of 15 in 2009), and then, from 2012, a more or less continuous rise to a record

---

to this communication when it rejected a request of the parties to meet and discuss the date of circulation of the report (see Appellate Body report, *US – Cool (Article 21.5 – Canada and Mexico)*, para. 1.27).

156 Speech by Roberto Azevêdo of 26 September 2014 before the DSB, minutes of meeting (WT/DSB/M/350), para. 1.2; also available at http://www.wto.org/english/news_e/spra_e/spra32_e.htm, including tables mentioned in the speech, but not contained in the minutes.

157 Speech by Roberto Azevêdo of 28 October 2015 before the DSB, minutes of meeting (WT/DSB/M/369), para. 11.2; also published in the Appellate Body Annual Report for 2015, March 2016 (WT/AB/26), pp. 124 – 127, including an Annex with statistical data mentioned in the speech, but not contained in the minutes.

158 Graham (2016), in particular pp. 112 – 115; see also former Appellate Body member Sacerdoti (2017), pp 153 – 158.

159 For instance in the annual reports of the DSB and of the Appellate Body (e.g., DSB, Annual Report 2018, 30 November 2018 [WT/DSB/76], paras. 13.1 – 13.2; Appellate Body, Annual Report for 2018, March 2019 [WT/AB/29], pp. 13 – 15, 141 – 143). Furthermore, from the DSB meeting of 25 November 2015 until that of 27 March 2018, the DSB chairperson had reported in the regular DSB meetings on the dispute settlement workload (e.g., minutes of the DSB meetings of 25 November 2015 [WT/DSB/M/370], paras. 8.1 – 8.3, and 27 March 2018 [WT/DSB/M/410], paras. 12.1 – 12.2).

160 See, for instance, https://www.wto.org/english/tratop_e/dispu_e/dispustats_e.htm, Dispute settlement activity – some figures.

161 See Appellate Body Annual Report for 2018, March 2019 (WT/AB/29), p. 142 (Annex 8: Percentage of panel reports appealed by year of adoption: 1996 – 2018).

number of 42 cases in 2018.[162] Focusing on appellate proceedings, a similar pattern emerges. With regard to the number of appeals filed each year, at the beginning the numbers rose sharply from four in 1996 to 13 in 2000, followed by a general downward trend until 2013 (which saw only two appeals) interrupted by a few spikes (in 2005, 2008 and 2011), and after that, since 2014, a consistently high level of appeals (13 in 2014, eight a year from 2015 to 2017, and 12 in 2018).[163]

The recent upsurge in dispute settlement activity that is expressed in these figures goes some way to explain why the delays in appellate proceedings have grown worse since 2011, the year in which the practice of the Appellate Body regarding the 90-day deadline changed. However, they cannot explain the change in 2011 itself because at that time the number of appeals was not higher than in many years in the earlier period (compare, for instance, the years 1999 and 2000, in which nine and 13 appeals were filed, respectively, with 2010 and 2011, which saw three and nine appeals, respectively). To explain that change, one has to consider not only the total number of cases but also their complexity. Indicators of complexity include, among others, the number of claims as well as requests for procedural rulings (legal complexity), the number of exhibits (factual complexity), the number of parties (main parties and third parties), the length of submissions, and the length of reports. The communication of the Appellate Body of May 2013 mentioned above looks at these (and other) figures and compares the first 10 appeals filed at the start of the system with the last 10 appeals decided by the end of 2012, i.e., only a year after the change of 2011.[164] As to the panels whose reports were appealed, the communication states, for instance, that the average number of exhibits rose from 62 to 552 and that the average length of panel reports more than doubled to 364 pages. On the appellate level, the average number of issues raised increased from about eight to more than 13, the average number of third parties almost tripled to eight, the average number of pages of submissions filed more than doubled to 450, and the average length of Appellate Body reports more than quadrupled to almost 210.

---

162 https://www.wto.org/english/tratop_e/dispu_e/dispustats_e.htm, Dispute settlement activity – some figures, Chart 9: Average annual number of active proceedings per month 1995 – 2018.

163 Appellate Body, Annual Report for 2018, March 2019 (WT/AB/29), p. 140.

164 All the following figures can be found in the communication from the Appellate Body (supra, fn. 155), pp. 33 – 38.

With these facts on the practice under Art. 17.5 of the DSU and the workload of the dispute settlement system in mind, we now turn to the criticism by the US. From the very beginning of the Appellate Body's new approach to delays, namely first not mentioning consultations or agreements with the parties in its communications to the DSB and the report, and then no longer even consulting with or seeking the agreement of the parties, the US denounced this new approach. In the meetings in which the delayed Appellate Body reports circulated between June 2011 and June 2015 were adopted, the US criticized, in some cases sharply, that the Appellate Body no longer involved the parties in its decisions regarding the delays, demanding a return to the pre-2011 practice.[165] Some member states, such as Japan, supported the position of the US, whereas others, such as the EU, argued that the Appellate Body had no obligation to consult the parties or seek their agreement.[166] Importantly, though, the US did not criticize the delays as such, but only the lack of consultation and the failure to seek the agreement of the parties. Indeed, the US usually expressed understanding for the delays and emphasized that it would have agreed to a circulation of the report outside the 90-day deadline.[167]

165 See the minutes of the DSB meetings of 15 July 2011 (WT/DSB/M/299), para. 11; 28 July 2011 (WT/DSB/M/301), para. 11; 5 October 2011 (WT/DSB/M/304), paras. 4 – 6; 22 February 2012 (WT/DSB/M/312), para. 106; 23 March 2012 (WT/DSB/M/313), para. 74; 13 June 2012 (WT/DSB/M/317), para. 17; 23 July 2012 (WT/DSB/M/320), para. 97; 18 June 2014 (WT/DSB/M/346), para. 7.8; 19 December 2014 (WT/DSB/M/354), para. 1.12; 16 January 2015 (WT/DSB/M/355), paras. 1.16 – 1.17; 26 January 2015 (WT/DSB/M/356), para. 5.6; 29 May 2015 (WT/DSB/M/362), para. 1.19; and 19 June 2015 (WT/DSB/M/364), para. 7.8.

166 See, for instance, minutes of the DSB meetings of 5 October 2011 (WT/DSB/M/304), paras. 11 – 14 (Japan); 23 July 2012 (WT/DSB/M/313), paras. 101 (EU) and 103 (Japan); and 26 January 2015 (WT/DSB/M/356), paras. 5.9 (Japan) and 5.23 (EU).

167 See, for instance, minutes of the DSB meetings of 18 June 2014 (WT/DSB/M/346), para. 7.8 („*While the 90-day deadline in the DSU text was categorical, Members had an understanding of the workload challenges faced by the Appellate Body, and had been willing to agree to receive a report after this deadline*"); 19 December 2014 (WT/DSB/M/354), para. 1.13 („*The Appellate Body, of course, had good reason to go beyond 90 days in this dispute.*"); 16 January 2015 (WT/DSB/M/355), para. 1.16 („*Given the size and complexity of this dispute, as well as many other ongoing appeals, the United States of course would have been willing to positively consider a request from the Appellate Body to exceed the time-limit.*"); 29 May 2015 (WT/DSB/M/362), para. 1.19 („*The United States fully understood the difficulty that the Appellate Body had in meeting this 90-day deadline in this dispute, which was in part due to the fact that the disputing parties had requested a modified timeline for their submissions, among other legitimate reasons.*").

Then, for a period of almost three years, between June 2015 and May 2018, the delays were no longer criticized or discussed in the DSB meetings, neither by the US nor by any other member states (with one exception concerning the reasons stated by the Appellate Body for a delay),[168] despite the fact that delays were still continuously increasing. This changed in the DSB meeting of June 2018, when the US made an extended statement, which runs to six pages in the minutes of the meeting, on the 90-day deadline.[169] Subsequently, starting with the DSB meeting of 27 August 2018, the US cited the disregard of the 90-day deadline regularly as one of the reasons for blocking the appointment of Appellate Body members.[170] Moreover, in its statement of June 2018 the US altered the basic thrust of its criticism regarding Art. 17.5 of the DSU. While it repeated its earlier criticism that the Appellate Body no longer sought the agreement of the parties to a delay, the US now focused on the delays itself, and, contrary to its earlier statements in the DSB, no longer accepted that the delays were justifiable: *„The Appellate Body has for many years apparently considered that it is not possible to issue reports within the 90-day deadline. The United States has two reactions to that notion: first, we do not see objective evidence to support it; second, and more importantly, that it is not within the Appellate Body's authority to disregard or amend the DSU.“*[171] Concerning the first point the US did not mention any of the reasons for delays discussed above, but instead explained that it would have been well within the power of the Appellate Body to comply with the 90-day deadline if it had limited itself to dealing only with issues necessary to resolve the specific dispute rather than with all issues raised by the parties.[172] In other words, the US claimed that the main, if not the only reason for the delays was the Appellate Body's failure to refrain from unnecessary considerations.

In sum, the US criticism is based on three arguments: first, the Appellate Body could have avoided the delays if it had limited itself to addressing the issues necessary to resolve the dispute, second, regardless of the reasons of the delays the Appellate Body does not have the power to disregard Art. 17.5 of the DSU,

168 See minutes of the DSB meeting of 28 October 2015 (WT/DSB/M/369), paras. 9.4 – 9.6 and 9.9 – 9.12.
169 Minutes of the DSB meeting of 22 June 2018 (WT/DSB/M414), paras. 5.1 – 5.22.
170 See supra, fn. 84 – 85 and accompanying text.
171 Minutes of the DSB meeting of 22 June 2018 (WT/DSB/M414), para. 5.16.
172 Minutes of the DSB meeting of 22 June 2018 (WT/DSB/M414), paras. 5.16 – 5.19.

and, third, it should in any case have sought the agreement of the parties for issuing a report beyond the stipulated deadline.

The first argument is not only plainly implausible in the face of all the evidence discussed above, none of which the US even mentions in its statement of June 2018, but is also belied by the statements the US had made itself in the past. Before June 2018, it had never questioned that the delays were justified by legitimate reasons to a large degree beyond the control of the Appellate Body, and sometimes even had said so explicitly.[173] Similarly, when the Director-General made his presentation in September 2014 before the DSB on the increased workload of the dispute settlement system, in which he concluded, as far as the Appellate Body is concerned, that „*[a]ll these factors explain ... why the Appellate Body will need more than 90 days to complete some appeals over the coming months*",[174] the US supported the presentation and said that „*[i]t demonstrated in a graphical and numerical way what Members had known intuitively*".[175] And, again, after the presentation of the Director-General in October 2015 on the same topic before the DSB, in which he mentioned, among other things, that „*[t]he increased breadth and complexity of disputes over the last 20 years has changed the face of WTO dispute settlement completely*",[176] the US did not object, but rather commented that „*[g]iven resource constraints on the WTO and the projected level of activity for the WTO dispute settlement system going forward, it was the US sense that Members would all need to be creative in considering solutions to the problem of delays, in order to maintain an efficient and high-quality mechanism.*"[177]

Concerning the second argument, i.e., that it is not for the Appellate to decide whether to comply with the DSU's deadline, suffice it to say no one, including the Appellate Body, can be obligated to do the impossible („ultra posse nemo obligatur"). As Brazil put it in the DSB meeting of June 2018, „*[i]f Members were to add too much weight to the work of the Appellate Body and simply requested ‚prompt compliance', but would not compensate it with either additional time, better institutional conditions or a change in the way Members themselves would*

173 See for examples supra, fn. 167.
174 Minutes of the DSB meeting of 26 September 2014 (WT/DSB/M/350), para. 1.2, p. 3.
175 Minutes of the DSB meeting of 26 September 2014 (WT/DSB/M/350), para. 1.7.
176 Minutes of the DSB meeting of 28 October 2015 (WT/DSB/M/369), para. 11.2, p. 22.
177 Minutes of the DSB meeting of 28 October 2015 (WT/DSB/M/369), para. 11.16.

conduct their cases, Members would find out that something would have to give."[178]

The third argument, i.e., that an extension of the 90-day deadline should only be possible with the consent of the parties, has two problems. First, it would not address the ostensible concern of the US about strict compliance with the DSU because even with the consent of the parties Art. 17.5 of the DSU would still not be complied with. Neither Art. 17.5 of the DSU nor any other provision of the DSU provides for an exemption from the deadline if the parties so agree. Only a formal amendment of the DSU by the Ministerial Council or the General Council deciding with unanimity could accomplish that.[179] Second, as pointed out by the EU, Brazil and China in the DSB meeting of June 2018,[180] requiring that the parties would have to consent to any delay would undermine the negative consensus rule of Art. 17.14 of the DSU, i.e., the rule that panel and Appellate Body reports will be adopted unless there is a consensus of all members not do so. If a party would refuse to consent after the 90-day deadline had passed, it could in effect block the adoption of the report. Moreover, knowing that, a party who is threatened to lose its case before the Appellate Body would have an incentive to delay the appellate proceedings in order to get them past the 90-day deadline and thus enable it to veto the report. Already before June 2018, the possible impact on Art. 17.14 of the DSU had been one of the reasons for a number of member states to reject the US demand for party consent.[181] Additionally, in 2012 it had forced the US, Canada, and Mexico as parties in the appellate proceedings in the case *US – COOL* to withdraw a proposal for a DSB decision authorizing a delay that had occurred in those proceedings,[182] even though these three countries had tried to allay

178 Minutes of the DSB meeting of 22 June 2018 (WT/DSB/M/414), para. 5.30.

179 Art. X:8 of the WTO Agreement, second sentence, in conjunction with, as far as the General Council is concerned, Art. IV:2 of the WTO Agreement, second sentence.

180 Minutes of the DSB meeting of 22 June 2018 (WT/DSB/M/414), paras. 5.25 (EU), 5.31 (Brazil), and 5.56 (China).

181 See minutes of the DSB meetings of 23 July 2012 (WT/DSB/M/320), paras. 101 (EU), 106 (Brazil) and 108 (China); 18 June 2014 (WT/DSB/M/346), paras. 7.9 (Guatemala) and 7.9 (EU); 26 January 2015 (WT/DSB/M/356), para. 5.23 (EU); and 19 June 2015 (WT/DSB/M/364), para. 7.14 (India).

182 See communication of 28 June 2012 from Canada, Mexico and the US, *US – COOL*, Joint request for a decision by the DSB (WT/DS/384/15 and WR/DS386/14); minutes of the DSB meeting of 10 July 2012 (WT/DSB/M/319), p. 1 (withdrawal of the draft decision) and paras. 10 – 16 (statements by the US, Canada and Mexico on the draft decision); minutes

fears about Art. 17.14 of the DSU by stating that „*[t]o be clear, there had never been any question that the three sponsors of the draft decision wished to cast doubt on one of the most important features of the WTO dispute settlement system – negative consensus for the adoption of reports.*“[183] By contrast, in the DSB meeting of June 2018 the US attacked Art. 17.14 of the DSU head-on, by claiming, for the first time, that „*[t]he consequence of the Appellate Body choosing to breach DSU rules and issue a report after the 90-day deadline would be that this report no longer qualifies as an Appellate Body report for purposes of the exceptional negative consensus adoption procedure of Article 17.14 of the DSU.*“[184] Of the 14 members who took the floor at the meeting in response to the US statement, not one supported the US position that a failure to meet the 90-day deadline would change the adoption procedure, and nine explicitly rejected it.[185] The opponents rightly observed that Art. 17.5 of the DSU does not specify any consequence for failing to comply with the deadline, and Art. 17.14 of the DSU does not make the negative consensus rule dependent on any conditions, such as meeting the deadline of Art. 17.5 of the DSU. In any event, the „*conclusions [drawn by the US regarding Art. 17.14 of the DSU] were vastly disproportionate to the issue at hand*“, i.e., the failure to observe the deadline of Art. 17.5 of the DSU.[186]

In summary, the Appellate Body has indeed failed to comply with the 90-day deadline of Art. 17.5 of the DSU, rarely until 2010, frequently between 2011 and 2015, and consistently since 2015. However, the reasons for this failure were largely beyond the control of the Appellate Body, namely the increased workload due to the increased number and especially the increased complexity of disputes. This has been repeatedly acknowledged by the membership, including the US. It was only in June 2018 that the US changed course and

of the DSB meeting of 22 June 2018 (WT/DSB/M/414), para. 5.48 (statement of Mexico on the reasons for the withdrawal of the draft decision in 2012).

183 Minutes of the DSB meeting of 10 July 2012 (WT/DSB/M/319), para. 14 (statement of Canada).

184 Minutes of meeting (WT/DSB/M/414), paras. 5.21. On the US arguments and actions regarding Art. 17.14 of the DSU, see further supra, fn. 61 and accompanying text.

185 Minutes of the DSB meeting of 22 June 2018 (WT/DSB/M/414), paras. 5.23 – 5.62; the nine members who explicitly opposed the US view on Art. 17.14 of the DSU were the EU (para. 5.25), Brazil (para. 5.32), New Zealand (para. 5.34), Canada (para. 5.40), Norway (para. 5.41), Mexico (para. 5.51), Uruguay (para. 5.59), Guatemala (para. 5.60) and Thailand (para. 5.62).

186 Minutes of the DSB meeting of 22 June 2018 (WT/DSB/M/414), para. 5.32 (statement of Brazil).

suddenly claimed, without even mentioning the workload problems, that the Appellate Body could have complied with the deadline if only it had wanted to. Before June 2018, the only complaint of the US had been that the Appellate Body in 2011 had changed its practice of asking the parties to consent to an extension of the deadline. However, the DSU does not allow the parties to extend the deadline, so their consent would not address the alleged concern of the US with strict compliance with the DSU. For all these reasons, the failure of the Appellate Body to observe the 90-day deadline of Art. 17.5 of the DSU cannot justify the blockage of appointments to the Appellate Body.

3. Advisory opinions

In the DSB meeting of 29 October 2018, the US made an extended statement on the issuance of advisory opinion on issues not necessary to resolve the dispute.[187] It defined advisory opinion as „*a non-binding statement on a point of law given by* [*an adjudicator*] *before a case is tried or with respect to a hypothetical situation.*“[188] It argued that advisory opinions „*breached WTO rule*“[189] and that the Appellate Body had repeatedly issued such advisory opinions in violation of WTO law.[190] In case a party should appeal an issue that is not necessary to resolve the dispute, the Appellate Body is, according to the US, under an obligation to exercise judicial economy, that is, to refuse to rule on the issue. The US raised the question of advisory opinions not only in the

187 Minutes of the DSB meeting of 29 October 2018 (WT/DSB/M/420), paras. 4.2 – 4.19. Sometimes the US also uses the term obiter dicta instead of advisory opinions (see, e.g., idem, para. 4.17). For a discussion of the concept of obiter dicta in the context of WTO dispute settlement, see Gao (2018) and Sacerdoti (2018) (both arguing against the US position on obiter dicta).

188 Minutes of the DSB meeting of 29 October 2018 (WT/DSB/M/420), para. 4.2, quoting Oxford Dictionaries, „advisory opinion“ (https://en.oxforddictionaries.com/definition/advisory_opinion).

189 Minutes of the DSB meeting of 29 October 2018 (WT/DSB/M/420), para. 4.2.

190 Minutes of the DSB meeting of 29 October 2018 (WT/DSB/M/420), paras. 4.2 and 4.13 – 4.18; as examples of such alleged breaches the US names five Appellate Body reports, namely *US – Continued Suspension / Canada – Continued Suspension* (paras. 4.15 – 4.16), *China – Publications and Audiovisual Products* (para. 4.17), *Argentina – Financial Services* (para. 4.17), *Indonesia – Import Licensing Regimes* (para. 4.17) and *EC – PET (Pakistan)* (para. 4.18).

current appointment crisis, it was also one of the major reasons why the US had vetoed the reappointment of Appellate Body member Chang in 2016.[191]

For a better understanding of the US criticism, we will briefly set out three of the instances that the US considers to be illegitimate advisory opinions. In *China – Publications and Audiovisual Products*,[192] the US had challenged certain Chinese measures regulating the importation and distribution of publications and audiovisual products.[193] In particular, the US had claimed that some of these measures violated trading commitments undertaken by China in its Accession Protocol. In its defense, China had argued that any inconsistency of its measures with the trading commitments under its Accession Protocol could be justified as being necessary to protect public morals pursuant to Art. XX(a) of the GATT. The US in turn had stated that Art. XX of the GATT could not be invoked as a defense to a breach of the trading commitments under China's Accession Protocol. The panel had left open the question whether Art. XX of the GATT was available as a defense and had instead addressed the question whether, assuming the availability of the defense (ad arguendo argument), the conditions of Art. XX(a) of the GATT were met in this case. Finding that these conditions were not met anyway, it then declared that it would not be necessary to rule on the availability of Art. XX of the GATT as a defense, that is, it exercised judicial economy. On Art. XX of the GATT, China appealed the panel's finding that the conditions of Art. XX(a) of the GATT were not satisfied, and, furthermore, asked the Appellate Body to complete the analysis and find that Art. XX of the GATT was available for justifying breaches of trading commitments of China's Accession Protocol. Unlike the panel, the Appellate Body decided to start its analysis with the availability of Art. XX of

191 See minutes of the DSB meeting of 23 May 2016 (WT/DSB/M/379), statement of the US, paras. 6.2 – 6.7 („*The role of the Appellate Body as part of the WTO's dispute settlement system was to decide appeals of panel reports to help achieve ‚[t]he aim of the dispute settlement mechanism ... to secure a positive solution to a dispute', as set out in DSU Article 3.7. ... Yet the reports on which this member [i.e., Chang] had participated did not accord with the role of the Appellate Body.*" [para. 6.3]; „*WTO adjudicators should be focused on addressing those issues necessary to resolve the dispute.*" [para. 6.7]); see further on the US veto of the reappointment of Chang supra, Chapter II.

192 For US criticism of the Appellate Body report in this case, see minutes of the DSB meetings of 29 October 2018 (WT/DSB/M/420), para. 4.17; and 19 January 2010 (WT/DSB/M/278), para. 77.

193 For a summary of the facts of the case and the decision of the panel, see Appellate Body report, *China – Publications and Audiovisual Products*, paras. 1 – 10.

the GATT as a defense,[194] and only afterwards addressed the conditions of Art. XX(a) of the GATT. It found that the defense was available,[195] but, like the panel, concluded that its conditions were not met.[196] In light of this conclusion, the finding on the availability of the defense was not relevant for the question whether China had violated its WTO obligations.

The second example is the report of the Appellate Body in the case *Argentina – Financial Services.*[197] In that case, Panama had challenged a number of measures by Argentina which restricted certain financial services from Panama.[198] According to Argentina, these measures were aimed at preventing tax evasion, tax avoidance and fraud, and Panama had been subject to these measures because it had been qualified by Argentina as non-cooperative in Argentina's campaign to protect its tax base. Panama claimed that the measures violated Art. II:1 of the GATS (most-favored nation principle) and Art. XVII of the GATS (national treatment) because its services were treated less favorably than like services from countries qualified as cooperative and like domestic Argentinian services. Argentina not only denied a violation of Arts. II:1 and XVII of the GATS, but also argued that even if there were such violations, they could be justified either by Art. XIV(c) of the GATS as measures necessary to secure compliance with its tax laws or by the prudential carve-out of Paragraph 2(a) of the GATS Annex on Financial Services. The panel found that although there was no violation of Art. XVII of the GATS, all measures were inconsistent with Art. II:1 of the GATS, and that these inconsistencies could not be justified by either Art. XIV(c) of the GATS or by Paragraph 2(a) of the GATS Annex on Financial Services. The parties appealed the panel's findings on „likeness" and „treatment no less favorable" under Arts. II:1 and XVII of the GATS as well as on the justifications of Art. XIV(d) of the GATS and Paragraph 2(a) of the GATS Annex on Financial Services. On „likeness", the Appellate Body reversed the panel's findings that the financial services and service suppliers of non-cooperative countries, such as Panama, were like such services and services suppliers from cooperative countries, in the sense of Art. II:1 of the GATS, or

194 *China – Publications and Audiovisual Products,* paras. 205 – 213.

195 *China – Publications and Audiovisual Products,* paras. 214 – 233.

196 *China – Publications and Audiovisual Products,* paras. 234 – 337.

197 For US criticism of this Appellate Body report, see minutes of the DSB meetings of 29 October 2018 (WT/DSB/M/420), para. 4.17; 23 May 2016 (WT/DSB/M/379), para. 6.4; and 9 May 2016 (WT/DSB/M/378), para. 2.6.

198 For a summary of the facts of the case and the decision of the panel, see Appellate Body report, *Argentina – Financial Services,* paras. 1.1 – 1.7.

from Argentina, in the sense of Art. XVII of the GATT.[199] Since there was no likeness, there could be no violation of Art. II:1 of the GATS or Art. XVII of the GATT. Consequently, any findings on „treatment no less favorable“ under Art. II:1 or Art. XVII of the GATS as well as on the justifications for inconsistencies with Art. II:1 or Art. XVII of the GATS were no longer required for the overall conclusion that there was no breach of WTO law by Argentina. Accordingly, the Appellate Body explicitly declared moot all findings of the panel on „treatment no less favorable“ and on the justifications pursuant to Art. XIV of the GATS and Paragraph 2(a) of the GATS Annex on Financial Services.[200] However, it then moved on and ruled on the appeals of all these moot panel findings anyway.[201]

The first two examples were about cases in which the Appellate Body made findings on issues that were not necessary for determining whether a member state had violated WTO law. The final example, *EU – PET (Pakistan)*, pertains to a situation in which, despite a finding of a breach of WTO law, no recommendation under Art. 19.1 of the DSU that the member state concerned should bring the WTO-inconsistent measure into compliance with WTO law is required. In that dispute, Pakistan had challenged the imposition of countervailing duties on PET from Pakistan by the EU as being inconsistent with the WTO Agreement on Subsidies and Countervailing Measures (SCMA).[202] After the panel in this case had been established by the DSB in March 2015, the EU in March 2016 had asked the panel to cease its work because the challenged measure had expired in September 2015. Pakistan had acknowledged the expiration of the measure, but still insisted that the panel rule on whether the

199 *Argentina – Financial Services*, paras. 6.1 – 6.80.

200 *Argentina – Financial Services*, para. 6.83.

201 *Argentina – Financial Services*, paras. 6.84 (explanation why it addressed an appeal of findings which it had declared to be moot) and 6.85 – 6.272 (analysis of „treatment no less favorable“, Art. XIV(c) of the GATS, and Paragraph 2(a) of the GATS Annex on Financial Services). Pablo Bentes, who was one of the attorneys representing Argentina in this appeal, later claimed that in the oral hearing of this appeal it had been the US that had urged the Appellate Body to rule on Paragraph 2(a) of the GATS Annex on Financial Services, a ruling the US later condemned as an advisory opinion (Bentes [2017], p. 2). However, according to that oral hearing's opening statement by the US that is made available on the USTR website, the US explicitly asked the Appellate Body not to rule on that issue (https://ustr.gov/sites/default/files/enforcement/DS/US.3rd.Ptcpt.Oral.Statement.pdf, paras. 1 – 5).

202 For a summary of the facts of the case and the decision of the panel, see Appellate Body report, *EU – PET (Pakistan)*, paras. 1.1 – 1.11.

measure had violated the SCMA. The panel denied the EU's request, and in its report found a number of violations of the SCMA, but, given that the measure had already expired, made no recommendation pursuant to Art. 19.1 of the DSU that the EU should bring the measure into conformity with the SCMA. On appeal, the EU argued that the panel should not have made findings on a measure that had already expired, and asked the Appellate Body to reverse the panel report in its entirety. The Appellate Body rejected that request, and found that the expiration of a measure in itself is not sufficient to deprive a panel of jurisdiction to make findings on the consistency of that measure with WTO law.[203] Then it addressed the parties' appeals on issues regarding the SCMA, but, although it upheld certain of the panel findings on violations of the SCMA, it, like the panel, made no recommendation pursuant to Art. 19.1 of the DSU because of the expiration of the challenged measure.[204] Even though in this case there was no question that the Appellate Body's findings were necessary for a determination whether WTO law had been breached, the US nevertheless criticized them as illegitimate advisory opinions because due to the expiration of the measure Pakistan had not asked for a recommendation according to Art. 19.1 of the DSU, a fact which the US read as confirmation that there was no longer a dispute between the parties.[205]

Based on these examples, what the US considers illegitimate advisory opinions by panels and the Appellate Body can be defined as any rulings on legal issues *„that would not assist the DSB in making a recommendation [under Art. 19.1 of the DSU] to bring a WTO-inconsistent measure into compliance with WTO rules“,*[206] in particular rulings on issues that are not necessary for a finding on whether a member state has violated WTO law.

Why does the US believe that such rulings are prohibited by the DSU? It offers a number of arguments. It states that the primary purpose of the DSU is the settlement of specific disputes between member states, rather than the abstract clarification of legal issues, and in support of that proposition it invokes

203 *EU – PET (Pakistan)*, paras. 5.1 – 5.53, followed by a dissenting opinion on this issue by one member of the Appellate Body division, paras. 5.54 – 5.61.

204 *EU – PET (Pakistan)*, paras. 6.10 (upholding a panel finding on violations of the SCMA) and 6.16 (no recommendation under Art. 19.1 of the DSU).

205 See minutes of the DSB meetings of 29 October 2018 (WT/DSB/M/420), para. 4.18; and 28 May 2018 (WT/DSB/M/413), paras. 10.5 – 10.9

206 Minutes of the General Council meeting of 12 December 2018 (WT/GC/M/175), statement of the US, para. 6.166.

several DSU provisions that emphasize dispute resolution, in particular Art. 3.3 („*prompt settlement [of disputes] is essential to the effective function of the WTO*"), Art. 3.4 („*[r]ecommendations or rulings made by the DSB shall be aimed at a satisfactory settlement of [disputes]*") and Art. 3.7 („*[t]he aim of the dispute settlement mechanism is to secure a positive solution to a dispute*"). Furthermore, the US points out that the DSU does not explicitly provide for the possibility of advisory opinions, in contrast to founding agreements of other international tribunals, such as the International Court of Justice[207] or the European Court of Human Rights.[208] In addition, it stresses that while the dispute settlement system, including the Appellate Body, should be focused on settling disputes, the task of abstract interpretations has explicitly been reserved to the Ministerial Conference and the General Council, i.e., the members themselves.[209] According to Art. IX:2 of the WTO Agreement, „*[t]he Ministerial Conference and the General Council shall have the exclusive authority to adopt interpretations of this Agreement and of the Multilateral Trade Agreements.*" This exclusive power of the members under Art. XI:2 of the WTO Agreement is confirmed in Art. 3.9 of the DSU.[210] Finally, the US highlights that in the early case *US – Wool Shirts and Blouses* of 1997, the Appellate Body itself had declared that panels are allowed to practice judicial economy,[211] meaning that they are not under an obligation „*to examine all legal claims made by the complaining parties.*"[212] Like the US, the Appellate Body emphasized that „*the basic aim of dispute settlement in the WTO is to settle disputes*", and, even though Art. 3.2 of the DSU states that the dispute settlement system „*serves ... to clarify the existing provisions of [the WTO agreements]*", the Appellate Body famously pronounced in that case that „*[g]iven the explicit aim of dispute settlement that permeates the DSU, we do not consider that Article 3.2 of the DSU is meant to encourage either panels or the Appellate Body to „make law" by clarifying existing provisions of the WTO Agreement outside the context of resolving a particular dispute. A panel need only address those claims which must*

207 See Art. 96 of the Charter of the United Nations and Arts. 65 – 68 of the Statute of the International Court of Justice.

208 See Art. 47 of the European Convention of Human Rights.

209 Minutes of the DSB meeting of 29 October 2018 (WT/DSB/M/420), para. 4.3.

210 „*The provisions of this Understanding are without prejudice to the rights of Members to seek authoritative interpretation of provisions of a covered agreement through decision-making under the WTO Agreement ... .*"

211 Minutes of the DSB meeting of 29 October 2018 (WT/DSB/M/420), para. 4.8.

212 *US – Wool Shirts and Blouses*, p. 339.

be addressed in order to resolve the matter in issue in the dispute."[213] In addition to these legal arguments, the US also makes policy arguments against advisory opinions. For instance, it points out that such advisory opinions increase the time required for appellate proceedings, which goes against the objective of speedy dispute resolution.[214]

What are the merits of these arguments? To begin with, it is worth emphasizing that no one, including the Appellate Body, claims that panels or the Appellate Body have the power to give advisory opinions independently of any specific dispute. The controversy is only about the more limited question whether the Appellate Body may make findings on legal issues that arise in a specific dispute between member states, but that are not necessary for determining whether WTO law was violated and whether a recommendation under Art. 19.1 of the DSU should be issued. As to this more limited question, there are at least five counterarguments to the position of the US: First, Art. 17.12 of the DSU obligates the Appellate Body to address each issue raised by the parties; second, contributing to a positive resolution to a dispute might go beyond the finding of a WTO violation and making a recommendation under Art. 19.1 of the DSU; third, according to Art. 3.2 of the DSU the dispute settlement system is a central element in providing security and predictability and serves to clarify the provisions of the WTO Agreements; fourth, there is no conflict between Art. IX:2 of the WTO Agreement and Appellate Body findings on issues not necessary to resolve a dispute; and, fifth, the US arguments regarding recommendations under Art. 19.1 of the DSU are at least partly self-contradictory. We will address each of these arguments in turn.

Starting with the first counterargument, the DSU provision most directly addressing the question which issues the Appellate Body should or could deal with is Art. 17.12 in conjunction with Art. 17.6. Art. 17.12 of the DSU stipulates that „*[t]he Appellate Body shall address each of the issues raised in accordance with paragraph 6 during the appellate proceeding*", and Art. 17.6 of the DSU, to which Art. 17.12 of the DSU refers, states „*[a]n appeal shall be limited to issues of law covered in the panel report and legal interpretations developed by the panel.*" A plain reading of these provision indicates that the Appellate Body is under an obligation („*shall*") to deal with any legal issue contained in a panel report and appealed by a party. This would mean that the Appellate Body is not

213 *US – Wool Shirts and Blouses*, p. 340.

214 Minutes of DSB meeting of 29 October 2018 (WT/DSB/M/420), para. 4.19.

allowed to refuse to rule on such an issue appealed by a party, even if it is not necessary to decide that issue in order to make a finding on whether there was a violation of WTO law. In other words, these provisions seem to prohibit the practice of judicial economy at the appellate level. This finds support in the history of the Uruguay Round negotiations, during which a proposal that would have given the Appellate Body the power to decline ruling on an appeal was considered, but not accepted.[215] And, apparently, this was also the view of the early Appellate Body. Notably, in its first ruling on the practice of judicial economy in *US – Wool Shirts and Blouses*, on which the US relies, the Appellate Body referred to the exercise of judicial economy by a panel, not by the Appellate Body itself, and, in contrast to Art. 17.12 of the DSU, there is no provision in the DSU that obliges a panel to address every issue raised by a party.[216] James Bacchus, one of the Appellate Body members who sat on the division of *US – Wool Shirts and Blouses*, said in a roundtable discussion in 2005 that „*there's the issue of judicial economy and there is a very real contrast between the discretion that is allowed under the DSU to panels not to rule on all of the legal issues that have been raised in particular claims in a particular dispute, and the absence of any such discretion on the part of the Appellate Body in an automatic appeal.*"[217] Bacchus's view was supported in that roundtable by former Appellate Body member Mitsuo Matsushita, who also sat on the *US – Wool Shirts and Blouses* division.[218] Moreover, as far as panels are concerned,

---

215 See communication of 28 June 1990 from Canada (MTN.GNG/NG13/W/41), p. 4: „*The Appellate Body would examine the questions raised by the appellant and would decide whether the case merited an appellate review.*" This proposal did not find its way into the final agreement.

216 Art. 7.2 of the DSU states that „[*p*]*anels shall address the relevant provisions in any covered agreement or agreements cited by the parties to the dispute*". This obligation of panels is narrower in at least two respects than that of the Appellate Body under Art. 17.12 of the DSU, namely, first, it refers only to „*provisions*" and not to the broader concepts of „*issues*", and, second, panels only have to address those provisions cited by the parties which are „*relevant*", whereas Art. 17.12 of the DSU does not limit the appealed issues to be addressed to the relevant ones.

217 American Society of International Law (ASIL), Annual Meeting, 1 April 2005, WTO Appellate Body Roundtable, transcript, pp. 28 – 29.

218 ASIL (supra, fn. 217), pp. 27 – 28: „*Now about the judicial economy: The DSU says that the Appellate Body needs to address each issue that was raised. Thus, compared with panels, the Appellate Body needs to deal with every issue. So judicial economy is not a privilege of the Appellate Body, at least in theory. But as far as the practical aspect is concerned, if you have say 20 issues, you might deal with some important issues heavily and deal with some other issues lightly.*"

even though the Appellate Body declared that panels are under no obligation to address all issues raised by the parties, it did not go so far as to say that panels are under an obligation to exercise judicial economy whenever a finding is not necessary for determining whether there was a violation of WTO law. In its report in *Australia – Salmon* of 1998, the Appellate Body emphasized that panels have discretion to decide which findings might be helpful in resolving a dispute between the parties[219] and it warned against the use of *„false judicial economy"*.[220] And in its report in *US – Lead and Bismuth II* of 2000, the Appellate Body explicitly rejected the argument of the US in that case that the Appellate Body's *„[r]eport in United States – Shirts and Blouses sets forth a general principle that panels may not address any issues that need not be addressed in order to resolve the dispute between the parties."*[221] It was only in the report in *US – Upland Cotton* of 2005, ten years after the establishment of the WTO dispute settlement system, that the Appellate Body for the first time explicitly addressed the question whether it was allowed to exercise judicial economy of its own, and, contrary to the views of the founding Appellate Body members mentioned above (which in 2005 were no longer on the Appellate Body), found that it had this power (although, like the panels, no obligation to exercise it).[222] In a recent report of 2018, the Appellate Body summarized its jurisprudence on this issue as follows: *„[W]hile the Appellate Body is required to address each issue on appeal, it has the discretion not to rule on an issue when doing so is not necessary to resolve the dispute, but the Appellate Body may rule*

219 *Australia – Salmon*, paras. 219 – 226.

220 *Australia – Salmon*, para. 223.

221 *US – Lead and Bismuth II*, para. 71; see also Appellate Body report, *Canada – Wheat Exports and Grain Imports*, para. 133: *„Although the doctrine of judicial economy allows a panel to refrain from addressing claims beyond those necessary to resolve the dispute, it does not compel a panel to exercise such restraint."*

222 See Appellate Body report, *US – Upland Cotton*, paras. 508 – 511, 743 – 748 and 761 – 762; see on the development of the Appellate Body's jurisprudence on judicial economy at the appellate level Alvarez-Jimenez (2009). Even before *US – Upland Cotton*, there are few cases in which the Appellate Body exercised judicial economy, without though, explicitly addressing the question whether it was allowed to do so (see, for instance, *Japan – Agricultural Products II*, paras. 139 and 143, and *Canada – Diary*, para. 124). Presumably, in these early cases the parties who had appealed the issues on which the Appellate Body exercised judicial economy had not insisted on a ruling, whereas in *Upland – Cotton*, the parties, the US and Brazil, had disagreed on whether the Appellate Body was allowed (or obligated) to exercise judicial economy (see, in particular, paras. 743 – 748 of that report).

on such an issue in light of the specific circumstances of a given dispute."[223] This practice of judicial economy at the appellate level has been described in the literature as „*difficult to reconcile ... with the provisions of Article 17 [of the DSU]*",[224] or even as „*judge-made*" and not „*rest[ing] on the provisions of the treaties*".[225]

The US is, of course, well aware of the requirement of Art. 17.12 of the DSU that the Appellate Body „*shall address*" each issue appealed by a party. However, relying on the dictionary definition of the word „address" as „*to [t]hink about and begin to deal with (an issue or problem)*",[226] it argues that „*to address an issue was not necessarily to resolve that issue*", and points to the fact that „*panels and the Appellate Body had often „addressed" an issue through the exercise of judicial economy*".[227] In support, the US quotes from the Appellate Body report in *US – Wool Shirts and Blouses* that „*[a] panel need only address those claims which must be addressed in order to resolve the matter in issue in the dispute.*"[228] The quoted sentence itself shows, though, that, at least at that time, the Appellate Body understood exercising judicial economy as *not* addressing an issue. Put differently, addressing an issue meant for the Appellate Body ruling on or resolving that issue. And, indeed, reading the language „*shall address*" an issue as permitting the Appellate Body to say nothing about the issue apart from saying that it is not necessary to say anything about it seems an exceedingly narrow understanding of that term. A more natural way to read Art. 17.12 of the DSU is that intends to give each party to a case the right to have any issue of law covered by the panel addressed in a meaningful fashion, i.e., to rule on it, rather than leaving it to the Appellate Body to decide whether

223 *US – Tuna II (Mexico) (Article 21.5 – US) / US – Tuna II (Mexico) (Article 21.5 – Mexico II)*, para. 6.138.

224 Roessler (2017), p. 112.

225 McRea (2006), pp. 361 – 362; see also Babu (2016), p. 508.

226 Minutes of the DSB meeting of 29 October 2018 (WT/DSB/M/420), statement of the US, para. 4.8, citing Oxford Dictionaries, „address" (third definition) (https://en.oxforddictionaries.com/definition/address); other common dictionaries define the relevant meaning of address not as „to begin to deal with", but simply as „to deal with" (see Merriam-Webster dictionary, definition 2b, „to deal with : treat", https://www.merriam-webster.com/dictionary/address; Cambridge dictionary, definition C1, „to give attention to or deal with a matter or problem", https://dictionary.cambridge.org/dictionary/englisch/address).

227 Minutes of the DSB meeting of 29 October 2018 (WT/DSB/M/420), statement of the US, para. 4.8; see for a similar argument Van den Bossche/Zdouc (2017), p. 243.

228 *US – Wool Shirts and Blouses*, p. 340.

it thinks it necessary to deal with the issue. To quote again from the 2005 statement of former Appellate Body member James Buchanan referred to above: „*The parties themselves choose the legal issues that are raised on appeal. ... They make their own decisions about what issues they want to raise on appeal and then when those issues are raised under Article 17 of the DSU. Under that provision, the Appellate Body is required – ‚shall address' – every legal issue that is raised on appeal. I have heard one or two law professors argue that the Appellate Body, despite this clear language, is not required to address those issues. But I do not know of any member of the WTO that feels that way. If the European Union or Japan or the United States raised a legal issue on appeal and the Appellate Body refused to rule on it, I think you would hear about that in the DSB meeting afterwards, and rightfully so.*“[229] Finally, the narrow reading propagated by the US can create a conflict with Art. 17.13 of the DSU, i.e., the paragraph following right after Art. 17.12 of the DSU, which states: „*The Appellate Body may uphold, modify or reverse the legal findings and conclusions of the panel*“. Upholding, modifying or reversing a legal finding requires forming a view on whether that finding is right or wrong. However, since exercising judicial economy means not ruling on the substance of a legal finding, there is no such judgment. Consequently, in cases in which the Appellate exercises judicial economy with regard to a legal finding of a panel, it does not uphold, modify or reverse that finding, but rather declares it to be „*moot and having no legal effect*“, which is contrary to the wording of Art. 17.13 of the DSU.[230]

Turning to the second counterargument, even if one accepts the US argument that the Appellate Body is not allowed to rule on every issue appealed by the parties, but only on those necessary to resolve the dispute, it does not follow that the Appellate Body may only make findings on those issues that are necessary for determining whether WTO law was violated and whether a recommendation under Art. 19.1 of the DSU is called for. This would only be true if any other finding could not make any contribution to the resolution of a dispute. This is obviously not the case, though. The dispute *China – Publications and Audiovisual Products*, which has been briefly outlined above, serves as a good illustration of this point. As explained, the question of whether Art.

229 ASIL (supra, fn. 217), p. 9. See also Bacchus (2005), p. 507: „*Nor does the Appellate Body have the authority under the DSU to refuse to 'address' a legal issue when it is appealed. ... A refusal by the Appellate Body to rule on a legal issue raised on appeal in dispute settlement would not help 'secure a positive solution to a dispute'.*“

230 WTO (2017), p. 119, fn. 307; Roessler (2017), p. 112.

XX of the GATT was available as a defense to China did not matter for a finding of violation of WTO law, since the conditions of Art. XX of the GATT were not met anyway. However, this question did matter for China's implementation of the resulting DSB recommendation. The panel and the Appellate Body had found that China had violated the trading commitments under its Accession Protocol. If the defense was not available, the only way for China to comply with the DSB ruling would have been to open its market and thus to honor its trading commitments. By contrast, if the defense was available, China could have alternatively focused on changing its restrictions in a way that ensured compliance with the conditions of Art. XX of the GATT. And indeed, in support of its decision to rule on the availability of the defense, the Appellate Body emphasized that leaving this issue open „*may not assist in the resolution of this dispute, in particular because such an approach risks creating uncertainty with respect to China's implementation obligations.*"[231] Such uncertainty might have led to a continuation of the dispute, in particular if China had chosen to implement the ruling by adapting its measure so that it met the conditions of Art. XX of the GATT, and the US had insisted that the defense was not available.

The third counterargument is based on Art. 3.2 of the DSU, which provides, in relevant part: „*The dispute settlement system of the WTO is a central element in providing security and predictability to the multilateral trading system. The Members recognize that it serves ... to clarify the existing provisions of* [*the WTO*] *agreements*". These statements strongly indicate that the purpose of rulings of panels and the Appellate Body is not only to resolve specific disputes, but also to clarify the meaning of WTO law more generally, for all WTO member states, and thereby make WTO law and thus the multilateral trading system more secure and predictable. Clarifying the law going forward is, indeed, a general function of adjudicatory bodies, in addition to the function of resolving specific disputes. This is particularly true for higher adjudicatory bodies within a hierarchical system, such as the Appellate Body as the second and final instance of adjudication within the WTO dispute settlement system. If one ac-

231 *China – Publications and Audiovisual Products*, para. 215. For another example see Appellate Body report, *Indonesia – Import Licensing Regimes*, para. 5.63: „[*W*]*hile our ruling on Article XI:2*(*c*) *may not directly change the recommendations and rulings by the DSB ... , the question as to whether Indonesia can in the future invoke Article XI:2*(*c*)(*ii*) *... could affect the manner in which it can comply with the recommendations and rulings by the DSB.*"

cepts this additional function of the WTO dispute settlement system and particular its Appellate Body, then it is entirely proper for the Appellate Body to rule on issues that are not necessary to resolve the dispute, as long as they have been raised by a party pursuant to Art. 17.12 of the DSU, and make a contribution to clarifying open issues of WTO law, such as, for example, in the case *Argentina – Financial Services* outlined above. It is noteworthy that even the US itself in the past has sometimes explicitly asked for such clarification on issues not necessary to resolve the dispute at hand. For instance, in the case *US – Steel Safeguards*, the Appellate Body explained: „*[N]one of the participants appeared to disagree that ... it would not be necessary for us to rule on the claims raised on causation. Nevertheless, several participants expressed an interest in having us rule on causation as it would provide guidance to Members on applying safeguard measures in the future consistently with their WTO obligations. The United States expressed a strong preference for us to rule on causation, stating that ‚[it would] be important for us in terms of understanding what our obligations are under the Agreement [on Safeguards] and what we have to do to comply with them'.*"[232]

Fourth, what about the argument of the US that, pursuant to Art. IX:2 of the WTO Agreement, only the member states, sitting as Ministerial Conference or as General Council, have the power to adopt abstract interpretations? The US seems to imply that rulings on issues that are not necessary for a determination of whether WTO law was breached and whether a recommendation according to Art. 19.1 of the DSU should be made are like abstract interpretations under IX:2 of the WTO Agreement and thus illegitimately interfere with the powers of the member states. However, such Appellate Body rulings are still made in the context of a specific dispute, based on the facts and circumstances of that case, and are thus not abstract interpretations like those under IX:2 of the WTO Agreement.[233] Furthermore, no one, including the Appellate Body, contends that panels and the Appellate Body would not be bound by authoritative interpretations adopted pursuant to Art. IX:2 of the WTO Agreement. For these reasons there is no conflict between Art. IX:2 of the

232 *US – Steel Safeguards*, para. 484. For another example see Appellate Body report, *China – Publications and Audiovisual Products*, para. 238: „*In response to questioning at the oral hearing in this appeal, the United States clarified that it is not raising a claim of error with respect to the way in which the Panel applied the ‚necessity' test. Instead, the United States stated that it would welcome clarification from the Appellate Body that an Article XX analysis should be approached in an integrated fashion.*"

233 Cf. Appellate Body report, *EU – PET (Pakistan)*, paras. 5.31 – 5.32.

WTO Agreement and any of the Appellate Body rulings criticized by the US as advisory opinions. At best one can read Art. IX:2 of the WTO Agreement as an implicit admonition to panels and the Appellate Body to interpret WTO law only within the confines of the specific disputes before them, but, as explained, staying within the confines of a specific dispute does not mean that one may only rule on issues necessary for the resolution of the dispute as understood by the US.

Fifth, and finally, in the case *EU – PET (Pakistan)*, referred to above, the US took the view that Appellate Body findings on WTO law made without the need of a recommendation under Art. 19.1 of the DSU are impermissible advisory opinions. However, the arguments of the US in support of that position suffer from internal contradictions. To recall, in that case the EU had contended that the panel should not have ruled on the measure challenged by Pakistan because that measure had already expired before the ruling of the panel. The reasoning of the EU bore striking similarities to that of the US against advisory opinions. The EU called the panel report *„a mere ‚advisory opinion'"*,[234] posited *„that WTO dispute settlement proceedings are intended to secure a positive solution to a dispute and should not serve as a vehicle to obtain ‚advisory opinions' on legal matters"*,[235] relied on the fact that Arts. 3.3, 3.4 and 3.7 of the DSU emphasized the settlement of disputes,[236] and pointed to Art. 3.9 of the DSU with its reference to Art. IX:2 of the WTO Agreement to show *„that there are other procedures that allow Members to obtain an authoritative interpretation of particular provisions of a covered agreement."*[237] Despite these similarities, though, the US did not support the EU, but rather the complainant, Pakistan. As a third party in this case, the US argued that since the measure had expired only after the panel's establishment, the panel was obligated to make findings on the measure's WTO consistency, and, furthermore, in case of a finding of inconsistency, a recommendation under Art. 19.1 of the DSU.[238] In addition, in an earlier dispute about a measure that had expired during the panel proceedings, *EU – Fatty Alcohols (Indonesia)*, the

234 Appellate Body report, *EU – PET (Pakistan)*, Annex A-1, European Union's notice of appeal, p.1.

235 Appellate Body report, *EU – PET (Pakistan)*, para. 5.31.

236 Appellate Body report, *EU – PET (Pakistan)*, paras. 5.22 – 5.26.

237 Appellate Body report, *EU – PET (Pakistan)*, para. 5.31.

238 Appellate Body report, *EU – PET (Pakistan)*, Annex C-1, Executive summary of the United States' third participant's submission, paras. 1 – 4.

US had not only made similar arguments as a third party,[239] but had also harshly criticized the Appellate Body's reliance on another prior ruling on expired measures, *US – Certain EC Products*. In that report, the Appellate Body had declared that a panel may not issue a recommendation under Art. 19.1 of the DSU regarding a measure found to be expired, reasoning *„that there is an obvious inconsistency between the finding of the Panel that ‚[the measure at issue] is no longer in existence' and the subsequent recommendation of the Panel that the DSB request that the United States bring [that measure] into conformity with its WTO obligations.*"[240] In the DSB meeting at which the Appellate Body report in *EU – Fatty Alcohols (Indonesia)* was adopted, the US stated *„that Article 19.1 of the DSU set out, in mandatory terms, the requirement that a panel or the Appellate Body ‚shall recommend' that any measure found to be WTO-inconsistent be brought into conformity with WTO rules*", and that „*[i]n the face of [such] clear, mandatory language in the DSU*" the refusal to issue such a recommendation regarding an expired measure amounted to adding to or diminishing rights provided in the WTO agreements in breach of Arts. 3.2 and 19.2 of the DSU.[241]

In view of this insistence of the US that panels and the Appellate Body are under a legal obligation to rule on expired measures, as long as they expired only after the establishment of the panel, how could the US at the same time condemn the ruling of the Appellate Body on the measure in *EU – PET (Pakistan)*, which had expired after the establishment of the panel, as an impermissible advisory opinion? According to the US, what turned the ruling into an advisory opinion was the fact that Pakistan had not asked for a recommendation under Art. 19.1 of the DSU, thereby confirming, in the view of the US, that there was no longer a dispute between the parties.[242] However, Pakistan had explained its failure to request a recommendation not with the

239 Appellate Body report, *EU – Fatty Alcohols (Indonesia)*, Annex C-1, Executive summary of the United States' third participant's submission, paras. 8 – 11.

240 Appellate Body report, *US – Certain EC Products*, para. 81; confirmed in the Appellate Body reports in *US – Upland Cotton*, para. 272; *EC – Bananas III (Article 21.5 – Ecuador II) / EC – Bananas III (Article 21.5 – US)*, para. 271; and *China – Raw Materials*, para. 263. For an analysis of WTO jurisprudence on panel recommendations for expired measures, see Bhardwaj (2019).

241 See minutes of the DSB meeting of 29 September 2017 (WT/DSB/M/402), statement of the US, paras. 5.9 – 5.10.

242 See minutes of the DSB meeting of 28 May 2018 (WT/DSB/M/413), statement of the US, paras. 10.5 – 10.8.

absence of an ongoing dispute with the EU, but rather with the argument that *„[l]ogically, measures cannot be brought into conformity if they no longer exist"*,[243] following the rational of the Appellate Body in *US – Certain EC Products.* It is difficult to see how that acknowledgement by Pakistan of such a point of logic could make any difference with regard to the question whether there was still a dispute between the parties. Moreover, in its third party submission the US had asserted that while Pakistan was entitled under the DSU to a ruling on the WTO consistency of the EU's expired measure, there was no need for a recommendation if *„the parties agree[d] that not issuing a recommendation [would] assist them in securing a positive resolution to this dispute."*[244] Such an agreement of the parties existed in this case, given that *„neither the European Union nor Pakistan question[ed] the Panel's decision not to make a recommendation to the DSB"*.[245] Therefore, according to arguments of the US itself, the panel and the Appellate Body in this dispute were right in ruling on the WTO consistency of the expired measure without also issuing a recommendation after a finding of inconsistency.

In conclusion, although there might be good policy reasons for the Appellate Body to limit itself to ruling only on those issues that are necessary for determining whether WTO law was violated and whether a recommendation pursuant to Art. 19.1 of the DSU is required, and thus to exercise judicial economy, the practice of judicial economy as demanded by the US is difficult to reconcile with the language of the provision that most directly deals with the question what the Appellate Body has to address, namely Art. 17.12 of the DSU. Other provisions, which speak indirectly to the issue, such as provisions which emphasize the settling of specific disputes as the main function of the dispute settlement system, at best support the view that the Appellate Body has discretion to use judicial economy, but do not contain any clear prescription that the Appellate Body has to use judicial economy whenever possible. In addition, the emphasis of Art. 3.2 of the DSU on *„security and predictability"* and *„clarif[ication] of the existing provisions"* counsels against a strict prohibition of ruling on issues not necessary to resolve the dispute.

243 Pakistan's response to the European Union's preliminary ruling request, para. 4.19, as quoted by the US in the minutes of the DSB meeting of 28 May 2018 (WT/DSB/M/413), para. 10.5, fn. 16.

244 Appellate Body report, *EU – PET (Pakistan)*, Annex C-1, Executive summary of the United States' third participant's submission, para. 4.

245 Appellate Body report, *EU – PET (Pakistan)*, para. 5.36.

Consequently, the position of the Appellate Body is at the very least defensible in light of the DSU, and certainly not a clear breach of the DSU that would justify blocking all appointments to the Appellate Body.

4. Appellate review of facts and of municipal law

In an extended statement at the DSB meeting of 27 August 2018, the US made two related, but legally quite distinct claims regarding Art. 17.6 of the DSU, which limits appeals to issues of law.[246] The US accused the Appellate Body of violating Art. 17.6 of the DSU by, first, reviewing not only panel findings of law but also panel findings of fact, and, second, characterizing panel findings on municipal law as issues of law rather than issues of fact, and reviewing them based on this characterization.

a. Review of facts

The first accusation of the US concerns the Appellate Body's practice of a limited review of factual findings based on Art. 11 of the DSU, which the Appellate Body introduced in 1998 in its report *EC – Hormones.* In that case, the respondent, the European Communities (EC), had claimed on appeal that the panel had disregarded or distorted certain factual evidence, thereby violating Art. 11 of the DSU. That provision states, in relevant part, that „*a panel should make an objective assessment of the matter before it, including an objective assessment of the facts of the case.*" The complainants, the US and Canada, had argued that by asking the Appellate Body to review whether the panel's findings were consistent with Art. 11 of the DSU, the EC were, in effect, asking for a review of factual findings, which was prohibited by Art. 17.6 of the DSU.[247] The Appellate Body opened its analysis by emphasizing that under Art. 17.6 of the DSU „*[fi]ndings of fact, as distinguished from legal interpretations or legal conclusions, by a panel are, in principle, not subject to review by the Appellate*

246 Minutes of the DSB meeting of 27 August 2018 (WT/DSB/M/417), paras. 4.1 – 4.17 (statement by the US) and 4.18 – 4.39 (subsequent discussion within the DSB). In addition to the discussion of the US statement at the DSB meeting of 27 August 2018, at the next regular DSB meeting of 26 September 2018 China made a separate statement in response to the earlier US statement (minutes [WT/DSB/M/419], paras. 4.2 – 4.6 [statement of China] and paras. 4.7 – 4.27 [subsequent discussion within the DSB]).

247 Appellate Body report, *EC – Hormones*, paras. 44 (US) and 61 (Canada).

Body."[248] It then added, though, that „[*t*]*he consistency or inconsistency of a given fact or set of facts with the requirements of a given treaty provision is, however, a legal characterization issue. It is a legal question. Whether or not a panel has made an objective assessment of the facts before it, as required by Article 11 of the DSU, is also a legal question which, if properly raised on appeal, would fall within the scope of appellate review.*"[249] As a matter of logic, this conclusion seems not objectionable. However, it raises the problem that a review of whether a panel has made an objective assessment of the facts under Art. 11 of the DSU might undermine the limitation of appellate review to legal issues under Art. 17.6 of the DSU. If every shortcoming in a panel's fact finding were to be considered as failure to make an objective assessment of the facts under Art. 11, then there would be nothing left of the limitation of appellate review to issues of law under Art. 17.6. The Appellate Body avoided this result by narrowing the types of errors that constitute a failure of making an objective assessment of the facts in the sense of Art. 11: „*Clearly, not every error in the appreciation of the evidence ... may be characterized as a failure to make an objective assessment of the facts. ... The deliberate disregard of, or refusal to consider, the evidence submitted to a panel is incompatible with a panel's duty to make an objective assessment of the facts. The wilful distortion or misrepresentation of the evidence put before a panel is similarly inconsistent with an objective assessment of the facts.*"[250] In later cases, the Appellate Body emphasized that in view of the different roles of the Appellate Body and the panels with regard to fact finding under Art. 17.6, the Appellate Body „*cannot base a finding of inconsistency under Article 11 simply on the conclusion that we might have reached a different factual finding from the one the panel reached*"[251] and „*will not ‚interfere lightly' with the panel's fact-finding authority.*"[252] In that way, the Appellate Body harmonized the potentially contradictory requirements of Arts. 11 and 17.6 of the DSU.[253]

248 *EC – Hormones*, para. 132.

249 *EC – Hormones*, para. 132.

250 *EC – Hormones*, para. 133.

251 *US – Wheat Gluten*, para. 151.

252 *EC and certain member States – Large Civil Aircraft*, para. 881.

253 On the development of the Appellate Body's jurisprudence on the review of factual findings under Art. 11 of the DSU, see Oesch (2003), pp. 157 – 166; see further WTO (2017), pp. 84 – 88 (on the review of facts by panels under Art. 11 of the DSU) and 108 (on the review of panel fact finding by the Appellate Body under Art. 11 of the DSU); and Voon/ Yanovich (2006).

In contrast to the Appellate Body's compromise between Arts. 11 and 17.6 of the DSU, the US argues that Art. 17.6 should trump Art. 11, i.e., that the Appellate Body should not be allowed to review at all whether a panel complied with its obligation under Art. 11 to make an objective assessment of the facts in order not to fall foul of Art. 17.6. Its main argument for this predominance of Art. 17.6 over Art. 11 is the fact that Art. 11 uses the word „should" rather than „shall": „*Key to this text [of Art. 11] was the word ‚should.' … [T]he decision of WTO Members to use the term ‚should' indicates that Members did not intend to create a legal obligation subject to review, a conclusion that is directly reinforced by the limitation on appeals to issues of law in Article 17.6.*"[254] Although „should" and „shall" can certainly carry different meanings, both generally[255] and in the WTO agreements,[256] it seems a bit of a stretch to follow from these nuances in meaning that Art. 11 has no legal binding effect on panels whatsoever. Furthermore, in other contexts the US relies heavily on Art. 11 as support for accusations of overreach against the Appellate Body, despite the use of „should" rather than „shall".[257] In that sense, the US claims are internally inconsistent. In any event, regardless of how one might evaluate the competing arguments of the US and the Appellate Body on Arts. 11 and 17.6, the US argument is certainly not so strong that it would justify calling the alternative interpretation by the Appellate Body an obvious, clear breach of the DSU.

Finally, there is an even more important point to make than substance in evaluating the argument of the US. That is that before its statement at the DSB meeting of 27 August 2018, the US had never criticized the fact that the Appellate Body engages in a limited review of a panel's fact finding based on Art. 11 of the DSU, neither at the DBS meeting at which the *EC – Hormones* report, which first recognized this power of the Appellate Body, was adopted,

---

254 Minutes of the DSB meeting of 27 August 2018 (WT/DSB/M/417), para. 4.5; see also minutes of the DSB meeting of 26 September 2018 (WT/DSB/M/419), para. 4.8.

255 Compare, for instance, the definitions of „should" and „shall" on https://en.oxforddictionaries.com, in particular, as far as our context is concerned, meaning 1 of „should" („*Used to indicate obligation, duty, or correctness, typically when criticizing someone's actions*", https://en.oxforddictionaries.com/definition/should) with meaning 3 of „shall" („*Expressing an instruction, command, or obligation*", https://en.oxforddictionaries.com/definition/shall).

256 For instance, the US points out that in the DSU „should" is used 21 times, compared to 259 instances in which „shall" is chosen; see minutes of the DSB meeting of 27 August 2018 (WT/DSB/M/417), para. 4.5.

257 See infra, text at fn. 353.

nor at any later DSB meeting. In fact, there have been occasions where the US not only explicitly acknowledged that power of the Appellate Body,[258] but even praised the balance struck and the restraint exercised by the Appellate Body in its review of findings of fact under Art. 11 of the DSU.[259] This lack of criticism is confirmed by the fact that in its statement at the DSB meeting of 27 August 2018, the US does not mention any earlier criticisms of this practice, neither by itself nor by other member states.[260] In addition, in various cases in the past the US has challenged the fact finding of panels on appeal by invoking Art. 11 of

---

258 See, for instance, the statement of the US in the DSB meeting of 1 February 2001 (WT/DSB/M/119) on the Appellate Body report in *US – Section 211 Appropriations Act*, para. 27: „*The meaning and operation of municipal law fell within the panel's role as finder of fact, and was outside the scope of appellate review unless the finding was inconsistent with the obligation to make an objective assessment of the facts, in accordance with Article 11 of the DSU.*"

259 See, for instance, the statement of the US in the minutes of the DSB meeting of 28 July 2011 (WT/DSB/M/301) on the Appellate Body report *EC – Fastener (China)*, para. 10: „*The United States said that it would also like to draw Members' attention to the Appellate Body's articulation of the standard of review for a claim of error under Article 11 of the DSU. ... The United States agreed with these statements and believed that they were a useful reminder to Members regarding the proper scope of Article 11, as well as reflecting the limited scope of appellate review under Article 17.6 of the DSU.*" See also the statement of the US in the minutes of the DSB meeting of 22 April 2015 (WT/DSB/M/360) on the Appellate Body report in *US – Shrimp II (Viet Nam)*, para. 8.6.

260 In the DSB meeting of 26 September 2018 the US rejected the allegation that it had raised its concern regarding appellate review of factual findings for the first time at the DSB meeting of 27 August 2018. In response to Mexico's comment at the DSB meeting of 26 September 2018 „*that this was the first time, after more than 500 disputes and more than 20 years, that the United States took the view that there had been ‚an invention of an authority to review fact-finding'*" (minutes [WT/DSB/M/417], para. 4.23), the US stated: „*One Member had suggested that US concerns with appellate review of panel fact-finding were new and had been only recently raised by the United States. In its statement made at the 27 August 2018 DSB meeting, the United States had quoted from a statement it had made in 2002 that expressed concerns on this issue. That Member's assertion therefore did not reflect reality.*" (minutes [WT/DSB/M/417], para. 4.26). The US refers here to a quote from a statement it had made at the DSB meeting of 1 February 2002 on the Appellate Body report in *US – Section 211 Appropriation Act* (see minutes of the DSB meeting of 27 August 2018 [WT/DSB/M/417], para. 4.12). However, in that statement the US had only criticized the Appellate Body's qualification of municipal law as an legal issue for purposes of Art. 17.6 of the DSU, and not the Appellate Body's power to review factual findings under Art. 11 of the DSU. Indeed, in that statement the US had explicitly acknowledged that power (see the quote from that statement in fn. 258 above).

the DSU, without questioning the legal validity of such a claim.[261] The relative weakness of its legal arguments combined with the fact that the US made its allegations for the first time 20 years after the establishment of the practice at issue and after it had blocked appointments to the Appellate Body for more than a year, raises serious doubts as to whether the position of the US is the result of good faith interpretation.

b. Review of municipal law

The second accusation the US makes concerning Art. 17.6 of the DSU refers to the Appellate Body's review of panel findings on municipal (domestic) law of the member states. The US argues that for purposes of the distinction between issues of law and issues of fact under Art. 17.6 of the DSU, municipal law should be treated as an issue of fact, and, accordingly, a panel's findings on the meaning of municipal should not be subject to review by the Appellate Body. This raises the question as to what kind of law Art. 17.6 of the DSU refers to in its term „*issues of law covered in the panel report and legal interpretations developed by the panel.*" The US asserts that legal issues in the sense of Art. 17.6 of the DSU are only issues of WTO law, i.e., excluding municipal law. As textual DSU basis for this assertion, the US cites Arts. 6.2, 11 and 12.7.[262] The first of these, Art. 6.2 of the DSU, refers to the request for the establishment of a panel and requires that this request must „*identify the specific measure at issue*", which is usually a measure of municipal law, and „*provide a summary of the legal basis of the complaint*", the legal basis being some provision(s) of WTO law which are alleged to be violated by the measure of municipal law. Art. 11 of the DSU calls on panels to make an objective assessment of the matter before it, and distinguishes in that respect an objective assessment of, on the one hand, „*the facts of the case*", and, on the other hand, „*the applicability of and*

261 This was pointed out by China in the DSB meeting of 26 September 2018, with reference to various examples (minutes [WT/DSB/M/417], para. 4.4). In response, the US stated, not unreasonably, that even if it disagreed with the Appellate Body's review of factual findings, the US could not be expected, once the Appellate Body had established this practice, „*not [to] avail itself of that opportunity even if other Members had been making use of that second bite at the apple*" (minutes [WT/DSB/M/417], para. 4.10). However, if opportunism had been the only reason why the US had appealed factual findings in reliance on Art. 11 of the DSU, then one would have expected the US to express its reservations in some other way or at other occasions, which it never did before the start of the appointment crisis.

262 Minutes of the DSB meeting of 27 August 2018 (WT/DSB/M/417), para. 4.8.

conformity with the relevant covered agreements", i.e., the WTO agreements. This juxtaposition of facts and of issues of WTO law implies that issues of municipal law are considered to be factual issues. Finally, Art. 12.7 of the DSU states that in its written report a panel has to set out „*the findings of fact*" and „*the applicability of the relevant provisions*", which, when read together with Art. 11 of the DSU, in particular, again implies that legal issues only include issues of WTO law. Based on these three provisions, the US concludes that „*the DSU made clear that the measure at issue was the core fact to be established by a complaining party, and the WTO consistency of that measure was the issue of law.*"[263] In addition, the US claims that the proposition that municipal law is to be qualified as fact rather than law is not only recognized by WTO law, but also by international law in general.[264] Finally, the US quotes statements from 10 WTO panels and statements made by members as parties in 15 WTO cases, all in favor of viewing municipal law as fact rather than law.[265]

The Appellate Body first addressed this question in 1997, in the case *India – Patents (US)*. At issue in that case was whether certain provisions of Indian law were compliant with Art. 70.8(a) of the TRIPS Agreement, i.e., with WTO law. India had asserted that the panel should have treated Indian municipal law as a fact to be established by the party relying on it, in this case the US, rather than as law to be interpreted by the panel, and should have given India the benefit of the doubt as to the meaning it ascribed to its own laws before the panel.[266] In response, the Appellate Body stated: „*In public international law, an international tribunal may treat municipal law in several ways. Municipal law may serve as evidence of facts and may provide evidence of state practice. However, municipal law may also constitute evidence of compliance or non-compliance with international obligations.*"[267] In support of these statements, it then quoted from a judgment of the Permanent Court of International Justice concerning whether a Polish law had violated international law: „*From the standpoint of International Law and of the Court which is its organ, municipal laws are merely facts which express the will and constitute the activities of States ... The Court is certainly not called upon to interpret the Polish law as such; but there is nothing to prevent the Court's giving judgment on the question whether*

263 Minutes of the DSB meeting of 27 August 2018 (WT/DSB/M/417), para. 4.8.
264 Minutes of the DSB meeting of 27 August 2018 (WT/DSB/M/417), para. 4.9.
265 Minutes of the DSB meeting of 27 August 2018 (WT/DSB/M/417), paras. 4.9 – 4.10.
266 Appellate Body report, *India – Patents (US)*, para. 64.
267 *India – Patents (US)*, para. 65.

or not, in applying that law, Poland is acting in conformity with its obligations ... under [international law]."[268] From this the Appellate Body followed that the panel in this case had been right to examine the Indian law at issue in detail because without an understanding of the meaning of that law it could not have determined whether India had complied with its obligations under WTO law.[269] As to its own role in reviewing the panel's findings on India's municipal law, the Appellate Body stated: „*And, just as it was necessary for the Panel in this case to seek a detailed understanding of the operation of [the Indian municipal law at issue] in order to assess whether India had complied with Article 70.8(a) [of the TRIPS Agreement], so, too, is it necessary for us in this appeal to review the Panel's examination of the same Indian domestic law.*"[270]

Two points are noteworthy in this argument of the Appellate Body. First, the Appellate Body seems to agree with the notion that within the WTO system issues of law are, at least in principle, issues of WTO law. Municipal law is only relevant insofar as its understanding it necessary for a proper application of WTO law, and in particular for determining whether a member state complied with WTO law. In that sense, municipal law is no different than ordinary facts, such as, for instance, the exact increase of imports in a given period (issue of fact), an understanding of which is required for a determination of whether a member state fulfills the conditions for taking a safeguard action against such imports under the WTO Agreement on Safeguards (issue of law). Second, the Appellate Body claims that there is no difference between itself and the panel as a far as the examination of municipal law is concerned, i.e., that it, like the panel, has to examine municipal on its own in order to get a detailed understanding of it, rather than just to take the panel's finding on the meaning of municipal law as given. However, if one accepts, as the Appellate Body seems to do, that issues of law within the WTO system are issues of WTO law only, then the Appellate Body's equalization of its role and that of the panel with regard to the review of municipal law disregards the different roles of Appellate Body and panels under Art. 17.6 of the DSU, which limits the power of the Appellate Body to reviewing issues of law. As the US correctly observes, „*many factual issues in WTO dispute settlement required ‚detailed understan-*

268 *India – Patents (US)*, para. 65, quoting from the judgment on the merits in *Case concerning certain interests in Polish Upper Silesia*, 1926, Publications of the Permanent Court of International Justice, Series A, No. 7, p. 19.

269 *India – Patents (US)*, para. 66

270 *India – Patents (US)*, para. 68.

ding.' But that provided no basis for treating those factual issues as issues of law to be decided de novo by the Appellate Body on appeal."[271]

It has to be added that in *India – Patents* (*US*), neither the parties nor the Appellate Body had referred to Art. 17.6 of the DSU and the relevance of that provision for the question of reviewing findings on municipal law on appeal.[272] That changed with the case *US – Section 211 Appropriations Act* in 2002. In dispute in that case was whether Section 211 of the US Appropriation Act violated certain provision of the TRIPS Agreements. Obviously, an answer to that question required an understanding of the meaning of Section 211. Accordingly, the panel determined the meaning of Section 211, and then rejected most of the EC claims. On appeal, the EC argued that the panel had read Section 211 erroneously, and asked the Appellate Body to reverse that reading of Section 211.[273] In response, the US contended that the Appellate Body was bound by the panel's reading of the measure at issue, i.e., Section 211, since a panel's review of municipal law was an issue of fact and thus under Art. 17.6 of the DSU outside the scope of appellate review.[274] In its analysis, the Appellate Body quoted at length the relevant passage from *India – Patents* (*US*) discussed above.[275] From that it followed that „*[u]nder the DSU, a panel may examine the municipal law of a WTO Member for the purpose of determining whether that Member has complied with its obligations under the WTO Agreement. Such an assessment is a legal characterization by a panel. And, therefore, a panel's assessment of municipal law as to its consistency with WTO obligations is subject to appellate review under Article 17.6 of the DSU.*"[276] Applying this reasoning to the question at hand, it found that the panel's assessment of Section 211 was „*an interpretation of the meaning of Section 211 solely for the purpose of determining whether the United States has fulfilled its obligations under the TRIPS Agreement. The meaning given by the Panel to Section 211 is,*

271 Minutes of the DSB meeting of 27 August 2018 (WT/DSB/M/417), para. 4.12.

272 The same was true for the 2001 Appellate Body report in *US – Hot-Rolled Steel*, para. 200, in which the Appellate Body repeated, in essence, its statement that not only the panels, but also the Appellate Body has „*to conduct a detailed examination of [domestic] legislation in assessing its consistency with WTO law*" (with reference to its earlier statement in *India – Patents* (*US*), paras. 66 – 67).

273 Appellate Body report, *US – Section 211 Appropriation Act*, para. 102.

274 Appellate Body report, *US – Section 211 Appropriation Act*, para. 101.

275 *US – Section 211 Appropriation Act*, para. 104.

276 *US – Section 211 Appropriation Act*, para. 105.

thus, clearly within the scope of our review as set out in Article 17.6 of the DSU."[277] However, as in *India – Patents* (*US*), the reasoning of the Appellate Body was based, as the US stated in the DSB meeting at which Appellate Body report in this case was adopted, on a „*logical misstep*".[278] While it is true that a panel's finding on whether a measure of municipal law complies with WTO law is an issue of WTO law, that does not make the meaning of municipal law itself an issue of WTO law because otherwise any finding of fact a panel makes in order to determine whether a member state complied with WTO law (and why else would a panel make a finding of fact in WTO dispute settlement?) would, ipso facto, become an issue of WTO law, thereby completely eradicating the distinction between issues of law and issues of fact in Art. 17.6 of the DSU.

In its subsequent case law, the Appellate Body has consistently confirmed its view that findings on municipal law made for the purpose of determining compliance with WTO law are issues of law under Art. 17.6 of the DSU, always relying on the logic first set out in *India – Patents* (*US*).[279] However, in *China – Auto Parts*, the Appellate Body seemed to say that this logic applied only to the text of the municipal legal instrument, but not to other elements relevant for the determination of its meaning. It stated „*that there may be instances in which a panel's assessment of municipal law will go beyond the text of an instrument on its face, in which case further examination may be required, and may involve factual elements.*"[280] As to what these factual elements were, it referred to its reports in *US – Carbon Steel* and *US – Corrosion-Resistant Steel Sunset Review*, which described them „*as evidence of the consistent application of such laws, the pronouncements of domestic courts on the meaning of such laws, the opinions of legal experts and the writings of recognized scholars.*"[281] Concerning the review of finding on such factual elements, the Appellate Body explained: „*With respect to such elements, the Appellate Body will not lightly*

277 *US – Section 211 Appropriation Act*, para. 106.

278 Minutes of the DSB meeting of 1 February 2002 (WT/DSB/M/119), para. 27.

279 See the following Appellate Body reports: *China – Auto Parts*, para. 225; *China – Publications and Audiovisual Products*, para. 177; *EC – Fasteners* (*China*), para. 295; *US – Countervailing and Anti-Dumping Measures* (*China*), para. 4.99; and *EU – Biodiesel* (*Argentina*), para. 6.155.

280 *China – Auto Parts*, para. 225; confirmed by the Appellate Body in *EC – Fasteners* (*China*), para. 296.

281 *US – Carbon Steel*, para. 157; *US – Corrosion-Resistant Steel Sunset Review*, para. 168.

interfere with a panel's finding on appeal."[282] By declaring that it would not lightly interfere with a panel's findings on these factual elements, it indicated that it would review them like other factual findings under Art. 11 of the DSU, without, though, mentioning Art. 11 explicitly. To distinguish for purposes of the scope of appellate review between one element of interpretation, the text of a legal instrument, and other elements, such as application by administrative agencies or interpretations by domestic courts, might have some practical value, in that the text is usually the most easily available fact, but it lacks any discernible basis in Art. 17.6 of the DSU. And, indeed, the Appellate Body gave up this distinction in *US – Countervailing and Anti-Dumping Measures (China)*. There it emphasized that all elements of interpretation can have both factual and legal aspects for purposes of Art. 17.6 of the DSU. In particular, the text of an instrument, like the other elements, may have factual elements, e.g., „*the individuation of the text and of some associated circumstances*", „*[f]or example, whether the text is official in more than one language, its date of enactment, publication and enforcement, the issuing authority, etc.*", and the other elements may not only include factual elements (such as, for instance, „*whether or when a domestic court ruling has been rendered and finalized, or what a writing by a recognized scholar contains*"), but also legal elements, in particular „*the examination of the legal interpretation given by a domestic court or by a domestic administering agency as to the meaning of municipal law with respect to the measure being reviewed for consistency with the covered agreements [i.e., WTO law]*".[283] In short, whether a certain element of interpretation, like the text of a measure, the practice of an administrative agencies or the ruling of a court, actually exists and what it consists of (e.g., which words it contains) is an issue of fact, but the meaning of such an element is an issue of law.

The weakness of the Appellate Body's basic argument in *India – Patents (US)* has also been pointed out in academic literature.[284] And, unlike in the case of

282 *US – Auto Parts*, para. 225; confirmed by the Appellate Body in *China – Publications and Audiovisual Products*, para. 177, and *EC – Fasteners (China)*, para. 296.

283 *US – Countervailing and Anti-Dumping Measures (China)*, para. 4.101; confirmed by the Appellate Body in *EU – Biodiesel (Argentina)*, para. 6.156.

284 See Lester (2018) („*Most people I talk to about this agree that the Appellate Body got it wrong.*"); Lester (2012), pp. 142 – 144 and 148 – 149 (p. 149: „*Arguably, the Appellate Body's decision to consider the panel's construction of the challenged measures, outside the context of WTO obligations, as a law application issue stretches the boundaries of [Art. 17.6 of the DSU].*"); Bohanes/Lockhart (2009), pp. 416 – 421 (p. 421: „*[T]he logic of the Appellate Body's*

the limited review of factual findings under Art. 11 of the DSU, the US has criticized the Appellate Body's review of municipal law not merely in the context of the appointment crisis, but it had done so early on, starting with *US – Section 211 Appropriations Act* in 2002,[285] and it has been consistent in its criticism ever since.[286]

If the Appellate Body's position on appellate review of municipal law is indeed so weak, what might explain it? Of course, one can only speculate, but one reason might be that, as a judicial body, the Appellate Body feels qualified not only to interpret WTO law, but other law as well.[287] However, although the Appellate Body's qualification as a judicial body might be a good policy reason for appellate review of municipal law, it is not enough to overcome the legal arguments against it under the DSU.

If one agrees that the Appellate Body went beyond the limits of Art. 17.6 of the DSU by reviewing on appeal findings on municipal law, in effect, as an issue of law rather than fact, the follow-up question in the context of our examination is whether by doing so the Appellate Body committed a breach of the DSU so serious that it would justify blocking all appointments to the Appellate Body. The answer is no, for at least three reasons.

---

finding [in India – Patents (US) and US – Section 211 Appropriations Act] is difficult to understand.").

285 See statement of the US in the minutes of the DSB meeting of 1 February 2002 (WT/DSB/M/119), para. 27.

286 See statements of the US in the minutes of the DSB meetings of 12 January 2009 (WT/DSB/M/261), para. 5, on the Appellate Body report in *China – Auto Parts*; 10 July 2014 (WT/DSB/M/347), paras. 7.7 – 7.8, on the Appellate Body report in *US – Countervailing and Anti-Dumping Measures (China)*; and 26 October 2016 (WT/DSB/M/387), paras. 8.9 – 8.15, on the Appellate Body report in *EU – Biodiesel (Argentina)*.

287 Cf. the statement of China in the DSB meeting of 12 January 2009 (at which the Appellate Body report in *China – Auto Parts* was adopted) in defense of the Appellate Body's review of municipal law: „*The process of interpreting municipal law was not materially different than the process of interpreting the covered agreements, at least where municipal law was interpreted on its face. The Appellate Body was, of course, eminently qualified in matters of legal interpretation. Therefore, the general principle that the Appellate Body should give some degree of deference to the factual determinations of a panel was not implicated by a panel's interpretation of a Member's municipal law.*" (minutes [WT/DSB/M/262], para. 9); see also Bohanes/Lockhart (2009), p. 421: „*A possible explanation for this finding is that the Appellate Body would like to retain the ability to review a panel's finding on municipal law even in the absence of errors that rise to the level of an Article 11 DSU violation. Although formally a factual matter, municipal law nevertheless remains law, and judges intuitively want to assess the meaning of law, whether it is municipal or international.*"

First, the question of whether and, if so, to what extent findings on municipal law are reviewable on appeal is not an easy one, and one that it is not explicitly answered in the DSU. Art. 17.6 of the DSU merely states that only issues of law can be reviewed by the Appellate Body, but the DSU does not say anything explicit on how municipal law has to be treated for purposes of Art. 17.6 of the DSU. Another indication of the difficulty of the question is the very textbook on international law on which the US relies in support of the proposition that municipal is always to be considered an issue of fact in international law, namely Ian Brownlie's Principles of Public International Law.[288] That textbook not only quotes, like the Appellate Body in *India – Patents* (*US*), the statement of the Permanent Court of Justice that „*municipal laws are merely facts which express the will and constitute the activities of States*", but also qualifies this statement with the assertion that „*the general proposition that international tribunals take account of municipal laws only as facts 'is, at most, a debatable proposition the validity and wisdom of which are subject to, and call for, further discussion and review'.*"[289] Similarly, while the Appellate Body's approach to municipal law has been criticized in academic literature,[290] there are also scholars who support the Appellate Body on this point,[291] again indicating that this is not a clear-cut issue.

Second, the US view that the Appellate Body's case law on municipal law is a clear breach of the DSU finds little resonance with other WTO members. Before August 2018, the US had criticized the Appellate Body on this issue on four occasions in the DSB, at the adoptions of the Appellate Body reports in *US – Section 211 Appropriations Act*, *China – Auto Parts*, *US – Countervailing and Anti-Dumping Measures* (*China*), and *EU – Biodiesel* (*Argentina*).[292] The review of municipal law in these four reports garnered altogether only four comments by other members in the DSB, two by China and one each by Japan and Korea, and each of them supported the Appellate Body.[293] The extended statement of

288 Minutes of the DSB meeting of 27 August 2018 (WT/DSB/M/417), statement of the US, para. 4.9, quoting Brownlie (1998), p. 39.

289 Brownlie (1998), p. 38, quoting Jenks (1964), p. 552.

290 See supra, fn. 284.

291 See, for instance, Howse (2003), pp. 21 – 22.

292 See supra, fn. 285 and 286.

293 Minutes of the DSB meetings of 12 January 2009 (WT/DSB/M/262), para. 9 (statement of China on the Appellate Body report in *China – Auto Parts* [„*China welcomed the finding of the Appellate Body that a panel's interpretation of a Member's municipal law was a matter of legal interpretation to be reviewed by the Appellate Body under Article 17.6 of the DSU*"]);

the US at the DSB meeting of 27 August 2018 prompted comments by nine members, immediately at the meeting of 27 August 2018[294] and at the following regular DSB meeting of 26 September 2018.[295] Of these nine members, four rejected the US allegations against the Appellate Body regarding municipal law (Brazil, China, the EU, and Mexico), three did not take a position on the issue (Canada, Chile, and the Philippines), and only two raised doubts as to the approach of the Appellate Body, and that only cautiously (Australia and Japan). This lukewarm reception of the US criticism by other members both before and after the start of the appointment crisis hardly suggests an egregious misinterpretation of the DSU by the Appellate Body.

Third, the consequences of, on the one hand, reviewing municipal law on appeal in (arguable) breach of Art. 17.6 of the DSU and, on the other hand, blocking all appointments to the Appellate Body in (clear) breach of Art. 17.2 of the DSU are vastly disproportionate. According to the US, the main practical disadvantage of the Appellate Body's review of findings of municipal law is that it *„represents a serious waste of the limited resources of the WTO dispute settlement system, adding complexity and delay to the process"*[296] because issues of municipal law have to be argued and decided twice, first by a panel and then by the Appellate Body. The US also contends that *„no purpose* [*is*] *served"* by such a review on appeal.[297] Of course, any review of first instance findings by a second instance adds time and costs to legal proceedings, and the review

22 July 2014 (WT/DSB/M/348), paras. 7.3 and 7.10 (statements on the Appellate Body report in *US – Countervailing and Anti-Dumping Measures* (*China*) by China [*„China welcomed, in particular, the Appellate Body's recognition that the baseline of prior municipal law was to be determined in accordance with the standard that the Appellate Body had previously articulated in its Report in the ‚US – Carbon Steel' dispute."*] and Japan [*„Japan agreed with the Appellate Body's previous findings* [*on municipal law*] *which were also reaffirmed in the present report."*]); and 22 June 2016 (WT/DSB/M/380), para. 11.8 (statement of Korea on *US – Countervailing and Anti-Dumping Measures* (*China*) [*„Korea believed that this approach* [*of the Appellate Body on municipal law*] *was no less valid than the one argued by a Member* [*i.e., the US*]"]).

294 See minutes of the DSB meeting of 27 August 2018 (WT/DSB/M/417), paras. 4.18 (Chile), 4.19 – 4.21 (Japan), 4.22 (Australia), 4.23 (Canada), 4.24 – 4.30 (Brazil), 4.31 – 4.32 (China), 4.33 – 4.36 (Philippines), 4.36 (Mexico) and 4.37 (EU).

295 See minutes of the DSB meeting of 26 September 2018 (WT/DSB/M/419), paras. 4.2 – 4.6 (China), 4.12 (Japan), 4.13 – 4.21 (Brazil), 4.22 (Canada), 4.23 (Mexico), 4.24 (EU), and 4.25 (Chile).

296 Minutes of the DSB meeting of 27 August 2018 (WT/DSB/M/417), para. 4.16.

297 Minutes of the DSB meeting of 27 August 2018 (WT/DSB/M/417), para. 4.16.

of panel findings on municipal law by the Appellate Body is no exception. However, usually, a review by an appeal instance also produces benefits in terms of an increased likelihood of a correct outcome, and one may safely assume that this applies to the Appellate Body, too. Therefore, the US assertion that „*no purpose* [*is*] *served*" by reviewing findings of municipal law on appeal is somewhat overstated. Be that as it may, the consequence of adding some time and costs to proceedings in which a party appeals panel findings on municipal law pales in comparison to the consequences of blocking all appointments to the Appellate Body. The resulting reduction of the number of Appellate Body members has already prolonged appellate proceedings to an unprecedented degree, exceeding any delays caused by appellate review of municipal law, and will soon, in December 2019, when the number of Appellate Body members will fall below three, freeze all work on new appeals.

Summarizing, there is a case to be made that by reviewing panel findings on municipal law the Appellate Body has gone beyond what is permissible under Art. 17.6 of the DSU. However, such misinterpretation cannot justify blocking all appointments to the Appellate Body because, first, given the difficulty of the legal question it is not an obvious breach of the DSU, second, no other member apart from the US considers it a serious breach, and, third, the consequences of a breach of Art. 17.6 of the DSU by reviewing municipal law are far less serious than those of a breach of Art. 17.2 of the DSU by blocking all appointments to the Appellate Body.

5. Precedential effect of Appellate Body reports

The US accuses the Appellate Body of illegitimately claiming precedential effect for its own reports and rulings.[298] Precedential effect of an adjudicatory body's ruling on a legal issue means[299] that this ruling is binding for a later decision on the same legal issue, i.e., that the legal issue in the later case has to

298 The issue of precedential effect in WTO dispute settlement has generated a substantial amount of discussion in academic literature; see, for instance, Gao (2018), pp. 523 – 528; Beshkar/Chilton (2016), pp. 385 – 388; Pauwelyn (2016); Pelc (2016); Kucik/Pelc (2016); Hsiang/Nyarko (2015); Piérola (2014); Luanratan/Roman (2014); Pelc (2014); Brewster (2011); Bhala (1999a), (1999b), and (2001); and Chua (1998).

299 On the definition of precedential effect, see, for instance, Brewster (2011), p. 193, and Murrill (2018), p. 4.

be decided in the same way than in the earlier ruling. Such precedential effect is also called stare decisis. One can distinguish between horizontal and vertical precedential effect. Horizontal precedential effect means that an adjudicatory body is bound by its own earlier rulings. Vertical horizontal effect refers to a hierarchical adjudicatory system in which a lower adjudicatory body is bound by rulings of a higher adjudicatory body within that system. Another relevant distinction for our purpose is that between de jure and de facto precedential effect. In the former case there is an legal obligation to follow prior rulings, whereas in the latter there is no such obligation, but prior rulings are followed nevertheless, as a matter of practice.

The US is particularly concerned about claims that panels should be bound by Appellate Body rulings (horizontal direct effect), but it is also opposed to any binding effect of earlier Appellate Body rulings on later Appellate Body decisions (vertical horizontal effect). In a lengthy statement at the DSB of 18 December 2018 *„on the precedential value of panel or Appellate Body reports under the WTO Agreement and DSU"*, the US gave its most detailed account so far of its views on this subject.[300] In that statement the US criticized *„the Appellate Body's misguided insistence that its reports had to serve as precedent ‚absent cogent reasons'"*[301] and set out a number of reasons why it believes that WTO law, and the DSU in particular, accords no precedential effect to Appellate Body rulings (and not to panel rulings, either). To evaluate this criticism, we will first look at what the Appellate Body has said on the issue, and to what extent panels and the Appellate Body actually rely on existing Appellate Body case law. Based on that, we will describe and analyze the arguments of the US.

The most important statements of the Appellate Body on precedential effect are to be found in its reports in the cases *Japan – Alcoholic Beverages II* (1996), *US – Shrimp (Article 21.5 – Malaysia)* (2001), *US – Oil Country Tubular Goods Sunset Reviews* (2004), *US – Stainless Steel (Mexico)* (2008), and *US – Continued Zeroing* (2009).

300 Minutes of the DSB meeting of 18 December 2018 (WT/DSB/M/423), paras. 4.2 – 4.25 (statement by the US) and 4.26 – 4.38 (discussion of the statement within the DSB); see for an earlier US statement on the issue minutes of the DSB meeting of 20 May 2008 (WT/DSB/M/250), paras. 50 – 55 (criticism of the Appellate Body's views on precedent in its report in *US – Stainless Steel (Mexico)*, paras. 154 – 162).

301 Minutes of the DSB meeting of 18 December 2018 (WT/DSB/M/423), para. 4.2.

In *Japan – Alcoholic Beverages II*, the panel, after declaring that interpretation of the WTO provision at issue in the case was governed by Arts. 31 and 32 of the VCLT,[302] had found that adopted GATT panel reports were subsequent practice of the GATT contracting parties in the sense of Art. 31(3)(c) of the VCLT and thus had to be taken into account, and, furthermore, that they were decisions of the GATT contracting parties in the sense of Art. 1(b)(iv) GATT 1994 and therefore part of GATT 1994.[303] The Appellate Body rejected both of these findings.[304] It argued that under the GATT 1947 panels were not „*legally bound by the details and reasoning of a previous panel report*“ and that such reports did not „*constitute a definitive interpretation of the relevant provisions of GATT 1947*“.[305] That this understanding also prevails under the GATT 1994 followed for the Appellate Body in particular from the power of the Ministerial Conference and the General Council to adopt exclusive interpretation pursuant to Art. IX:2 of the WTO Agreement and the confirmation of that power in Art. 3.9 of the DSU. Still, the Appellate Body also emphasized that adopted panels reports are not meaningless, since they belong to the „*legal history and experience under the GATT 1947*“,[306] which was incorporated into the WTO by Art. XVI:1 of the WTO Agreement (according to which „*the WTO shall be guided by the decisions, procedures and customary practices*“ under GATT 1947). From all of this the Appellate Body concluded: „*Adopted panel reports are an important part of the GATT acquis. They are often considered by subsequent panels. They create legitimate expectations among WTO Members, and, therefore, should be taken into account where they are relevant to any dispute. However, they are not binding, except with respect to resolving the particular dispute between the parties to that dispute.*“ [307]

In *US – Shrimp (Article 21.5 – Malaysia)* the complainant, Malaysia, had objected to the fact that the panel in that case had relied heavily on the earlier Appellate Body report *US – Shrimp*. In response, the Appellate Body not only endorsed the right of the panel to rely on Appellate Body rulings, but added that it „*would have expected the Panel to do so.*“[308] Furthermore, it quoted its passage from *Japan – Alcohol Beverages II* that adopted panel rulings create

302 Panel report, *Japan – Alcoholic Beverages II*, para. 6.8.
303 Panel report, *Japan – Alcoholic Beverages II*, para. 6.10.
304 Appellate Body report, *Japan – Alcohol Beverages II*, pp. 106 – 108.
305 *Japan – Alcoholic Beverages II*, p. 107.
306 *Japan – Alcoholic Beverages II*, p. 108.
307 *Japan – Alcoholic Beverages II*, p. 108.
308 *US – Shrimp (Article 21.5 – Malaysia)*, para. 107.

legitimate expectations and should be taken into account, and stated that „*[t]his reasoning applies to adopted Appellate Body Reports as well.*“[309] The thrust of *US – Shrimp (Article 21.5 – Malaysia)* was affirmed and strengthened in *US – Oil Country Tubular Goods Sunset Reviews*, in which again reliance of the panel on an earlier Appellate Body case on a similar issue was before the Appellate Body. It declared that „*following the Appellate Body's conclusions in earlier disputes is not only appropriate, but is what would be expected from panels, especially where the issues are the same.*“[310]

The Appellate Body's most detailed and arguably most relevant statement to date on precedential effect was made in the case *US – Stainless Steel (Mexico)*. At issue in this case was the US practice of „zeroing“ in anti-dumping proceedings, an issue that has spawned more WTO disputes than any other single practice of a member state.[311] The panel in this dispute had, after careful consideration, explicitly rejected and disregarded the reasoning of the Appellate Body in two earlier cases, *US – Zeroing (EC)* and *US – Zeroing (Japan)*, on the same type of zeroing that was before the panel.[312] On appeal, the claimant Mexico had argued that by refusing to follow these Appellate Body precedents the panel had violated its obligations under Art. 11 of the DSU, which describes the function of panels. In its analysis, the Appellate Body considered that the function of panels pursuant to Art. 11 of the DSU is informed by Art. 3 of the DSU, which states, among other things, that „*[t]he dispute settlement system of the WTO is a central element in providing security and predictability to the multilateral trading system*“ (first sentence of Art. 3.2 of the DSU) and that it serves „*to clarify the existing provisions of those agreements in accordance with customary rules of interpretation of public international law*“ (second sentence of Art. 3.2 of the DSU).[313] The Appellate Body then summarized its earlier statements on precedential effect in *Japan – Alcoholic Beverages II*, *US – Shrimp (Article 21.5 – Malaysia)* and *US – Oil Country Tubular Goods Sunset Reviews*.[314] As to the practical effect of existing case law, it said that „*[d]ispute settlement practice demonstrates that WTO Members attach significance to reasoning provided in previous panel and Appellate Body re-*

309 *US – Shrimp (Article 21.5 – Malaysia)*, paras. 108 – 109.

310 *US – Oil Country Tubular Goods Sunset Reviews*, para. 188.

311 For an overview of the zeroing disputes, see, for instance, Mavroidis/Prusa (2018), pp. 244 – 247, Nedumpara (2012), and Bown/Prusa (2011).

312 Panel report, *US – Stainless Steel (Mexico)*, para. 7.106.

313 *US – Stainless Steel (Mexico)*, para. 157.

314 *US – Stainless Steel (Mexico)*, paras. 158 – 159.

ports."[315] Relying on the first sentence of Art. 3.2 of the DSU, it then made its core statement on horizontal stare decisis: „*Ensuring ,security and predictability' in the dispute settlement system, as contemplated in Article 3.2 of the DSU, implies that, absent cogent reasons, an adjudicatory body will resolve the same legal question in the same way in a subsequent case.*"[316] The Appellate Body drew further support for precedential effect from the „[*c*]*larification ... envisaged in* [*the second sentence of*] *Article 3.2 of the DSU*": „[*T*]*he relevance of clarification contained in adopted Appellate Body reports is not limited to the application of a particular provision in a specific case.*"[317] Regarding the relationship between the Appellate Body and the panels, that is, the issue of vertical stare decisis, the Appellate Body explained that „[*i*]*n the hierarchical structure contemplated in the DSU, panels and the Appellate Body have distinct roles to play.*"[318] It pointed out that the Appellate Body is a standing body (whereas the panels are ad-hoc bodies), and that it has the power on appeal to overturn legal interpretations by the panels (Arts. 17.6 and 17.13 of the DSU), from which it followed that „[*t*]*he creation of the Appellate Body by WTO Members to review legal interpretations developed by panels shows that Members recognized the importance of consistency and stability in the interpretation of their rights and obligations*" and that a panel's disregard of applicable Appellate Body precedent „*undermines the development of a coherent and predictable body of jurisprudence ... as contemplated under the DSU.*"[319] In conclusion, the Appellate Body declared that it was „*deeply concerned about the Panel's decision to depart from well-established Appellate Body jurisprudence clarifying the interpretation of the same legal issues*", but, since it had overturned the panel's finding on zeroing anyway, it did not make an additional finding on whether the panel had violated Art. 11 of the DSU.[320]

Finally, in *US – Continued Zeroing*, the Appellate Body was presented with the question whether its statement in *US – Stainless Steel (Mexico)* that „*absent cogent reasons, an adjudicatory body will resolve the same legal question in the same way in a subsequent case*" meant that only the Appellate Body or also panels could deviate from earlier Appellate Body rulings if there were „*cogent*

315 *US – Stainless Steel (Mexico)*, para. 160.

316 *US – Stainless Steel (Mexico)*, para. 160; on the genesis of the term „*cogent reasons*", see Lester (2019) (attributing the first use of the term to the EU).

317 *US – Stainless Steel (Mexico)*, para. 161.

318 *US – Stainless Steel (Mexico)*, para. 161.

319 *US – Stainless Steel (Mexico)*, para. 161.

320 *US – Stainless Steel (Mexico)*, para. 162.

reasons" for such deviation. The panel in that dispute had to decide a legal issue – again zeroing in anti-dumping proceedings – on which it agreed with the respondent, the US, and earlier panels who had addressed the same issue, but on which the Appellate Body had repeatedly ruled to the contrary.[321] After reviewing the case law of the Appellate Body on precedential effect,[322] the panel indicated that a panel had the power and indeed the obligation to disregard Appellate Body precedent if that was warranted.[323] However, in the end the panel nevertheless followed the Appellate Body, in particular because refusing to do so in the face of repeated and consistent Appellate Body rulings on an issue, like in the case before it, would run contrary to the DSU's objective of prompt settlement of disputes (Art. 3.3 of the DSU).[324] On appeal, the EC argued „*that, if the Panel Report is construed as finding that a panel can invoke ‚cogent reasons' for departing from previous Appellate Body rulings on the same issue of legal interpretation,*" then the Appellate Body should reverse that finding.[325] The Appellate Body noted that since the panel had, despite its reservations, followed Appellate Body precedent, it did „*appear to have acceded to the hierarchical structure contemplated in the DSU.*"[326] Therefore, the Appellate Body saw no need to address the EC's appeal, i.e., it left the issue open.[327] Since then, several panels have declared with regard to specific Appellate Body rulings that they would follow them because there were no

321 Panel report, *US – Continued Zeroing*, paras. 7.162 – 7.169.

322 Panel report, *US – Continued Zeroing*, paras. 7.170 – 7.177.

323 Panel report, *US – Continued Zeroing*, paras. 7.180: „*In our view, ... a panel cannot simply follow the adopted report of another panel, or of the Appellate Body, without careful consideration of the facts and arguments made by the parties in the dispute before it. To do so would be to abdicate its responsibilities under Article 11. By the same token, however, neither should a panel make a finding different from that in an adopted earlier panel or Appellate Body report on similar facts and arguments without careful consideration and explanation of why a different result is warranted, and assuring itself that its finding does not undermine the goals of the system.*"

324 Panel report, *US – Continued Zeroing*, paras. 7.182.

325 Appellate Body report, *US – Continued Zeroing*, para. 358. Notably, in the earlier *US – Stainless Steel (Mexico)* case, the EC as third party had made the opposite argument, namely that a „*rule whereby panels must follow Appellate Body findings on legal questions would not prevent panels from departing from earlier decisions, provided there are ‚cogent reasons' for doing so*" (Appellate Body report, *US – Stainless Steel* [*Mexico*], para. 51 [from the summary of the position of the EC as third party]).

326 *US – Continued Zeroing*, para. 365.

327 *US – Continued Zeroing*, para. 365.

„cogent reasons" to do otherwise,[328] thereby, on the one hand, accepting precedential effect as the general rule, but, on the other hand, implying that they have the power to deviate from Appellate Body rulings should *„cogent reasons"* exist. So far, the Appellate Body has not had the opportunity to finally settle that question.

After having established what the precedential value of the Appellate Body rulings should be according to the Appellate Body, we will also briefly look at the empirical record, i.e., to what extent panels and the Appellate Body actually consider and follow earlier Appellate Body rulings. Concerning references by the Appellate Body to its own earlier reports (i.e., horizontal precedential effect), Jost Pauwelyn conducted a comprehensive citation analysis of all Appellate Body reports issued until the end of 2013.[329] He found that *„[f]rom its creation, the Appellate Body has opted for a strong de facto rule of precedent: in 108 reports [up to the end of 2013], the Appellate Body has dropped a total of 2,957 cross-references to earlier reports for an average of 27.4 cross-references per report ... (indeed, this trend began with the second report ...); ... this strong de facto rule of precedent has continued unabated over time and, if anything, an upward trend can be detected"*.[330] This confirms the anecdotal evidence from reading Appellate Body reports and the results of qualitative studies.[331] There are no comparable empirical studies for citations of panels to Appellate Body reports.[332] However, not only is every regular reader of panel

328 See the following panel reports: *China – Rare Earths*, paras. 7.61, 7.72, 7.99, 7.104 and 7.114 – 7.115; *US – Countervailing and Anti-Dumping Measures (China)*, paras. 7.316 – 7.317, 7.326, 7.342, and 7.351 – 7.352; *EU – Biodiesel (Argentina)*, para. 7.276; *Canada – Welded Pipe*, paras. 7.22 and 7.37; *EU – Biodiesel (Indonesia)*, para. 7.26; *US – Supercalendered Paper*, para. 7.306; and *EU – Energy Package*, para. 7.1350.

329 Pauwelyn (2016).

330 Pauwelyn (2016), p. 143.

331 See, for instance, the early qualitative study Bhala (1999b) (analyzing the Appellate Body's case law on procedural issues inaugurated in *US – Wool Shirts and Blouses* and *EC – Bananas III* and on substantive issues in the areas of Art. XX of the GATT, like product determinations, and Art. XIII of the GATT).

332 There are at least two empirical studies on citation of precedent by WTO panels, namely Pelc (2014) and Hsiang/Nyarko (2015), but both have a different focus. Pelc is interested in the commercial value a dispute has as precedent for the complaining party in that dispute. Hsiang/Nyarko analyze how the background of the panel chairs (lawyer vs. non-lawyer and common law vs. civil law) influences the extent to which a panel cites to precedents. Neither study distinguishes between panel reports and Appellate Body reports.

reports aware of the prevalence of Appellate Body precedents in these reports, it is also noteworthy that panels almost never depart from applicable Appellate Body rulings. Indeed, in the more than 250 panel reports issued up to date, there are, as far as one can tell, only three instances of an outright refusal to follow the Appellate Body, all concerning the Appellate Body's controversial zeroing jurisprudence.[333]

Summarizing the Appellate Body's position and practice, the Appellate Body has, one the one hand, never claimed that either itself or panels are legally bound by earlier Appellate Body (or panel) rulings, i.e., according to the Appellate Body, there is no de jure precedential effect. Indeed, building on its case law, starting with *Japan – Alcoholic Beverage II*, the Appellate Body in its crucial *US – Stainless Steel* (*Mexico*) report explicitly confirmed that „*[i]t is well settled that Appellate Body reports are not binding, except with respect to resolving the particular dispute between the parties.*“[334] On the other hand, however, it is obvious that there is substantial de facto precedential effect. The Appellate Body expects panels to follow Appellate Body precedent (*US – Oil Country Tubular Goods Sunset Reviews*) and finds it deeply troubling if a panel fails to do so (*US – Stainless Steel* (*Mexico*)). Moreover, only (but at least) „*cogent reasons*“ can justify departure from precedent (*US – Stainless Steel* (*Mexico*)). As explained, it is not yet clear whether the Appellate Body deems such deviation from precedent for „*cogent reasons*“ permissible only for itself (limitation of horizontal precedential effect), or also for panels (limitation of vertical precedential effect). In any event, in practice both the Appellate Body and panels rely heavily on past Appellate Body rulings.

In contrast to the Appellate Body, the US argues that, under the DSU and the WTO Agreement, Appellate Body and panel rulings have no precedential effect whatsoever. In other words, each panel and each division of the Appellate

333 First, panel report in *US – Zeroing* (*Japan*), paras. 7.99 (refusal to follow Appellate Body precedent) and 7.143 (conclusion), reversed by the Appellate Body report in *US – Zeroing* (*Japan*), para. 138 (reversing the panel's finding in para. 7.143; however, the Appellate Body did not comment on the panel's refusal to follow Appellate Body precedent); second, panel report in *US – Stainless Steel* (*Mexico*), paras. 7.106 (refusal to follow Appellate Body precedent) and 7.43 (conclusion), reversed by the Appellate Body report in *US – Stainless Steel* (*Mexico*), paras. 134 (reversing the panel's finding in para. 7.43) and 162 (expressing deep concern about the panel's refusal to follow Appellate Body precedent) (discussed above); third, panel report in *US – Differential Pricing Methodology* (appealed by Canada on 4 June 2019, appeal still pending), para. 7.107.

334 *US – Stainless Steel* (*Mexico*), para. 158.

Body should decide any legal issue de novo, without any deference to prior rulings on the same issue. According to the US, panels and the Appellate Body may refer to prior panel or Appellate Body rulings only for their persuasive value, but not because of any precedential value.[335] That would mean that panel and Appellate Body reports would be no different in that respect than, for instance, „persuasive" academic literature. Furthermore, and consistent with that, the US strenuously objects to the notion that deviation from prior rulings should only be allowed for *„cogent reasons"*, rather than whenever a later panel or Appellate Body has a different view on an issue.[336] As an empirical matter, the US also claims that parties to dispute settlement proceedings indeed refer to prior rulings for their persuasive value only, contending that *„there was no support for the proposition that parties cited to reports because they considered them somehow binding on or precedential for subsequent panels and the Appellate Body"*.[337]

What are the legal arguments of the US for this complete rejection of any precedential effect? Three arguments stand out. First, the US posits that the function of panels and the Appellate Body is solely to assist the DSB in resolving specific disputes between member states, but not to provide guidance for the future through any system of precedent. It derives this in particular from Art. 3.7 of the DSU on the overall objective of the DSU, Arts. 11, 7.1, 19.1 and 3.2 of the DSU on the function of panels, and, finally, Arts. 17.6 and 17.13 of the DSU on the function of the Appellate Body.[338] Second, and complementary to the first, the task of adopting abstract interpretations that provide guidance for the future has been assigned by the member states to different bodies within the WTO, namely the Ministerial Conference and the General Council,

335 Minutes of the DSB meeting of 18 December 2018 (WT/DSB/M/423), paras. 4.7, 4.10 and 4.19.

336 See minutes of the DSB meeting of 18 December 2018 (WT/DSB/M/423), paras. 4.9 and 4.24; in addition, in recent dispute settlement proceedings the US has objected to the use of the notion of *„cogent reasons"* in panel reports, and has asked panels to strike that term and references to the relevant Appellate Body jurisprudence on precedential effect; see panel report in *US – Pipe and Tube Products (Turkey)*, paras. 2.45 – 2.48 and 2.51 – 5.52 (panel acceded to the request, but followed Appellate Body precedent), and panel report in *US – Differential Pricing Methodology*, paras. 7.106 – 7.107 and Annex A-5 (Interim Review), paras. 2.13 – 2.14 (panel rejected the request, but refused to follow Appellate Body precedent).

337 Minutes of the DSB meeting of 18 December 2018 (WT/DSB/M/423), para. 4.19.

338 See, in particular, minutes of the DSB meeting of 18 December 2018 (WT/DSB/M/423), para. 4.5 (*„function of panels and the Appellate Body under the DSU"*).

which, pursuant to Art. IX:2 of the WTO Agreement, have the exclusive authority to adopt interpretations of the WTO agreements, an authority explicitly acknowledged in Art. 3.9 of the DSU.[339] Third, since the Appellate Body can make mistakes, and in particular may engage in interpretations that, contrary to Arts. 3.2 and 19.2 of the DSU, *„add to or diminish the rights and obligations provided in the covered agreements“*, attributing precedential effect to Appellate Body rulings would make it impossible (or at least more difficult) to correct such mistakes and thus increase the likelihood of violations of Arts. 3.2 and 19.2 of the DSU.[340]

Turning to the evaluation of the US criticism and its arguments, the first point to note is that the US position of rejecting any precedential value of panel and Appellate Body reports is rather extreme. This becomes especially apparent if one compares the WTO disputes settlement system with the International Court of Justice (ICJ). The founding instrument of the ICJ, the Statute of the ICJ, contains, unlike the DSU, an explicit prohibition of de jure precedential effect. Art. 59 of the Statute stipulates that *„[t]he decision of the Court has no binding force except between the parties and in respect of that particular case.“* Nevertheless, in practice the ICJ usually follows its own settled jurisprudence,[341] and, indeed, has described its approach to precedent in terms stri-

339 See, in particular, minutes of the DSB meeting of 18 December 2018 (WT/DSB/M/423), paras. 4.3 – 4.4, 4.6 – 4.7, 4.10, 4.14 – 4.15, 4.21, and 4.25.

340 See minutes of the DSB meeting of 18 December 2018 (WT/DSB/M/423), paras. 4.6, 4.19, and 4.25.

341 On the treatment of precedent by the International Court of Justice, see Alschner/Charlotin (2018); Haynes (2014), pp. 515 – 518; Guillaume (2011), pp. 7 – 12; Shahabuddeen (1996) (see p. 239: *„[A] decision [of the ICJ] which cannot be distinguished on valid grounds will be followed in a latter case unless it is shown to have been clearly wrong“*); and Clemons (1996), pp. 1503 – 1504. Already in 1944, a United Nations Report of the Informal Inter-Allied Committee on the Future of the Permanent Court of International Justice pointed out that there is no necessary conflict between the prohibition of de jure stare decisis in Art. 59 of the then Statute of the Permanent Court of International Justice, which would become Art. 59 of the Statute of the International Court of Justice, and the practice of following precedent: *„The effect of [Art. 59] has, in our opinion, sometimes been misinterpreted. What it means is not that the decisions of the Court have no effect as precedents for the Court or for international law in general, but that they do not possess the binding force of particular decisions in the relations between the countries who are parties to the Statute. The provision in question in no way prevents the Court from treating its own judgments as precedents, and indeed it follows from Article 38 … that the Court's decisions are themselves ‚subsidiary means for the determination of rules of law.'“* (American Journal of International Law 39 [1945], Supplement: Official Documents, pp. 1 – 15, p. 20, para. 63).

kingly similar to those of the Appellate Body: „[*W*]*hile* [*its prior*] *decisions are in no way binding on the Court, it will not depart from its settled jurisprudence unless it finds very particular reasons to do so.*“[342] More generally, Gilbert Guillaume concludes after a review of how various international courts use their own precedents that although „*all the international jurisdictions distance themselves in principle from the rule of stare decisis* ... [,] *they construct an entire jurisprudence based on their own precedent.*“[343] On the national level, even civil law systems which reject, like the Statute of the ICJ, de jure stare decisis, still attribute a certain degree of weight to precedent through doctrines such as *jurisprudence constante.*[344] This ubiquity of at least some sort of de facto precedential effect is not surprising. Following precedent, at least as the general rule (unless there are „*very particular*“ [ICJ] or „*cogent*“ [Appellate Body] reasons to do otherwise), and thereby being consistent, serves important goals, notably, first, the rule-of-law principle of treating like cases alike, and,

342 *Application of the Convention on the Prevention and Punishment of the Crime of Genocide* (*Croatia v. Serbia*), Preliminary Objections, Judgment, 18 November 2008, ICJ Reports (2008), para. 53; confirmed in *Application of the Convention on the Prevention and Punishment of the Crime of Genocide* (*Croatia v. Serbia*), Merits, Judgment, 3 February 2015, ICJ Reports (2015), para. 125.

343 Guillaume (2011), p. 14; for similar statements, see Bederman (2016), p. 50: „*The decisions of these* [*international*] *tribunals are not, strictly speaking, binding precedent* (*or stare decisis*), *not even for the institution which issued the decision. ... Happily, the reality of judicial precedent does not coincide with the theory. The truth is that international tribunals almost invariably follow their precedents, especially on procedural issues, and it is very routine for international lawyers to rely heavily on judicial decisions to support their arguments.*“; Cohen (2015), p. 269: „*International law today, like international law a century ago, generally denies international precedents doctrinal force. ... And yet ..., the invocation of international decisions as precedent is ubiquitous. ... Across international law, practitioners invoke it and tribunals apply it.*“ The only international court which is bound by its founding instrument to de jure precedential effect is the Caribbean Court of Justice, see Revised Treaty of Chaguaramas Establishing the Caribbean Community including the CARICOM Single Market and Economy (signed on 5 July 2001 and entered into force on 4 February 2002), Art. 221 („*Judgments of the Court shall constitute legally binding precedents for parties in proceedings before the Court unless such judgments have been revised in accordance with Article 219*“); see on that Haynes (2014).

344 For the relevance of stare decisis and jurisprudence constante on the level of national constitutional law, see Lundmark (2017), p. 353 („*Stare decisis is not limited to the common law world. Convincing evidence of a similar process can be found in civil law jurisdictions like Germany.*“) and Camarena González (2016) (case study of Mexico and Columbia); for a broad comparative study of the role of precedent in different jurisdictions see MacCormick/Summers (1997) (with contributions on the role of precedent in Germany, Finland, France, Italy, Norway, Poland, Spain, Sweden, UK, US and the law of the EU).

second, the related objectives of stability, predictability, and clarity.[345] The objectives of stability, predictability, and clarity are particularly important in the area of economics and trade. Knowing clearly and in advance about a rule, which allows planning, is often more important for economic actors than the actual content of the rule.[346] Therefore, it is no accident that the DSU – unlike, for instance, the Statute of the ICJ – expressly emphasizes the values of stability, predictability and clarity. According to Art. 3.2 of the DSU, as highlighted by the Appellate Body in *US – Stainless Steel (Mexico)*,[347] „*[t]he dispute settlement system of the WTO is a central element in providing security and predictability to the multilateral trading system*", and „*[t]he Members recognize that it serves (..) to clarify the existing provisions*" of the WTO agreements. In sum, given the importance of consistency in judicial decision-making, as reflected in the prevalence of some form of de facto stare decision in international judicial fora, and the DSU's explicit emphasis on „*security and predictability*" and „*clarif[ication] of the existing provisions*", one would and should, contrary to the US position, expect panels and the Appellate Body to accord prior rulings a substantial degree of precedential value.[348]

Moreover, the empirical claim of the US that parties to dispute settlement proceedings cite to reports only because of their persuasive value lacks plausibility. Of course, and hopefully, persuasive value will be one reason, and an important reason, for referring to prior panel and Appellate Body reports.[349]

345 On rationales for following precedent, see, for instance, Cohen (2015), pp. 281 – 285.

346 Cf. Piérola (2014), p. 428.

347 *US – Stainless Steel (Mexico)*, para. 157.

348 Cf. the view on precedent in the influential Sutherland report on the future of the WTO (Sutherland et al. [2004]), para. 231: „*It is generally agreed that the strictest type of precedent … is not applicable in international proceedings … However, it is quite clear that some degree of ‚precedent' concepts motivates the WTO dispute settlement processes (as well as most other international law tribunals process). This reliance on prior cases, while not always determinative, and certainly not totally binding on subsequent panel cases, nevertheless provides a degree of consistency which, in turn, enhances the predictability of the whole system. That is called for by the DSU, when it stresses the goal of providing ‚security and predictability.'*"

349 On the importance of persuasive value, see former Appellate Body member Unterhalter (2015), pp. 471 – 473 („*[L]et us turn to a consideration of the decisions of the Appellate Body as a source of its authority. All the trappings of authority and the most thorough adherence to proper procedure will never salvage the reputation of a court or tribunal if its decisions, and the reasons that support them, do not command respect. Respect is not the same as agreement. Think about it this way: in every dispute, the party that does not prevail may not be expected to agree with the decision, but the question is whether the reasoning that is*

But persuasive value alone could never explain the dominance of citations to case law, as compared to, for instance, academic literature, in WTO dispute settlement proceedings.[350] Only persuasive value in combination with precedential value can do that, especially considering that many rulings of the Appellate Body have been quite controversial, that is, have not been persuasive to everyone.

After these general remark on the position of the US, we will now address the first of the three main US arguments against precedential effect, namely that the function of panels and the Appellate Body is only to resolve specific disputes, but not to provide guidance for the future through any system of precedent. We will examine the three DSU bases invoked by the US in support of this argument, namely Art. 3.7 on the aim of the DSU, Arts. 11, 7.1, 19.1 and 3.2 on the function of the panels, and Arts. 17.6 and 17.13 on the function of the Appellate Body.

Starting with the first basis, in support of its claim that *„fundamentally, the purpose of the WTO dispute settlement system was to resolve trade disputes between Members"*, the US quotes the second sentence of Art. 3.7 of the DSU, which reads: *„The aim of the dispute settlement mechanism is to secure a positive solution to a dispute"*.[351] Now, no one would deny that the core function of the WTO disputes settlement system, including panels and the Appellate Body, is to settle disputes between member states. However, contrary to the assertions of the US, it does not follow from this core function that the adjudicatory bodies should not give any precedential weight to their earlier rulings. This

---

offered nevertheless meets a threshold of persuasive reasonableness. ... I would suggest that the law developed by the Appellate Body exceeds this threshold."), and current Appellate Body member Graham (2014), p. 322 (*„Why do [governments] comply with our decisions? ... I would suggest there is a more fundamental reason why governments comply with Appellate Body decisions: Because our decisions are respected."*).

350 Apparently, there are no empirical studies yet on the use of academic literature and case law by the parties to WTO dispute settlement proceedings. However, the dominance of case law seems uncontested; see, for instance Unterhalter (2015), p. 473: *„[N]o observer of the practices of the dispute settlement system could fail to conclude that past decisions of the Appellate Body and the panels are central to the legal reasoning relied upon by litigants"*. As to the Appellate Body itself, references to academic literature are insignificant compared to references to its own reports; between 1996 and 2013, the Appellate Body has made on average only 1.4 citations per report to academic literature (Helmersen [2016], p. 344), compared to 27.4 citations per report to its own reports (Pauwelyn [2016], p. 143).

351 Minutes of the DSB meeting of 18 December 2018 (WT/DSB/M/423), para. 4.5.

can be illustrated by Art. 3.7 of the DSU itself. The US quotes only its second sentence. To understand the meaning of that sentence its context is important, though. Here, relevant context are the two sentences directly preceding and following it. The first sentence of Art. 3.7 of the DSU states that „[*b*]*efore bringing a case, a Member shall exercise its judgement as to whether action under these procedures would be fruitful*“, and the third sentence adds that „[*a*] *solution mutually acceptable to the parties to a dispute and consistent with the covered agreements is clearly to be preferred.*“ In other words, the emphasis of the first three sentences of Art. 3.7 of the DSU is on finding amicable solutions to disputes as opposed to needless litigation. However, if panels and the Appellate Body would accord prior rulings no precedential effect whatsoever, as demanded by the US, then litigation would become more likely, contrary to the objective of Art. 3.7 of the DSU, because even if a legal issue had already been settled in prior reports, a party that is not happy with that outcome would have an incentive to relitigate the issue.[352] In summary, the objectives of securing „*a positive solution to a dispute*“ (Art. 3.7 of the DSU) and providing „*security and predictability*“ (Art. 3.2 of the DSU) through following precedent are not in tension with each other, but usually go hand in hand.

Concerning the second element of the first main US argument, the function of the panels, the US states that, pursuant to the first sentence of Art. 11 of the DSU, the „*function of the panels is to assist the DSB in discharging its responsibilities*“ under the DSU, to which end, according to the standard terms of reference for panels in Art. 7.1 of the DSU and the second sentence of Art. 11 of the DSU, a panel is entrusted with (only) two tasks, namely, first, to examine the matter before it and, second, to make findings assisting the DSB in making the recommendations pursuant to Art. 19.1 of the DSU, i.e., the recommendation to the member state concerned, in case of a finding of breach of WTO law, to come into compliance.[353] The first task of the panel, the examination of the matter before it, includes, according to Art. 11 of the DSU, „*an objective assessment of … the applicability of and conformity with the relevant covered agreements*“. In order to determine how a panel is to undertake such „*objective*

352 See, to the same effect, statement of Brazil in the minutes of the DSB meeting of 19 December 2018 (WT/DSB/M/423), para. 4.29: „*Brazil could foresee a scenario where greater uncertainty in the dispute settlement system could provoke an increase in the number of cases brought to the dispute settlement system and a decrease in the willingness of Members to have recourse to mutually agreed solutions. This would undermine the clear preference for amicable settlement reflected in Article 3.7 of the DSU.*“

353 Minutes of the DSB meeting of 18 December 2018 (WT/DSB/M/423), para. 4.5.

assessment" of the relevant WTO agreements, the US looks to Art. 3.2 of the DSU, which, according to the US, „*further informed the function of a panel established by the DSB to assist it.*"[354] From the statement in Art. 3.2 of the DSU that „[*t*]*he Members recognize that* [*the dispute settlement system of the WTO*] *serves ... to clarify the existing provisions of those agreements in accordance with customary rules of interpretation of public international law*" the US follows that „*the DSU directed WTO adjudicators to apply „customary rules of interpretation of public international law", reflected in Articles 31 to 33 of the Vienna Convention on the Law of Treaties*",[355] and asserts that „[*t*]*hose rules of interpretation did not assign to interpretations given as part of dispute settlement a precedential value for purposes of discerning the meaning of agreement text.*"[356] The US concludes that „*were a panel to decide to simply apply the reasoning in prior Appellate Body reports alone, it would fail to carry out its function, as established by the DSB, under Articles 7.1, 11, and 3.2 of the DSU to make findings on the applicability of existing provisions of the covered agreements, as understood objectively through customary rules of interpretation.*"[357]

The problem with this argument of the US is that it paints only part of the picture. The US itself points out that Art. 3.2 of the DSU „*further informs the function of a panel established by the DSB to assist it*", very similar to the Appellate Body, which considers that „*the meaning of ‚*[*t*]*he function of panels' in the first sentence of Article 11 is informed by the general provisions contained in Article 3 of the DSU, which sets out the basic principles of the WTO dispute settlement system.*"[358] Of course, Art. 3.2 does not only refer, in its second sentence, to „*customary rules of interpretation*", the focus of the US in the reasoning above, but also, in its very first sentence, to „*security and predictability*", which calls for, as explained above, some degree of precedential effect. There is no reason to assume that only the second, but not the first sentence of Art. 3.2 „*informs the function of a panel*". In an attempt to negate the importance of the first sentence, the US claims that the Appellate Body's reliance on this provision „*rests on a misunderstanding of the text of Article 3.2.*"[359] It argues that because „[*t*]*here is no ‚shall' or ‚may' in this text*", the „*text*

354 Minutes of the DSB meeting of 18 December 2018 (WT/DSB/M/423), para. 4.5.
355 Minutes of the DSB meeting of 18 December 2018 (WT/DSB/M/423), para. 4.5.
356 Minutes of the DSB meeting of 18 December 2018 (WT/DSB/M/423), para. 4.4.
357 Minutes of the DSB meeting of 18 December 2018 (WT/DSB/M/423), para. 4.6.
358 Appellate Body report, *US – Stainless Steel* (*Mexico*), para. 157.
359 Minutes of the DSB meeting of 18 December 2018 (WT/DSB/M/423), para. 4.15.

of Article 3.2 is neither a directive to panels or the Appellate Body nor an authorization for them", but rather „*a statement of what Members have agreed flows from the system when it operates in accordance with the provisions agreed by Members in the DSU.*"[360] And since the US contends that the other provisions of the DSU do not permit any precedential effect, it considers that Art. 3.2 has no bearing on the issue. However, to deduce from the absence of „shall" or „may" that the first sentence of Art. 3.2 has, in essence, no normative force, is not only unconvincing, but also in contradiction to the US's own reliance on the second sentence of Art. 3.2, which does not contain „shall" or „may" either. Moreover, there are further provisions in Art. 3 of the DSU, informing the function of the panels, which back precedential effect. First, as mentioned above, the preference expressed by Art. 3.7 of the DSU of amicable settlements over litigation, increases the need for „*security and predictability*" and „*clarif[ication] of the existing provisions*" which settled jurisprudence provides. Second, Art. 3.3 of the DSU stipulates that „*[t]he prompt settlement [of disputes] is essential to the effective functioning of the WTO and the maintenance of a proper balance between the rights and obligations of Members*". However, if a panel refuses to follow clearly established Appellate Body precedent, the most likely result is that the losing party will appeal and that the Appellate Body will then overrule the panel, causing unnecessary delay, contrary to the objective of Art. 3.3 of the DSU.[361]

As to the „*customary rules of interpretation of public international law*", it is indeed true that Arts. 31 – 33 of the VCLT do not refer to precedent. However, that does not mean that they prohibit the use of precedent. This is indicated by the fact that, as described above, international adjudicatory bodies almost universally rely on precedent. It is difficult to argue that such a widespread practice in public international law violates the „*customary rules*" in that area.

---

360 Minutes of the DSB meeting of 18 December 2018 (WT/DSB/M/423), para. 4.15.

361 On Art. 3.3 of the DSU as support for precedential effect, see the position of Mexico as summarized in the Appellate Body report in *US – Stainless Steel (Mexico)*, para. 21, and the panel report in *US – Continued Zeroing*, para. 7.182 („*In addition to the goal of providing security and predictability to the multilateral trading system, we recall ... Article 3.3 of the DSU ... Given the consistent adopted jurisprudence on the legal issues that are before us ..., we consider that providing prompt resolution to this dispute in this manner will best serve the multiple goals of the DSU, and, on balance, is furthered by following the Appellate Body's adopted findings in this case.*"). The Appellate Body in its jurisprudence on prudential effect has, so far, mentioned „prompt settlement" only once in passing, and without explicit reference to Art. 3.3 of the DSU (*US – Stainless Steel [Mexico]*, para. 161).

Moreover, applying precedent does not mean that a panel could not or would not apply the interpretative criteria set out in Arts. 31 – 33 of the VCLT, especially the basic rule of Art. 31(1) that „*[a] treaty shall be interpreted in good faith in accordance with the ordinary meaning to be given to the terms of the treaty in their context and in the light of its object and purpose*" because legitimate precedent is itself the result of an interpretation using these criteria. Therefore, if a panel follows precedent rather than to adopt a possibly different interpretation it might have reached through applying the criteria of Arts. 31 – 33 of the VCLT without such precedent, it does not ignore Arts. 31 – 33, but rather choses the precedent's application of these interpretative rules, in consideration of the DSU's objectives of „*security and predictability*" and „*prompt settlement*", which it has to take into account in its „*objective assessment*" under Art. 11 of the DSU. Additionally, following precedent does not necessarily prevent a panel from a searching examination of the legal questions before it, not at least, as the panel in the case *China – Rare Earths* remarked, because „*where a party asks a panel to deviate from a prior Appellate Body finding on a question of law on the basis of novel legal arguments, a full exploration of those arguments may assist the Appellate Body in the event of an appeal, particularly where those arguments raise complex legal issues.*"[362]

On the third and final element of the first main argument of the US, the function of the Appellate Body, the US maintains that „*[t]he Appellate Body's task under the DSU was similarly [i.e., similar to that of the panels] limited to assisting the DSB in discharging its functions under the DSU, albeit more so than panels.*"[363] In substantiation of that claim the US quotes Art. 17.6 of the DSU („*An appeal shall be limited to issues of law covered in the panel report and legal interpretations developed by the panel*") and Art. 17.13 of the DSU („*The Appellate Body may uphold, modify or reverse the legal findings and conclusions of the panel*"). The US later repeats its emphasis on the limits of the Appellate Body's power in response to the Appellate Body's defense of vertical precedential effect. As set out above, in *US – Stainless Steel (Mexico)*, the Appellate Body justified vertical precedential effect with the „*hierarchical structure contemplated in the DSU*", i.e., the fact that the Appellate Body has the power on appeal to overturn legal interpretations of the panels (Arts. 17.6 and 17.13 of the DSU), and that a panel's failure to follow Appellate Body precedent „*undermines the development of a coherent and predictable body of jurisprud-*

362 Panel report, *China – Rare Earths*, para. 7.58.

363 Minutes of the DSB meeting of 18 December 2018 (WT/DSB/M/423), para. 4.5.

ence".[364] The US rejects the notion of a hierarchical structure and claims that *„[a]rticles 17.6 and 17.13 of the DSU do not ‚vest' the Appellate Body with broad authority to develop ‚a coherent and predictable body of jurisprudence.' … In fact, those articles are limitations on the parameters of appellate review and on the permissible actions of the Appellate Body."*[365] It is indeed the case that Arts. 17.6 and 17.13 of the DSU limit the Appellate Body to reviewing and, if necessary, overturning panels on legal issues only. However, as far as precedential effect is concerned, this is clearly the decisive power. If one wants to WTO dispute settlement system to develop *„a coherent and predictable body of jurisprudence"* (which, of course, the US refuses to acknowledge as an objective of the DSU), the main responsibility for that has to lay with the body that has, within the system, the final word on legal interpretation, namely the Appellate Body.[366] This is reinforced by the fact that the Appellate Body, in contrast to the panels, is a standing body, which facilitates a greater degree of continuity and consistency on the level of the Appellate Body than on that of the panels.[367] A second, but equally important argument in favor of vertical stare decisis is, as already mentioned, the DSU's objective of *„prompt settlement"* of disputes (Art. 3.3 of the DSU).[368]

---

364 *US – Stainless Steel (Mexico)*, para. 161.

365 Minutes of the DSB meeting of 18 December 2018 (WT/DSB/M/423), para. 4.21.

366 Formally, of course, it is the DSB who has the final word, since it has to adopt panel and Appellate Body reports (Arts. 16 and 17.14 of the DSU). However, since a report is adopted unless the DSB decides by consensus not to adopt it (Arts. 16.4 and 17.14 of the DSU), meaning that the consent of just one member, including the one that won the dispute, is enough for adoption, it is virtually impossible for the DSB to prevent adoption, and indeed has never happened yet. See also infra, fn. 436-437 and accompanying text.

367 China argues that the dissatisfaction with the lack of coherence in the pre-WTO case law of panels had been one of the reasons for creating the Appellate Body in the first place; see statement of China in the minutes of the DSB meeting of 18 December 2018 (WT/DSB/M/423), para. 4.35: *„During the GATT-era, Panels had issued reports with conflicting interpretations, and that had been seen as problematic. … The Appellate Body had been, in part, a deliberate response to the problem of inconsistent panel interpretations."*

368 Adjudicatory systems with more than one instance, like the WTO dispute settlement system, are rare in international law. One such example is the Court of Justice of the European Union, which is comprised of the General Court and the Court of Justice (Art. 19(1) of the TEU). Decisions of the former can be appealed to the latter (Art. 256(1) of the TFEU). Similar to the WTO dispute settlement system, there is no explicit rule on whether the General Court is bound by decisions of the Court of Justice. Nevertheless, in practice the General Court follows rulings of the Court of Justice, even if it disagrees with those rulings. See Bradley (2014) and the judgment of the General Court of 30 September 2010 in Case T-85/09 *Kadi* v *Commission*, paras. 112 – 121, in particular para. 121: *„[T]he*

Moving on to the second main argument of the US, concerning Art. IX:2 of the WTO Agreement and Art. 3.9 of the DSU, does the exclusive power of the Ministerial Conference and the General Council to adopt authoritative interpretations prevent the Appellate Body from treating its prior rulings as precedent? According to the US, the answer is yes because „*[t]o say that an Appellate Body interpretation in one dispute was precedent or controlling for later disputes would effectively convert that interpretation into an authoritative interpretation of the covered agreement*", which would „*directly contradict*" Art. IX:2 of the WTO Agreement.[369] There would indeed be a direct contradiction if the Appellate Body claimed a power equivalent to that granted under Art. IX:2 of the WTO Agreement. As pointed out approvingly by the US,[370] the Appellate Body itself acknowledged as much when it said in its very first case on precedential effect, *Japan – Alcoholic Beverages II*, that „*[t]he fact that such an ‚exclusive authority' in interpreting the treaty has been established so specifically in the WTO Agreement is reason enough to conclude that such authority does not exist by implication or by inadvertence elsewhere.*"[371] However, the assertion that the Appellate Body has usurped a power that under Art. IX:2 of the WTO Agreement belongs to the Ministerial Conference and the General Council is wrong on two levels. First, as already mentioned above in the section on advisory opinions, neither the Appellate Body nor anyone else has ever claimed that panels or the Appellate Body would not be bound by an authoritative interpretation adopted pursuant to Art. IX:2 of the WTO Agreement. Hence, the Appellate Body accepts that such an authoritative interpretation would trump any prior Appellate Body ruling to the contrary. Second, only legally binding precedents, or de jure stare decisis, would be a true equivalent to the legally binding interpretations adopted under Art. IX:2 of the WTO Agreement, whereas, as explained above, the Appellate Body has consistently held that its precedents are *not* legally binding. Of course, it is also true that, while it rejects de jure stare decisis, the Appellate Body stands for substantial de facto precedential effect, i.e., as stated in *US – Stainless Steel (Mexico)*, „*absent cogent reasons*", the Appellate Body „*will resolve the same legal question*

---

appellate principle itself and the hierarchical judicial structure which is its corollary generally advise against the General Court revisiting points of law which have been decided by the Court of Justice."

369 Minutes of the DSB meeting of 18 December 2018 (WT/DSB/M/423), para. 4.6.

370 See minutes of the DSB meeting of 18 December 2018 (WT/DSB/M/423), para. 4.10.

371 *Japan – Alcoholic Beverages II*, p. 107.

in the same way in a subsequent case.“[372] However, there is little reason to believe that by reserving the final word on interpretation for the Ministerial Conference and the General Council, the member states wanted to prevent the Appellate Body from deciding consistently and predictably, in particular since the same member states had declared, in Art. 3.2 of the DSU, that the dispute settlement system should be central in providing „*security and predictability*“. Contrary to the US allegation that „*the Appellate Body asserted a very different approach in the „US – Stainless Steel (Mexico)“ dispute [than in its report in Japan – Alcoholic Beverages II] (..), without explaining the basis for that changed approach*“,[373] this line of reasoning is entirely consistent with the argument of the Appellate Body in *Japan – Alcoholic Beverages II.* In that case, the Appellate Body concluded that prior panel reports, on the one hand, „*are not binding*“ (i.e., no de jure stare decisis), but, on the other hand, „*create legitimate expectations among WTO Members, and, therefore, should be taken into account where they are relevant to any dispute*“ (i.e., some degree of de facto stare decisis).[374] The US tries to deny the second part of the Appellate Body's conclusion by rephrasing the Appellate Body's words of „*should be taken into account*“ as „*could be taken into account*“, and stressing that a panel may only rely on prior reports „*to the extent a panel finds the reasoning persuasive*“,[375] but this is simply a distortion of what the Appellate Body has said.

The third argument of the US is based on Arts. 3.2 and 19.2 of the DSU, according to which rulings and recommendations of panels and the Appellate Body „*cannot add to or diminish the rights and obligations provided in the covered agreements.*“ The US claims that the Appellate Body's approach on precedent „*would set the system on a path of departing from the agreed rights and obligations of Members under the WTO Agreement*“[376] because „*given the probability that some interpretations [of the Appellate Body] might be in error*“[377] and disregard rights and obligations of members in violation of Arts. 3.2 and 19.2, such errors could not be corrected, and, moreover, „*would accumulate over time, and where the Appellate Body in a subsequent appeal built its interpretation on a flawed interpretation, the interpretations and resulting findings*

372 *US – Stainless Steel (Mexico)*, para. 160.

373 Minutes of the DSB meeting of 18 December 2018 (WT/DSB/M/423), para. 4.9; see also paras. 4.10 and 4.15.

374 *Japan – Alcoholic Beverages II*, p. 108.

375 Minutes of the DSB meeting of 18 December 2018 (WT/DSB/M/423), para. 4.10.

376 Minutes of the DSB meeting of 18 December 2018 (WT/DSB/M/423), para. 4.25.

377 Minutes of the DSB meeting of 18 December 2018 (WT/DSB/M/423), para. 4.19.

would become more and more removed from what Members had agreed."[378] It is certainly true that, first, the Appellate Body, like any adjudicative body, can and sometimes will make mistakes, and, second, attributing any precedential weight to prior rulings will make it more difficult to reverse such mistakes. There is, indeed, in any system of precedential effect a trade-off between the goals pursued by following precedent, such as, in the WTO context, in particular „*security and predictability*", and the objective of getting the „correct" answer in each individual case. Because of this, few, if any, legal systems follow a system of strict stare decisis, whether de jure or de facto, but rather allow deviations from past rulings under certain conditions, for example, when an earlier ruling has come to be considered as clearly erroneous.[379] As we have seen, the Appellate Body, too, allows such deviations for „*cogent reasons*". However, since the DSU puts such emphasis on not adding to or diminishing rights and obligation provided in the WTO agreements, why not be on the safe side and, as the US demands, remove any precedential effect and thereby allow unencumbered corrections of any past interpretive mistakes? The problem with such an approach is not only that it would ignore the commitment to „*security and predictability*" of Art. 3.2 of the DSU, but also that it implicitly assumes that it is easy to determine when an interpretation has been erroneous and in violation of Arts. 3.2 and 19.2 of the DSU. Obviously, that assumption is false. Many legal questions before panels and the Appellate Body are difficult and controversial, with good arguments on both sides, and on which reasonable people (and adjudicators) can reasonably reach different conclusions. And, even though members from time to time claim that interpretations by panels or the Appellate Body violate Arts. 3.2 and 19.2,[380] there is rarely anything even close to a consensus among members on such allegati-

378 Minutes of the DSB meeting of 18 December 2018 (WT/DSB/M/423), para. 4.25; see also para. 4.6.

379 For an example from national law, see the US Supreme Court, which will not overrule its own constitutional precedent unless justification is provided by „*some special reason*" (*Planned Parenthood* v. *Casey*, 505 U.S. 833 [1992], 864) or „*strong grounds*" (*Janus v. Am. Fed. of State, County, & Mun. Employees*, 585 U.S. __ [2018], slip opinion, at 34); one factor in deciding whether to overrule is the quality of the precedent's reasoning (*Franchise Tax Board of California* v. *Gilbert*, 587 U.S. __ [2019], slip opinion, at 17); see more generally Murrill (2018).

380 For a list of examples of such claims, see Stewart/McDonough/Smith/Jorgensen (2013), pp. 393 – 394 („*Examples of Statements by WTO Members Expressing Concern That the Appellate Body Is Creating Rights or Obligations by Overreaching*").

ons.[381] All too often, one member's clear example of a breach of Arts. 3.2 and 19.2 is another member's clearly correct interpretation.[382] In such a situation, denying any precedential effect to prior rulings simply risks a back-and-forth in the decisions of different panels and Appellate Body divisions with different compositions at different times, endangering *„security and predictability"* and *„prompt settlement"*, without any guarantee that one interpretation is better or more faithful to Arts. 3.2 and 19.2 of the DSU than the other.

In conclusion, the problem with the US position on precedential effect is not that it does not raise noteworthy points, or that the practice of the Appellate Body is beyond criticism, far from it. The main problem is the extremism of the US position, which the US takes in order to be able to depict the Appellate Body's stance on precedential effect as *„yet another example of a failure by the Appellate Body to follow the rules agreed by Members"*.[383] This extremism lies in the fact that the US argues that panels and the Appellate Body should decide legal questions always de novo, without any deference to prior rulings, and therefore without trying to decide consistently and predictably over time. This is not only contrary to the common practice of courts and other adjudicatory bodies on the national and international level, but, importantly, it also ignores the DSU's explicit focus on *„security and predictability"* and *„clarif[ication] of the existing provisions"* (Art. 3.2 of the DSU). As explained above, none of the

381 There is probably only one instance where almost all member states agreed that the Appellate Body had gone beyond its mandate, namely when it allowed the submission of *amicus curiae* briefs by private parties in dispute settlement proceedings (see, in particular, the minutes of the special meeting of the General Council of 22 November 2000 on that issue [WT/GC/M/60]; see more generally on the *amicus curia* dispute Lim [2005]). Notably, in that instance it was the US that, more or less alone, defended the interpretation of the Appellate Body as proper (see minutes of the General Council meeting of 22 November 2000 [WT/GC/M/60], paras. 74 – 77).

382 For instance, while the US considers the Appellate Body's practice on precedential effect a clear example of overreach, Costa Rica made the opposite claim already in 1997, accusing Appellate Body of violating Arts. 3.2 and 19.2 of the DSU by *not* following precedent without good reasons; see minutes of the DSB meeting of 25 June 1997, statement of Costa Rica, p. 12: *„Even in legal systems not based on common law, precedents had an undeniable value. They clarified the interpretation of the rules and provided security and predictability to the relations governed by those rules. In Costa Rica's view any divergence from the GATT and WTO precedents had to be supported by sound and convincing legal reasoning. This had not been so in this case [i.e. US – Wool Shirt and Blouses]. The observations of the Panel and the Appellate Body had diverged from past practice and had modified the balance of rights and obligations which they claimed to be seeking to protect."*

383 Minutes of the DSB meeting of 18 December 2018 (WT/DSB/M/423), para. 4.25.

provisions invoked by the US prohibit panels and the Appellate Body from attributing a certain degree of de facto precedential weight to prior decisions and thus serving the DSU's objectives of *„security and predictability"* and *„clarif[ication] of the existing provisions"*, neither a panel's obligation to make an objective examination (Art. 11 of the DSU), nor the power of the Ministerial Conference and the General Council to adopt authoritative interpretations (Art. IX:2 of the WTO Agreement), or the prohibition to add to or diminish the rights and obligations of member states (Arts. 3.2 and 19.2 of the DSU).

That the position of the Appellate Body on precedential effect is closer to *„the rules agreed by Members"* than that of the US is also indicated by the reactions of the other members to statements of the US on the issue. Both at the DSB meeting of May 2008, in which the US criticized the Appellate Body's views on precedential effect in *US – Stainless Steel (Mexico)* harshly, and at the DSB meeting of December 2018, in which the US gave its extended statement on precedential effect, the majority of members commenting on the issue supported the Appellate Body's approach.[384] Moreover, even those critical of the Appellate Body's practice and supportive of the US position did not go as far as the US in its statement of December 2018. For instance, Colombia, which was probably closest to the US in both these meetings,[385] stating that although it *„understood and shared the concerns [of the US] regarding the use of precedent at the WTO"*, it still *„recogniz[ed] the need to provide security and predictability to the multilateral trading system through the development of a consistent line of jurisprudence"* and *„believed that prior appellate and panel reports constituted important doctrine for clarifying and interpreting the legal standards established in WTO agreements."* Furthermore, Colombia added *„that these concerns, while valid, were not enough to justify blocking of the appointments of the AB members."* Notably, in the early years of WTO dispute settlement even the US itself had claimed that the DSU requires panels to follow Appellate Body rulings. In 2001, in the panel proceedings in the case *US – Shrimps (Article 21.5 – Malaysia)*, in which Malaysia had criticized an earlier ruling of the Appellate Body, the US had argued *„that Malaysia makes the rather extraordinary ar-*

384 See minutes of the DSB meeting of 1 July 2008 (WT/DSB/M/250), paras. 46 – 73 (discussion of the Appellate Body report in *US – Stainless Steel (Mexico)*), and of 18 December 2018 (WT/DSB/M/23), paras. 4.26 – 4.37 (discussion of the US statement on precedential effect).

385 Minutes of the DSB meetings of 20 May 2008 (WT/DSB/M/250), para. 72, and 18 December 2018 (WT/DSB/M/423), para. 4.26; all statements from Colombia quoted in the main text are taken from para. 4.26 of the latter minutes.

gument that the Appellate Body was wrong and the Panel should ignore the Appellate Body finding. Nowhere does the DSU grant dispute settlement panels the authority to overrule the Appellate Body.“[386]

Its extreme position of denying any form of de facto precedential effect prevents the US from engaging with the Appellate Body's practice in a more meaningful and productive way. It is not the basic question of whether an adjudicatory body should follow its own precedents at all that is interesting and challenging, but rather the details of how such precedential effect should work. For example, in the same way as it would be unreasonable to completely disregard any past decision (zero precedential effect), it would equally make little sense to bind oneself to never changing prior rulings (absolute precedential effect), in particular if there are no other readily available means of correction (e.g., by a legislature). In that vein, Harlan Grant Cohen remarks in a study of precedential effect in international law that the fact „*that few (if any) regimes explicitly provide for precedential effect ... suggests that for the states designing those regimes, the optimal level of clarity and predictability is greater than a system of de novo review but less than one of stare decisis.*“[387] Transferring that to the WTO dispute settlement system, it is not especially fruitful to argue about whether „*absent cogent reasons*“, the Appellate Body should „*resolve the same legal question in the same way in a subsequent case*“ (clearly, it should), but rather what constitutes „*cogent reasons*“ that could justify or even require departure from prior rulings, something the Appellate Body has not yet addressed.[388] Similarly, should the Appellate Body pursue quite a rigid approach

386 Panel report, *US – Shrimps (Article 21.5 – Malaysia)*, para. 3.14, concerning the admissibility of amicus curiae briefs.

387 Cohen (2015), p. 282.

388 On the panel level, a first attempt at explaining what such „*cogent reasons*“ could be has been made by the panel in the dispute *US – Countervailing and Anti-Dumping Measures (China)*: „*To our minds, ‚cogent‘ reasons, i.e. reasons that could in appropriate cases justify a panel in adopting a different interpretation [than that of the Appellate Body], would encompass, inter alia: (i) a multilateral interpretation of a provision of the covered agreements under Article IX:2 of the WTO Agreement that departs from a prior Appellate Body interpretation; (ii) a demonstration that a prior Appellate Body interpretation proved to be unworkable in a particular set of circumstances falling within the scope of the relevant obligation at issue; (iii) a demonstration that the Appellate Body's prior interpretation leads to a conflict with another provision of a covered agreement that was not raised before the Appellate Body; or (iv) a demonstration that the Appellate Body's interpretation was based on a factually incorrect premise.*“ (panel report, para. 7.317). This passage was later quoted approvingly by the panel in the dispute *EC and certain member States – Large Civil*

to stare decisis and change course only under extraordinary circumstances, or should it be more open to new arguments or to admitting mistakes?[389] Equally worth discussing is the level of transparency about changes of case law that do take place, e.g., whether the Appellate Body should explicitly acknowledge overruling precedent.[390] In that respect, after an examination of three areas in which the Appellate Body has changed its case law over time, Frieder Roessler concludes critically that in all these areas the Appellate Body has failed to „*acknowledge and cogently explain the change*", thereby creating legal uncertainty.[391] Finding answers to these and other important questions concerning the role of precedent in the WTO is hindered rather than furthered by the absolutist position taken by the US.

Aircraft (*Article 21.5 – US*) (panel report, para. 6.1143). In other legal systems, detailed criteria for changing jurisprudence exist, for instance in the US legal system regarding changes by the US Supreme Court of its own precedents on constitutional law; see for a recent example *Knick* v. *Township of Scott, Pennsylvania, et al.*, 587 U.S. ___ (2019) (slip opinion), opinion of the Court, pp. 20 – 23, and for an overview Murrill (2018).

389 For an argument to that effect, see the dissenting opinion (most likely by Thomas R. Graham) in the recent Appellate Body report in *US – Countervailing Measures* (*China*) (*Article 21.5 – China*), paras. 5.242 – 5.281, e.g., para. 5.244 („*I believe the continuing lack of clarity as to what is a ‚public body' represents an instance of undue emphasis on ‚precedent', which has locked in a flawed interpretation that has grown more confusing with each iteration, as litigants and Appellate Body Divisions repeated the original flaw while trying to navigate around it. That is what I believe the majority has done here.*").

390 On that question, the current chairman of the Appellate Body, Ujal Singh Bhatia, remarked in 2018: „[*T*]*hroughout more than two decades of case law, the Appellate Body has never overtly overruled its prior decisions. This, of course, does not mean that one cannot discern certain shifts in the Appellate Body"s orientation and sensibility. ... An examination of our jurisprudence should convince you that Appellate Body jurisprudence is not always monolithic and, indeed, leaves ample room for the accommodation of future changes of direction. Yet, in my view, change best occurs at a piecemeal pace, rather than through abrupt ruptures of well-established jurisprudential trends. The physiological evolution of case law should, in my view, look more like a slow tectonic shift than a sudden earthquake.*" (Bhatia [2018], pp. 126 – 127).

391 Roessler (2015), p. 142; the three areas of law analyzed by him are judicial economy (pp. 132 – 134), the measure to be examined under Art. XX of the GATT (pp. 134 – 140) and other duties and charges on importation under Art. II:1(b) of the GATT (pp. 140 – 142).

C. Conclusions

After having analyzed in some detail the six areas of US concern on issues of procedure and interpretative approach (Rule 15, 90-day deadline, advisory opinions, appellate review of facts and of municipal law, precedential effect), what is the picture that emerges? We have found that on five of those (Rule 15, 90-day deadline, advisory opinions, appellate review of facts, precedential effect) no case can be made for a clear breach of the DSU or other WTO agreements. What is more, the legal arguments of the Appellate Body on all of these issues are stronger than those of the US. Only with regard to one issue (appellate review of municipal law), the Appellate Body's has arguably gone beyond what is permissible under the DSU, namely Art. 17.6 of the DSU. But even that one issue does not reach the level of a breach that would justify the blockage of all appointments to the Appellate Body because the legal question is a difficult one without an obvious answer, no other member has supported the US allegation of a clear breach (indeed, almost all members who took a position on that issue in the DSB agreed with the Appellate Body), and, finally, the consequences of blocking all appointments to the Appellate Body in breach of Art. 17.2 of the DSU are vastly disproportionate to the consequences of a misinterpretation of Art. 17.6 of the DSU through appellate review of findings on municipal law.

As stated at the outset of our analysis, the US and the Appellate Body agree on the proper interpretative approach to the extent that they both put most emphasis on the wording of the relevant WTO provisions (grammatical interpretation).[392] However, they reach opposite conclusions in the application of this interpretative approach to the six issues discussed here. According to the US, *„the Appellate Body had been acting contrary to the unambiguous text of the DSU.“*[393] Our analysis has demonstrated, though, that only with regard to one of the six issues, the 90-day deadline, the Appellate Body has clearly disregarded the wording of the DSU, namely Art. 17.5 of the DSU, and it was forced to do so for reasons mainly beyond its control, a fact repeatedly acknowledged by the membership, including, at least until the appointment crisis, the US. As far as the other five issues are concerned, the text of the DSU is simply not as unambiguous as the US asserts, and certainly not unambiguously in favor of the US allegations of Appellate Body overreach.

392 See supra, fn. 105 and accompanying text.

393 Minutes of the General Council meeting of 7 May 2019 (WT/GC/M/177), para. 4.154.

In an attempt to strengthen its credibility and to portray its blocking of appointments to the Appellate Body as an ultima ratio, the US has repeatedly emphasized that its complaints are not new, stating *„that for more than 15 years, across multiple US Administrations, the United States had been raising serious concerns with the Appellate Body's disregard for the rules set by WTO Members.*"[394] Our examination has shown, however, that this is only partly true for the six issues of interest here. Regarding three of these (Rule 15, 90-day deadline, review of facts), the US voiced its criticism for the first time *after* it had begun to block the appointments. Before the blockage, the US had for decades acquiesced in the practices it now contests, at times even explicitly supporting them. This contradictory behavior makes it doubtful whether the US argues in good faith on these three issues.

In summary, a close analysis of the six issues on procedure and interpretative approach presented by the US as prime evidence of its case against the Appellate Body simply does not bear out its claim that the Appellate Body is as a *„rule-breaking"* runaway institution that has *„felt free to depart from what WTO Members agreed to"*.[395] Consequently, from a legal point of view these six issues, whether viewed individually or as a whole, do not even come close to justifying the US blockage of all appointments to the Appellate Body.

394 DSB meeting of 27 August 2018 (WT/DSB/M/417), para. 12.2; see similar or identical US statements in the DSB meetings of 29 October 2018 (WT/DSB/M/420), para. 20.5; 21 November 2011 (WT/DSB/M/421), para. 21.4; 18 December 2018 (WT/DSB/M/423), para. 9.4; 28 January 2019 (WT/DSB/M425), para. 7.5; 25 February 2019 (WT/DSB/M/426), para. 5.6; 26 April 2019 (WT/DSB/M428), para. 11.3; 28 May 2019 (WT/DSB/M/429), para. 8.3; and 24 June 2019 (WT/DSB7M/430), para. 8.4.

395 Minutes of the General Council meeting of 12 December 2018 (WT/GC/M/175), statement of the US, para. 6.169.

V. A broader explanatory framework for the US blockage

If our analysis of the issues of procedure and interpretative approach is correct, i.e., that these issues fall far short of legally justifying the blockage of appointments to the Appellate Body, what does that tell us about the US motives for the continued blockage? Are the US concerns regarding these issues genuine, despite the weakness of the legal arguments of the US, or have they just been contrived for political purposes? Furthermore, is it plausible that the US would be willing to bring down the Appellate Body, and thereby potentially the whole dispute settlement system, just because of complaints about these issues of procedure and interpretative approach?

The position taken here is that, on the one hand, some of the allegations do indeed appear to be contrived, most notably the Rule 15 issue, and, in addition, it is hard to imagine that these issues of procedure and interpretative approach are really as important to the US as it has made out in its statements in the DSB since the start of the appointment crisis. But, on the other hand, it is also difficult to deny that the concerns and even frustrations of many on the US side with the Appellate Body are authentic and long-running, especially on issues of substantive law. As John Magnus, a US trade remedy lawyer and long-time critic of the Appellate Body, put it in a colloquium on the appointment crisis at the end of 2017: „*[W]hile the specific tactics that are being deployed [by the US] might surprise some observers, the depth of feeling underneath those tactics cannot surprise anyone.*"[396] More specifically, many US critics believe that the Appellate Body has prevented the US from getting what it had bargained for in 1995. Jennifer Hillman, US-appointed Appellate Body member from 2007 to 2011, expressed this notion in the just-mentioned colloquium by stating that „*we got here [i.e., to the appointment crisis] because, in the end of the day, I think the system has not worked out how the United States anticipated that it would.*"[397] In the following we will discuss some of the ways in which the

396 Magnus (2017), p. 1.
397 Hillman (2017), p. 1.

WTO dispute settlement system, and in particular the Appellate Body, has developed differently than the US, and indeed most other members, had expected at the end of the Uruguay Round in 1995, leading to growing dissatisfaction of the US with that system. We will then ask what, if anything, has changed under the Trump administration, which has brought the festering conflict between the US and the WTO to a head.

A. Unfulfilled expectations

In at least three respects the WTO dispute settlement and the Appellate Body have developed differently than expected by the US in 1995, at the end of the Uruguay Round: first, the role the Appellate Body within the dispute settlement system, both quantitatively and qualitatively; second, the track record of the US as litigant before the Appellate Body; and, third, the relationship between the judicial and the legislative branches of the WTO, that is, between dispute settlement by panels and the Appellate Body, on the one hand, and treaty-making by WTO members, on the other. Together, these unfulfilled expectations go a long way towards explaining the dissatisfaction of the US with the system, and, ultimately, the current appointment crisis.

Starting with the first point, the role the Appellate Body within the dispute settlement system, the negotiating history of the Uruguay Round shows that, at the time, the negotiators had a far more limited role in mind for the Appellate Body than what later emerged, or, as Peter Van den Bossche has famously written, that the Appellate Body changed „*[f]rom afterthought to centrepiece*“ in the world trading system.[398] The idea of a „*standing review tribunal*“ was first proposed in December 1989,[399] appeared in a first draft of

398 Van den Bossche (2006).

399 Negotiating Group on Dispute Settlement, Meeting of 7 December 1989, Note by the Secretariat (MTN.GNG/NG13/17), p. 3 („*One delegation proposed that the Group consider various options for possible appellate review of panel reports. ... the delegation indicated that it was assessing the following ... options: ... the establishment of a standing review tribunal ...*“). Elsig/Eckhardt (2015), p. s25, attribute this proposal to Canada; however, according to a news bulletin issued by the GATT on 11 January 1990 (NUR 33), p. 14, the proposal was made by the US („*The United States [at the meeting of 7 December] put forward some tentative ideas on ... the creation of an appellate body to review panel reports*“).

revised provisions on dispute settlement in September 1990,[400] and was included, already in its more or less final form, in the draft Dispute Settlement Understanding that was part of the comprehensive „Dunkel Draft“ of the results of the Uruguay Round negotiations of December 1991.[401] In a proposal of April 1990 the US stated that such *„a review process could be established for extraordinary cases where a panel report contains legal interpretations that are questioned formally by one of the parties.*“[402] This notion that the proposed review process should be limited to *„extraordinary cases*“, *„truly exceptional cases*“[403] or *„rare cases*“[404] was widely shared among the negotiators. However, that is not what happened. From the very beginning appeals to the Appellate Body were the rule rather than the exception. Between 1996 and 2018, about two thirds (67 %) of all panel reports were appealed, oscillating between a low of 40 % in 2007 and a high of 100 % in 2008.[405]

Moreover, the Appellate Body assumed a different role than expected not only in quantitative but also in qualitative terms. Debra Steger, first Director of the Appellate Body Secretariat and senior negotiator for Canada of dispute sett-

400 Negotiating Group on Dispute Settlement, Draft text on dispute settlement, 21 September 1990 (MTN.GNG/NG13/W/45), pp. 3 – 4.

401 Trade Negotiations Committee, Draft Final Act Embodying the Results of the Uruguay Round of Multilateral Trade Negotiations, 20 December 1991 (MTN.TNC/W/FA), Section S: Understanding on Rules and Procedures on Dispute Settlement, pp. S.12-S.14.

402 Communication from the United States of 6 April 1990 (MTN.GNG/NG13/W/40), p. 5; see also p. 6: *„There are a number of questions, however, that arise in considering an appellate mechanism: How might we ensure that the review process is used only in extraordinary cases, rather than affording an automatic opportunity to delay the dispute settlement process?*“.

403 Negotiating Group on Dispute Settlement, Meeting of 5 April 1990, Note by the Secretariat (MTN.GNG/NG13/19), p. 4 (*„While some participants declared their opposition to any such mechanism [of appellate review], others considered that it might be useful in specific circumstances if appeals could be limited to truly exceptional cases.*“); Negotiating Group on Dispute Settlement, Profile on the Status of the Work in the Group, Report by the Chairman, 18 July 1990 (MTN.GNG/NG13/W/43), p. 3 (*„There is concern that appeals should be limited to only truly exceptional cases but work remains to be done on how this would be achieved in practice*“).

404 Communication from Canada of 28 June 1990 (MTN.GNG/NG13/W/41), p. 4 (*„In rare cases, where a party to a dispute considered, despite the review by the panel, that a report was so fundamentally flawed that it should not be accepted, the GATT dispute settlement system should provide for a means of correcting errors. The addition of an appellate mechanism would serve that purpose. The intent would not be to have appellate review become a quasi-automatic step in the dispute settlement process*“).

405 Appellate Body, Annual Report for 2018, March 2019 (WT/AB/29), p. 142.

lement in the Uruguay Round, noted that *„Uruguay Round negotiators did not intend to create a court“*,[406] and certainly not one with wide-ranging powers and influence. Similarly, Joseph H.H. Weiler observed in 2002, *„[f]rom interviews with many delegations that I have conducted it is clear that … they saw the logic of the Appellate Body as a kind of Super-Panel to give a losing party another bite at the cherry, given that the losing party could no longer block adoption of the Panel* [*report*]. *It is equally clear to me that they did not fully understand the judicial … nature of the Appellate Body.“*[407] That negotiators perceived the Appellate Body as more of a *„Super-Panel“* than a traditional international court, like the International Court of Justice, is reflected in many features of the Appellate Body set out in the DSU, such as the names of the institution (Appellate Body rather than court) and the persons sitting on it (Appellate Body members rather than judges), the fact that Appellate Body rulings, like those of panels, only become binding after formal adoption by a political body, the DSB (albeit with negative consensus), the comparatively small number of Appellate Body members (seven, only three of which sit on any given case), and the relatively short tenure of Appellate Body members (only four years, renewable once).[408] But, while, in the words of one former Appellate Body member, *„[g]overnments didn't want it to be really a judicial process“*,[409] the Appellate Body *„[f]rom the outset … has made the conscious choice to function as if it were a court.“*[410] For instance, the first Working Procedure of Appellate Review, which the first Appellate Body members drew up in early 1996, were based on a careful analysis of the working procedures of a number of international courts and one national supreme court.[411] The personalities and backgrounds of the first seven Appellate Body members played a large part in the transformation of the Appellate Body from a more panel-like institution,

406 Steger (2015), p. 447.

407 Weiler (2002), p. 201.

408 For a more detailed comparison of the Appellate Body with other international courts, see Van den Bossche (2006), pp. 294 – 300.

409 Terris/Romano/Swigart (2007), p. 106 (quoting from an interview with an unnamed Appellate Body member).

410 Van Damme (2009), p. 157.

411 The European Court of Justice, the European Court of Human Rights, the Central American Court of Human Rights, and the Supreme Court of the Philippines (the latter presumably because one of the first Appellate Body members, Florentino P. Feliciano, had been a justice of that court before joining the Appellate Body), in addition the International Centre for Settlement of Investment Disputes and the dispute settlement system of the North American Free Trade Agreement; see Steger (2015), p. 451, fn. 13.

still influenced by the diplomatic traditions of the old GATT, that many negotiators had in mind, to the fully-fledged court-like institution which the Appellate Body turned out to be. Unlike most panelists in the pre-WTO time, they were, with one exception, lawyers and not members of the close-knit GATT community.[412] Tellingly, one of the first seven Appellate Body members, Claus-Dieter Ehlermann, published an account of his experiences as Appellate Body member under the title „*Six Years on the Bench of the ‚World Trade Court*‘".[413] This self-understanding of the Appellate Body has persisted, as expressed more recently by a current Appellate Body member, Thomas R. Graham, who remarked that „*[f]or although they don't call us that, we are in effect judges, on what is in effect the highest appeals court for the rules of global trade.*"[414] The basic difference between viewing the Appellate Body as merely another kind of panel or, alternatively, as an international court is the source of much of the US criticism on issues of procedure and interpretative approach, especially on advisory opinions and precedent. In that vein, Gregory Shaffer argues that „*[t]he core U.S. complaint is the judicialization of WTO dispute settlement, where the AB has been operating as if it is an international court building a jurisprudence, rather than a modest body that issues ad hoc decisions to help WTO members resolve discrete disputes.*"[415]

---

412 See Terris/Romano/Sigart (2007), p. 107: „*Many also agree that had the first members of the Appellate Body not been mostly lawyers, but instead diplomats, as in the GATT system, the WTO process would have probably remained much closer to its diplomatic roots.*"; on the background of the first seven Appellate Body members, see their CVs on the WTO website (https://www.wto.org/english/tratop_e/dispu_e/ab_members_descrp_e.htm) and Appleton (2016), pp. 20 – 22. The one exception mentioned was Julio Lacarte-Muró from Uruguay, a career diplomat and consummate GATT insider, who, among other things, was Deputy Executive Secretary of the GATT in 1947 – 1948 and chairman of the Negotiating Group on Dispute Settlement in the Uruguay Round. Terris/Romano/Sigart (2007), p. 107, quote an unnamed Appellate Body member as saying „*Lacarte underwent a fundamental change of outlook and was won over by the lawyers' side.*"

413 Ehlermann (2002).

414 Graham (2014), p. 318.

415 Shaffer (2019), p. 7; see also McDougall (2018): „*At issue is a disagreement about what in fact WTO members expected from the Appellate Body when they founded the WTO. The US has long argued that it agreed only to a limited mandate that focuses on resolving specific disputes, avoiding unnecessarily sweeping interpretations of the trade rules, and deferring to the decisions of governments in cases of ambiguously worded obligations – even if it means leaving some trade restrictive measures in place. On the other hand, many other members, and in some ways the institution itself, consider the Appellate Body to be an independent world court charged with providing broad clarifications of the trade rules, even beyond what is necessary to resolve specific disputes as well as updating the rules as required to reflect*

The second case of unfulfilled expectations is the track record of the US as a litigant before the Appellate Body. The current United States Trade Representative (USTR), Robert E. Lighthizer, who had been Deputy USTR from 1983 to 1985 under President Reagan and had then worked in private practice as trade remedy lawyer until his appointment as USTR in 2017 by President Trump, said in 2000 that „*I was at USTR in the early '80s when the idea really began to take on currency that, well, we have a problem, we need binding resolution if a country can lose a panel decision and then block it. And that the U.S. at that time viewed itself as entirely the plaintiff, not really the defendant in any case.*"[416] This view of the US as plaintiff rather than defendant was echoed in 2017 by former Appellate Body member Jennifer Hillman: „[*W*]*hat were the expectations of the United States when the system went into place? I think, first of all, the expectation of the United States* [*was*] *that the vast majority of the time the United States would be on offense and only relatively rarely, if ever, on defense.*"[417] In line with these expectations, the US is the most active complainant in the WTO, with 124 cases it filed from 1995 to August 2019, followed by the EU with 102 and Canada with 39 complaints. But, contrary to US expectations, by an even greater margin the US is also the country most often sued in the WTO, with 154 cases brought against it, the next in rank being the EU with 85 and China with 43 times being a respondent.[418] And, similar to the experience of other WTO litigants, while the US wins most of its cases as complainant, it loses most of its cases as respondent.[419] Furthermore, not only has the US been

changing economic realities." These differences on the proper function of dispute settlement even predate the WTO, as John H. Jackson has pointed out: „[*T*]*hroughout the history of the GATT, and now in the WTO, there has been some ambivalence about the appropriate role of dispute settlement procedures. To over-generalize a bit, there were roughly two viewpoints: one favours a 'negotiation' or 'diplomacy'-oriented approach whereby dispute settlement procedures should not be juridical or 'legalistic', but should simply assist negotiators to resolve differences through negotiation and compromise. Another approach views the dispute settlement procedure as a relatively disciplined juridical process by which an impartial panel could make objective rulings about whether or not certain activities were consistent with GATT obligations.*" (Jackson [1998], p. 60).

416 Lighthizer (2000).

417 Hillman (2017), p. 1.

418 All figures from the WTO website, Disputes by member (https://www.wto.org/english/tratop_e/dispu_e/dispu_by_country_e.htm), including all disputes up to and including DS586.

419 According to Daku/Pelc (2017), p. 4, in all WTO disputes between 1995 and 2013 claimants prevailed on average with 74 % of their claims at the panel level and 69 % at the appellate level; defining a win as finding that respondent's measure is not in compliance

sued successfully more often than expected, there is a widespread perception among many in the US that it has been losing unjustly. To quote Appellate Body critic John Magnus again: „*The dissatisfaction [of the US] with the dispute settlement system is a sort of a bundle of items ... But, by far, the biggest item is that when on defense, we lose cases and claims we shouldn't lose.*"[420] The greatest concern to the US are loses in the area of trade remedies (anti-dumping duties, countervailing duties and safeguard measures),[421] which are designed to protect industries threatened by import competition.[422]

The third instance of unfulfilled expectations concerns the relationship between the judicial and legislative branches of the WTO. Whereas the judicial branch (i.e., the WTO dispute settlement system) has been, as described, very active, the legislative branch (i.e., treaty-making by members) has failed to produce significant results. Since the founding of the GATT in 1947 the world trading system has been further developed and adapted in successive trade rounds. The eighth and latest of these trade rounds was the Uruguay Round of 1986 – 1994. The expectation after the conclusion of the Uruguay Round was that, like in the past, further trade negotiations and treaty amendments would follow. To that effect, Art. III:2 of the WTO Agreement stipulates that „*[t]he WTO shall provide the forum for negotiations among its Members concerning their multilateral trade relations*". Consistent with these expectations, in November 2001, the WTO members started the ninth trade round, the so-called

with WTO law, Colares (2009), p. 403, concludes that for all WTO disputes until September 2007 the average win rate for complainants amounts to 89 % in trade remedy cases and 83 % in non-trade remedy cases; a study of the news agency Bloomberg of 2017 finds that the US success rates as WTO litigant as claimant as well as respondent are similar to, but slightly better than the average success rates („America Wins Often With Trade Referee That Trump Wants to Avoid", 27 March 2017, https://www.bloomberg.com/news/articles/2017-03-27/trump-isn-t-a-fan-of-the-wto-but-u-s-lawyers-often-win-there); in the DSB meeting of 24 June 2019, China put the US success rate as complainant at 85.7 % compared with a total average of 84.4 %, and as respondent at 25 % compared with a total average of 16.6 % (minutes [WT/DSB/M/430], para. 8.13).

420 Magnus (2017), p. 1.

421 See, e. g., former US trade diplomat and current WTO Deputy-Director General Wolff (2018): „*I can testify from interactions over an extended period of time with a number of officials in U.S. government and with other U.S. practitioners that they share the belief that the Appellate Body has narrowed the use of trade remedies, including antidumping, in a manner that was not anticipated at the inception of WTO dispute settlement. This is not, however, the view of many WTO Members.*"

422 See for an in-depth discussion of the law and economics of trade remedies Mavroidis/Messerlin/Wauters (2008).

Doha Development Round, or Doha Round for short, with an ambitious negotiating agenda covering almost all areas of WTO law.[423] The aim was to conclude the Doha Round until the end of 2005.[424] However, apart from the Trade Facilitation Agreement of 2013,[425] no major new agreement or treaty amendment was accomplished,[426] and in 2015 the US declared that the Doha Round should be abandoned and negotiations should take new directions.[427] This lack of progress at the negotiating table meant that not only could the WTO rules book not be adapted to new challenges and developments that had emerged since 1995, such as digitalization or the rise of China's state-led economy, but also that members were unable to correct through amendments any controversial interpretations of the existing rules by panels and the Appellate Body. Moreover, the failure of negotiations since 1995 has not only prevented changes to substantive WTO law, but also changes to the DSU, despite reform efforts from the very beginning.[428] The Final Act of the Uruguay Round of 1994 already contained a decision by the members to review the DSU within four years of the entry into force of the WTO Agreement, i.e., by the

423 See WTO Ministerial Conference, Fourth Session, Doha, 9 – 14 November 2001, Ministerial Declaration, adopted on 14 November 2001 (WT(MIN(01)/DEC/1) („Doha Declaration").

424 Doha Declaration (fn. 423), para. 45.

425 Ministerial decision of 7 December 2013, Agreement on Trade Facilitation (WT/MIN(1)/36 and WT/L/911) (conclusion of negotiations); General Council decision of 27 November 2014, Protocol amending the Marrakesh Agreement Establishing the World Trade Organization (WT/L/940) (submission for acceptance); the Trade Facilitation Agreement entered into force on 22 February 2017 after ratification by two-thirds of the WTO membership (https://www.wto.org/english/news_e/news17_e/fac_31jan17_e.htm); on the negotiating history of the Trade Facilitation Agreement, see Hassan (2014), pp. 33 – 65; Schott/Hufbauer (2014); and Kerr (2015).

426 In addition to the multilateral Trade Facilitation Agreement, there were since 1995 a few negotiating successes on the plurilateral level (i.e., agreements with less than full participation of the WTO membership), especially the Information Technology Agreement of 1995, the product coverage of which was substantially expanded in 2015, with currently 82 member states (see https://www.wto.org/english/tratop_e/inftec_e/inftec_e.htm), and the Revised Agreement on Government Procurement of 2012 with currently 48 member states (see https://www.wto.org/english/tratop_e/gproc_e/gp_gpa_e.htm).

427 See Froman (USTR at the time) (2015); statement of Froman at the Ministerial Conference in December 2015 in Nairobi (WT/MIN(15)/ST/121); Nairobi Ministerial decision, adopted on 19 December 2018 (WT/MIN(15)/DEC), para. 30.

428 See on the history of the DSU reform negotiations until 2004, Zimmermann (2006), pp. 91 – 125.

beginning of 1999.[429] After the negotiators had missed that deadline, they set at the start of the Doha Round in 2001 a new deadline, May 2003, for coming to an agreement on improvements and clarifications of the DSU,[430] but that deadline was not met either. Today, these negotiations on DSU reform are still ongoing, but without an end in sight.[431] The resulting imbalance between the judicial and the legislative branches of the WTO was highlighted by USTR Robert Lighthizer in his opening statement at the 11th WTO Ministerial Conference in 2017, in which he said, as cited previously, that *„many are concerned that the WTO is losing its essential focus on negotiation and becoming a litigation-centered organization. Too often members seem to believe they can gain concessions through lawsuits that they could never get at the negotiating table.*"[432]

In short, the US finds itself with an Appellate Body that has turned out to be more powerful than anticipated, has ruled against the US, especially US industries threatened by import competition, far more frequently than expected, and is not checked by members through treaty amendments, again contrary to expectations. It is not any one of these unfulfilled expectations alone but rather their combination that fuels to a large degree the current US opposition to the Appellate Body. For instance, it is not much of a stretch to assume that the US would be far less critical of the court-like approach of the Appellate Body and its ambition to develop *„a coherent and predictable body of jurisprudence clarifying Member's rights and obligations under the covered agreements*"[433] through relying heavily on its own precedents if the rulings of Appellate Body had generally been more favorable to the US.[434] Similarly, if the

429 Final Act Embodying the Results of the Uruguay Round of Multilateral Trade Negotiations, 15 April 1994 (UR-94-0083), p. 419: Decision on the application and review of the Understanding on Rules and Procedures Governing the Settlement of Disputes.

430 Doha declaration (supra, fn. 123), para. 30.

431 See for the latest state of the negotiations the report of 17 June 2019 of the chairman of the DSB in Special Session (TN/DS/31).

432 Supra, fn. 74.

433 Appellate Body report, *US – Stainless Steel (Mexico)*, para. 161.

434 Not surprisingly, for instance, the early US statement cited above (fn. 386) strongly in favor of precedential effect of Appellate Body reports was made regarding an Appellate Body ruling the US supported (on the admissibility of amicus curiae briefs), whereas the later US condemnations of precedential effect typically concerned Appellate Body rulings which the US vehemently opposed (in particular on zeroing, like in the crucial case *US – Stainless Steel (Mexico)*). In the same vein, Bacchus/Lester (2019), p. 4, argue that the *„true concern*" of the US regarding precedent is that it *„has long hoped that, in deciding new*

US had been more successful in treaty negotiations, including on issues on which it lost before the Appellate Body, the potential for US frustration with the Appellate Body would have been much reduced.

The link between these unfulfilled expectations and the current US opposition to the Appellate Body raises the question as to what extent the Appellate Body is to blame for the mismatch between what the US believed it had agreed to in 1995 and what happened afterwards.

As to the first point, the rise of the Appellate Body *„from afterthought to centrepiece"*, the quantitative aspect of that rise, i.e., the use of the appeal mechanism in the majority of cases right from the beginning, was, of course, due to the members themselves. And, as VanGrasstek pointed out, *„[i]n retrospect, it is clear that the expectation* [that the Appellate Body *„would be called upon only in rare instances"*] *was unrealistic"* because, for political reasons, governments usually have to demonstrate to their domestic constituents that they have defended their interests with all available legal means, including an appeal. *„That simple calculation seems to have evaded the DSU negotiators during the round."*[435]

The qualitative aspect of the Appellate Body's rise, meaning the self-perception of the Appellate Body as an international court rather than as a mere settler of individual disputes, is, on closer inspection, similarly a case of unrealistic expectations. Although, as described above, the Uruguay Round negotiators did not intend to create a court, and indicated that in various ways in the DSU, for example, by avoiding the words „court" and „judges", they nevertheless invested the Appellate Body with the core power of a court, especially of a highest court of appeal, namely the final word on interpretation. The fact that formally the DSB, i. e., the membership, adopts the reports of the Appellate Body was due to the negative consensus rule never more than a formality.[436] Equally, the power of the Ministerial Conference and the General Council to adopt interpretations pursuant to Art. IX:2 of the WTO Agreement, which figures so prominently the arguments of the US regarding

appeals, new members of the Appellate Body would overrule the judgments of previous members of the Appellate Body on an assortment of legal issues of political significance to the United States, particularly on antidumping, subsidies, and safeguards. ... Failing this, the United States wants WTO panels to disregard these previous Appellate Body rulings on trade remedies and rule differently in new disputes."

435 VanGrasstek (2013), p. 242.

436 Cf. supra, fn. 366.

advisory opinions and precedential effect, and which would allow members to overturn Appellate Body interpretations, has never been used by members. This is no surprise either because such an authoritative interpretation would require, according to Art. IX:2 of the WTO Agreement, a three-fourths majority of the members, and, in reality, as a consequence of the WTO's informal consensus principle, a unanimous decision, like the unanimous decision necessary to prevent the adoption of an Appellate Body report.[437] The late Julio Lacarte-Muró, who as chairman of the group that negotiated the DSU in the Uruguay Round and as one of the founding members of the Appellate Body probably had more knowledge about the genesis of the Appellate Body than anyone else, could therefore properly conclude that what the Uruguay Round negotiators had devised, whether intentionally or not, „*was, in effect, a new international court for the settlement of [trade] disputes, irrespective of the name given to it by WTO members*".[438] And the members reinforced the judicial nature of the Appellate Body in 1995 with the first appointments they made to it, namely, as mentioned above, they chose primarily GATT outsiders with legal or even judicial backgrounds rather than GATT insiders with diplomatic credentials (with the single exception of Lacarte-Muró). Thus, even though the Appellate Body's self-perception as a court differed from what many nego-

437 See Weiler (2001), p. 201: „*De jure the DSU leaves the final interpretation of the Agreements in the hands of the General Council and Ministerial Conference. De facto, unless the Organization is to break the hallowed principle of consensus, that power has shifted to the Appellate Body. The circumstances would have to be utterly unique to envisage a consensus in the General Council and/or Ministerial Conference to overturn an interpretation or decision of the Appellate Body.*" These practical limits upon Art. IX:2 of the WTO Agreement were well known at the time of the Uruguay Round, as indicated, for instance, by an early scholarly review of the DSU in 1994: „*Although the DSB is required to make decisions by consensus, the same matters, if they were to involve interpretations, could be referred to the WTO at the request of a disputing Member (paragraph 3. 9), and the relevant decisions could be made by a three-fourths majority of the Members [under Art. IX.2 of the WTO Agreement]. The general power of decision-making by consensus under Article IX.1 of the WTO is consistent with past GATT practice. Given the history of the GATT, the complex nature of international trade relations and the difficulties associated with implementing majority decisions in the international plane, it is unlikely that decision-making by majority vote would become a lightly used option for the WTO.*" (Kohona [1994], p. 31).

438 Lacarte-Muró (2015), p. 476; see further Weiler (2001), p. 201: „*In interviews many delegations would state, with some incredulity: ‚We have created a Court ....*'"; on the difference between the form and the substance of the Appellate Body, see also the founding Appellate Body member Matsushita (2015), pp. 547 – 549 („*Is the Appellate Body a court of international trade?*").

tiators had expected, it cannot be said that by behaving like a court the Appellate Body has acted contrary to the function it had been assigned to by these negotiators.

Regarding the second instance of unfulfilled expectations, the higher than expected loss rate of the US as respondent, the Appellate Body would indeed bear a large part of the blame if, as the US claims, many of these losses were caused by *„the Appellate Body adding to or diminishing rights or obligations under the WTO Agreement in areas as varied as subsidies, antidumping and countervailing duties, standards under the TBT Agreement, and safeguards.“*[439] As mentioned earlier, analyzing whether these US allegations of judicial overreach in the area of substantive law are justified would go far beyond the scope of the present study. However, if the result of our analysis of the corresponding US allegations regarding the six issues of procedure and interpretative approach is any guide, then one might assume that the performance of the Appellate Body in the area of substantive law is at least not as dire as the US proclaims.

Finally, as to the third case of unfulfilled expectations, the relationship between the judicial and legislative branches of the WTO, there are indeed some, especially among US trade remedy lawyers, who see a causal relationship between alleged judicial overreach in the dispute settlement system and the failure of WTO negotiators to conclude new agreements: *„A runaway dispute settlement system complicates – maybe even totally blocks – ongoing progress at the negotiating table. And I would suggest that anyone who doesn't see a link between what's been happening in dispute settlement since 1995 and what's been happening at the negotiating table, the paucity of negotiating outcomes during that same period, isn't looking very closely.“*[440] This view seems to be shared by

---

439 Minutes of the DSB meeting of 18 December 2018 (WT/DSB/M/423), statement of the US, para. 9.4.

440 Magnus (2017), p. 3; see also Stewart/McDonough/Smith/Jorgensen (2013), p. 392: *„A[ppellate] B[ody] activism may chill the ability/willingness of WTO Members to reach new agreements out of concern that any agreement will provide the opportunity for finding obligations that were never agreed to. ... The current Doha Round negotiations are moribund, and A[ppellate] B[ody] decisions have already led many governments to decide not to seek negotiations on issues that historically would have been subject to negotiation in the hope that they can get through dispute settlement that which they never achieved through negotiations.“*; see for an early discussion of the issue Tarullo (2003), pp. 373 – 393 (from the abstract, p. 373: *„If important trading countries like the United States believe that the Appellate Body will undermine provisions intended to preserve their ability to use trade*

USTR Lighthizer, who just recently said in a hearing before a US Senate committee in March 2019: „[*W*]*e're not a negotiating body anymore, the WTO, the litigation, these are all sort of link things. … It's a major-major change from what the WTO was supposed to do, and the result is we don't have* [*negotiation*] *rounds*".[441] However, if there were such a negative impact of the dispute settlement system on the progress of negotiations, it is at best a tangential one. Almost all accounts of the reasons for the demise of the Doha Round and the deadlock in the negotiations focus on fundamental political differences between the major players, such as the US, the EU, China and India, and rarely even mention the dispute settlement system as an explanatory factor, let alone attribute any great weight to it. That is not only true of accounts given by scholars,[442] but also by former US Trade Representatives.[443] And even the current US administration has, when discussing the Doha Round outside the context of the appointment crisis, explained its failure with basic political disagreements.[444] The dispute settlement system is better described as a victim rather than a cause of the stalemate in negotiations because if controversial issues cannot be resolved through negotiations, greater strain is put on that system, as the current crisis exemplifies.

---

remedies, they may decline to negotiate further disciplines on the use of these remedies or, possibly, to enter multilateral negotiations entirely.").

441 Transcript of Senator James Lankford's questions and Robert Lighthizer's answers at the hearing of 12 March 2019 of the Senate Finance Committee (https://www.lankford.senate.gov/news/press-releases/senator-lankford-attends-finance-committee-hearing-on-the-world-trade-organization).

442 See, for instance, Erixon (2014), Wolfe (2013), Kleinmann/Guinan (2011), and Evenett (2011).

443 See Froman (USTR from 2013 to 2017) (2015), and Schwab (USTR from 2006 to 2009) (2011).

444 See statement of the US at the General Council meeting of 24 July 2019, item 8: „*The Doha Round failed because the more advanced, wealthier, and most influential of the self-declared developing countries refused to contribute in a meaningful way.*" (https://geneva.usmission.gov/2019/07/24/statements-delivered-by-ambassador-dennis-shea-wto-general-council-meeting-geneva-july-24-2019).

B. Continuity and change under the Trump administration

The current Appellate Body crisis began shortly after the new US administration under President Donald Trump had come into office in January 2017. In this section, we will discuss to what extent the Trump administration's policy of blocking appointments to the Appellate Body is merely an extension and logical consequence of policies of past US administrations regarding WTO disputes settlement and the Appellate Body, or a sign of a fundamental policy shift. As we will see, there are elements of both continuity and change, but the latter dominates.

As to continuity, the US criticism of the Appellate Body certainly did not start with the Trump administration. Although, as mentioned earlier, some of the most recent criticisms are new, such as the Rule 15 issue or the claim that it is only the Appellate Body's fault that its reports are not issued within the 90-day deadline of Art. 17.5 of the DSU, for many years various US administration have, again and again, faulted the Appellate Body for overreach, for disregarding the text of the WTO agreements, and for adding to or diminishing the rights and obligations negotiated by members, most notably in the area of trade remedies. In all of this, the US has been the most outspoken and frequent critic among the members. The prominent role of the US as challenger of the Appellate Body is illustrated by a study by Terence P. Stewart, a US trade remedy lawyer and long-time Appellate Body opponent, who analyzed all DSB meetings up to 2017 for claims by WTO members of Appellate Body overreach.[445] He found that members raised such claims 55 times with respect to 45 of a total of 134 Appellate Body reports, ranging in time from 1997 to 2017. Of these 55 claims of overreach, 30, that is, more than half of them, were made by just one member, the US. The remaining 25 claims of overreach were spread across 16 members, none of which made more than three such claims, i.e., only one tenth of that of the US. Another indicator of continuity is a conversation in September 2018 of six former US trade representatives (USTRs), who held office between 1981 and 2013. In response to a question by the moderator as to whether the allegations of Appellate Body overreach made by the Trump administration were correct, there was general agreement among these former

445 Stewart (2018), pp. 5 – 6 and Attachment 1.

USTRs that they were.[446] Hostility toward the WTO dispute settlement system and the Appellate Body has also been expressed in the past by the US Congress. For example, in the Trade Act of 2002 Congress stated that „*the recent pattern of decisions by dispute settlement panels of the WTO and the Appellate Body to impose obligations and restrictions on the use of antidumping, countervailing, and safeguard measures by WTO members under the Antidumping Agreement, the Agreement on Subsidies and Countervailing Measures, and the Agreement on Safeguards has raised concerns*"[447] and demanded from the executive branch „*a report setting forth the strategy of the executive branch to address concerns of the Congress regarding whether dispute settlement panels and the Appellate Body of the WTO have added to obligations, or diminished rights, of the United States.*"[448] Such concerns were repeated 13 years later in another Congressional act on trade matters,[449] combined with a similar request for a report by the executive branch.[450] Moreover, like the Trump administration, previous US administrations have not limited themselves to just

446 Center for Strategic and International Studies, transcript of „A Conversation with Six Former USTRs" (William Brock [1981 – 1985], Carla Hills [1989 – 1993], Michael Kantor [1993 – 1996], Charlene Barshefsky [1996 – 2001], Susan Schwab [2006 – 2009], and Ronald Kirk [2009 – 2013]) on 17 September 2018 in Washington, D.C. (https://csis-prod.s3.amazonaws.com/s3fs public/event/180917_Conversation_Former_USTRs.pdf), pp. 19 – 21.

447 Sec. 2101(b)(3) of the Trade Act of 2002 (19 USC 3801(b)(3)).

448 Sec. 2105(b)(3) of the Trade Act of 2002 (19 USC 3805(b)(3)); on the fulfillment of this obligation, see Executive Branch Strategy Regarding WTO Dispute Settlement Panels and the Appellate Body, Report to Congress transmitted by the Secretary of Commerce on 30 December 2002.

449 Sec. 102(b)(16)(C)(i) of the Bipartisan Congressional Trade Priorities and Accountability Act of 2015 (19 USC 4201(b)(16)(C)(i)): „*The principal negotiating objectives of the United States with respect to dispute settlement and enforcement of trade agreements are ... to seek adherence by panels convened under the Dispute Settlement Understanding and by the Appellate Body to ... the mandate of those panels and the Appellate Body to apply the WTO Agreement as written, without adding to or diminishing rights and obligations under the Agreement*".

450 Sec. 106(b)(5) of the Bipartisan Congressional Trade Priorities and Accountability Act of 2015 (19 USC 4205(b)(5): The executive branch „*shall transmit to Congress a report setting forth the strategy of the executive branch to address concerns of Congress regarding whether dispute settlement panels and the Appellate Body of the World Trade Organization have added to obligations, or diminished rights, of the United States*"; on the fulfillment of this obligation, see the 2015 Executive Branch Strategy Regarding WTO Dispute Settlement Panels and the Appellate Body, Report to Congress transmitted by the Secretary of Commerce.

criticizing the Appellate Body, but also have taken actions aimed at changing the course of the Appellate Body. As described above in Chapter II, from early on the US has used the appointment process as a means to influence the Appellate Body, culminating, during the Obama administration, in the blocking of the reappointment of Appellate Body member Seung Wha Chang, which directly preceded the current appointment crisis. In addition, as part of the DSU reform negotiations, the US, mostly together with Chile, had already between 2002 and 2007 made proposals for increasing member control of the Appellate Body.[451]

With so much continuity, where is change? What has changed are the basic assumptions underlying US trade policy. Since the end the Second World War, the US, working from foundations that were laid in the wake of the Great Depression by President Roosevelt and his Secretary of State Cordell Hull, has been the main architect and defender of the multilateral trading system, a system build on the rule of law, openness and non-discrimination, and on the belief that trade promotes peace and prosperity. It is based on economic theories in the tradition of Adam Smith and David Ricardo, according to which free trade benefits all participating countries („win-win"), and, conversely, protectionism hurts not only the trading partners of a protectionist country, but also that country itself. The central institutional pillars of this system were first the GATT and then its successor, the WTO. This focus on free trade and multilateralism does not mean that during this period the US did not also engage in protectionism, far from it.[452] Like almost all countries, the US used, to a greater or lesser degree, protectionist instruments to shield domestic industries from foreign competition, such as voluntary export restraints, farm subsidies, and, most prominently, trade remedies. But these protectionist measures were always perceived and applied as exceptions to the general rule of free trade.[453]

451 Communication from 17 December 2002 from Chile and the US (TN/DS/W/28) (see Zimmermann [2006], pp. 112 – 116, on the background of that proposal and reactions by other members); communication of 11 March 2003 from Chile and the US (TN/DS/W/52); communication of 15 March 2005 from the US (TN/DS/W/74); communication of 21 October 2005 from the US (TN/DS/W/82); communication from 30 May 2007 from Chile and the US (TN/DS/W/89).

452 See Williams (2019); for protectionist measures imposed by the US on China since 1980, see Bown (2019), pp. 6 – 11.

453 See Irvin (2017) for an in-depth treatment of the history of US trade policy and the relative weight of free trade and protectionism.

The trade policy of the Trump administration constitutes a sharp break with this prevailing US trade paradigm of the post-war era.[454] For a better understanding of the Appellate Body crisis, three closely related elements of this break are of particular importance.

First, Trump views international trade not as a „win-win" but, in the tradition of mercantilism, as a „zero-sum" game, where one country's trade win is another country's trade loss. In this world view, protectionist measures are not potentially dangerous, self-defeating exceptions, but crucial tools to further national interest. Trump stated this belief forcefully in his Inaugural Address of January 2017: „*We must protect our borders from the ravages of other countries making our products, stealing our companies, and destroying our jobs. Protection will lead to great prosperity and strength.*"[455] Consistently, Trump is also an ardent supporter of the traditionally most important protectionist instrument, tariffs, which the GATT and the WTO successfully strove over decades to reduce: „*I am a Tariff Man. When people or countries come in to raid the great wealth of our Nation, I want them to pay for the privilege of doing so.*"[456]

Second, Trump prefers power-based over rule-based international trade relations.[457] This goes hand in hand with his mercantilist convictions. In the free trade paradigm, a rule-based trading system makes sense because it provides security and predictability for traders, and, importantly, serves as bulwark against protectionist domestic interests, which would hurt the overall economic welfare of a country. By contrast, in the mercantilist zero-sum world, binding international rules prevent a powerful country such as the US from using its power to the fullest extent possible in its economic struggles with other countries.[458]

454 On this break, see Kerr (2018), Charnovitz (2018b), VanGrasstek (2017), and Fidler (2017).

455 https://www.whitehouse.gov/briefings-statements/the-inaugural-address.

456 Tweet by Trump of 4 December 2018 (https://twitter.com/realdonaldtrump/status/1069970500535902208); see also tweet by Trump of 10 May 2019: „*Tariffs will make our Country MUCH STRONGER, not weaker. Just sit back and watch!*" (https://twitter.com/realdonaldtrump/status/1126816259851673601).

457 See, for instance, Charnovitz (2018b), pp. 228 – 229: „*The Trump Administration sees power rather than law as the most important principle of international relations. ... Trump seems to endorse raw power without any control by law. Nowhere can this been seen more clearly than in Trump's trade policy.*"

458 See Kerr (2018), p. 77: „*If one perceives international trade relations as a largely adversarial zero sum game where a country can win only if benefits arise from concessions garnered from trading partners by the exercise of superior economic power or guile, then trade policy*

Third, Trump is opposed to multilateral institutions and instead prefers bilateral deals or unilateral actions. He made this clear right at the beginning of his presidency, in January 2017, when he withdrew from the 12-country Trans-Pacific Partnership (TPP) that had been negotiated by his predecessor Obama. In his Withdrawal Memorandum he declared: „*[I]t is the intention of my Administration to deal directly with individual countries on a one-on-one (or bilateral) basis in negotiating future trade deals.*“[459] Again, this ties in with his mercantilist philosophy because in bilateral relations the US has a better chance of bringing its power to bear than in large multilateral negotiations, where even the US is only one party among many. The most important multilateral institution in international trade is, of course, the WTO, for which Trump has again and again expressed his disdain, calling it „*a catastrophe*“[460] and „*a disaster for this country*“.[461] He also showed his antipathy toward multilateralism in a speech before the General Assembly of the United Nations in September 2017: „*For too long, the American people were told that mammoth multinational trade deals, unaccountable international tribunals, and powerful global bureaucracies were the best way to promote their success. But as those promises flowed, millions of jobs vanished and thousands of factories disappeared.*“[462]

The Trump administration's new approach to trade is not limited to words, but has also been translated into action. The withdrawal from the TPP has

making needs to be pro-active and unfettered.“; VanGrassteck (2017), pp. 60 – 61, describes the logic of the Trump administration's „*mercantilist approach to international economic relations*“ as follows: „*Governments should use their power to intervene in domestic and international markets in order to maximize exports, minimize imports and promote a positive trade balance, and the state should not restrict its freedom of action via agreements that limit its sovereignty.*“

459 https://www.whitehouse.gov/presidential-actions/presidential-memorandum-regarding-withdrawal-united-states-trans-pacific-partnership-negotiations-agreement.

460 Remarks by President Trump at the 2018 White House Business Session with Governors on 26 February 2018, transcript available at https://www.whitehouse.gov/briefings-statements/remarks-president-trump-2018-white-house-business-session-governors.

461 Remarks by President Trump in Listening Session with Representatives from the Steel and Aluminum Industry on 1 March 2018, transcript available at https://www.white-house.gov/briefings-statements/remarks-president-trump-listening-session-representatives-steel-aluminum-industry.

462 https://www.whitehouse.gov/briefings-statements/remarks-president-trump-72nd-session-united-nations-general-assembly.

already been mentioned. Other noteworthy trade policy measures include,[463] especially, first, in March 2018, the imposition of tariffs on steel and aluminum imports, at rates of 25 % and 10 %, respectively,[464] and, second, in successive steps since July 2018, the levying of tariffs on Chinese imports, which, effective as of December 2019, will cover Chinese imports in an amount in excess of $500 billion, at rates between 15 % and 30 %.[465] As a reaction to these tariffs, a number of targeted states retaliated with tariffs of their own against the US,[466] and initiated WTO dispute settlement proceedings.[467] China, in particular, imposed retaliatory tariffs on more than $100 billion worth of US imports, at rates between 5 % and 25 %, and filed four WTO cases against the US.[468]

Under WTO law, the Trump administration justified the tariffs on steel and aluminum with the national security exception of Art. XXI(b) of the GATT, and argued that under the terms of that exception such measures are not subject to review by the WTO dispute settlement system.[469] Since most observers consider the national security justification of the US as merely pretextual,[470] the implication of the US action is that any country can take purely protec-

463 For an overview of the various protectionist trade measures of the Trump administration, see Bown/Kolb (2019) and Williams/Hammond (2019a) as well as (2019b).

464 See Lester/Zhu (2019), pp. 1457 – 1461; Bown/Kolb (2019), pp. 3 – 6; Williams/Hammond (2019a), p. 3; and Williams/Hammond (2019b), p. 2 – 3.

465 For the official announcements in the US Federal Register of all these tariff actions against China, see the USTR website at https://ustr.gov/issue-areas/enforcement/section-301-investigations/tariff-action; see further Bown/Kolb (2019), pp. 7 – 12; Williams/Hammond (2019a), p. 4 – 5; and Williams/Hammond (2019b), p. 2 – 4.

466 See Williams/Hammond (2019b), p. 3, and Bown/Kolb (2019), pp. 3 – 12.

467 With regard to the steel and aluminum tariffs, see DS544 (China), DS547 (India), DS548 (EU), DS550 (Canada), DS551 (Mexico), DS552 (Norway), DS554 (Russia), DS556 (Switzerland), and DS564 (Turkey) (on the WTO consistency [or lack thereof] of these retaliatory measures, see Lee [2019], pp. 491 – 496 and 500 – 501); with regard to the tariffs against China, see DS543, DS565, and DS587. The US, in turn, brought WTO cases against a number of retaliatory tariffs, see DS557 (Canada), DS558 and DS565 (China), DS559 (EU), DS560 (Mexico), DS561 (Turkey), DS566 (Russia), and DS585 (India).

468 See supra, fn. 466 – 467.

469 See, for instance, statements of the US at the DSB meeting of 29 October 2018 (WT/DSB/M/420), paras. 9.3, 10.3 – 10.4, 11.3, 12.3, 13.3, and 14.3. The first report of a WTO panel on the national security exception was issued in April 2019 in the case *Russia – Traffic in Transit* (see paras. 7.27 – 7.149 of that report). For detailed discussions of the exception, see Lee (2018), Lester/Zhu (2019), and Voon (2019).

470 See Kho/Petersen (2019); Lester/Zhu (2019), p. 1458; Lee (2019), pp. 489 – 490 and 500; Lee (2018), pp. 302 – 303; Anuradha (2018), pp. 318 – 319; and Alden (2018).

tionist measures in breach of its WTO obligation without fear of legal consequences as long as it invokes reasons of national security, no matter how spurious such claims may be.[471]

The justification proffered by the Trump administration for its tariffs against China, as far as WTO law is concerned, was even less convincing than that for the tariffs on steel and aluminum. The tariffs against China are based on Section 301 of the US Tariff Act of 1974, which allows unilateral US trade sanctions against countries which violate trade agreements or otherwise unjustifiably interfere with US trade.[472] In 2018, the USTR had determined in a Section 301 investigation that China was engaged in certain policies aimed at illegitimate technology transfers from the US to China.[473] With the tariffs the US wanted to force China to change these policies.[474] Section 301, described as *„the classic embodiment of unilateralism"*,[475] had been a major factor in the Uruguay Round negotiations of the DSU.[476] The threat of unilateral US trade sanctions under Section 301, which had been significantly strengthened by Congress during the Uruguay Round negotiations, had induced the other negotiating countries to give in to US demands for a more effective multilateral enforcement system. In return, as mentioned in Chapter I,[477] the US had

471 Furthermore, in a White House press briefing on 6 June 2018, the Director of the National Economic Council, Lawrence Kudlow, indicated that the US would, in any case, refuse to comply with WTO dispute settlement rulings against the US on these tariffs (*„Q ... since a lot of countries now are ... taking their cases to the WTO, will this administration respect the decisions that come out of the WTO on this? KUDLOW: You know, the United States – the President has said this many times: We are bound by the national interests here more than anything else. All right? ... international multilateral organizations are not going to determine American policy. I think the President has made that very clear."* [https://www.whitehouse.gov/briefings-statements/press-briefing-nec-director-larry-kudlow-g7-summit-060618]).

472 On the history of and practice under Section 301, see Claussen (2019).

473 See Office of the USTR, Findings of the investigation into China's acts, policies, and practices related to technology transfers, intellectual property, and innovation under Section 301 of the Trade Act of 1974, 22 Mach 2018.

474 See US statements in the minutes of the DSB meetings of 27 March 2018 (WT/DSB/M/410), paras. 11.2 – 11.3; 27 April 2018 (WT/DSB/M/412), paras. 5.5 – 5.11; 18 December 2018 (WT/DSB/M/413), paras. 8.3 – 8.7; and 28 January 2019 (WT/DSB/M/425), para. 5.3.

475 Silverman (1996), p. 235.

476 On the role of Section 301 in the Uruguay Round's DSU negotiations, see Stewart (1993), pp. 2760 – 2763, 2777 – 2779, 2786, 2788 – 2789, 2792, and 2795; Elsig/Eckhard (2015), pp. s24-s25 and s30.

477 Supra, fn. 7 and accompanying text.

to commit itself to abstaining from unilateral trade sanctions. This US commitment was enshrined in Art. 23 of the DSU, which obligates members that *„seek the redress of a violation of obligations or other nullification or impairment of benefits under"* the WTO agreements to resort to WTO dispute settlement rather than to act unilaterally. In 1998, the EC had initiated WTO proceedings against the US, claiming that the continued existence of Section 301 and related provisions of US law violated Art. 23 of the DSU. The panel rejected this claim, but only after the US had affirmed before the panel that it would not employ Section 301 against another WTO member it considered to be in breach of WTO law without a prior finding in WTO dispute settlement proceedings confirming such a breach.[478] Relying on this panel decision, China argued that the US tariffs against it violated Art. 23 of the DSU.[479] The US retorted that it *„had made no findings in the Section 301 investigation that China had breached its WTO obligations"*, and, *„[a]ccordingly, China's argument that the United States had somehow acted inconsistently with Article 23 of the DSU was completely lacking in foundation"*, leaving it free to respond to such *„unfair"* and *„trade-distorting"*, but WTO-compliant measures with unilateral trade sanctions.[480] The problem with that argument is that the tariffs undisputedly violate the tariff commitments of the US (Art. II of the GATT) and the most-favored national principle (Art. I of the GATT). If the tariffs are not retaliation against breaches of WTO law, as the US claims, then another legal justification is required for the violations of Arts. I and II of the GATT. However, until very recently, the US offered no such justification,[481] apart from calling the complaints by China *„hypocritical"* and *„pointless"* because with its retaliatory ta-

478 Panel report, *US – Section 301 Trade Act*, paras. 7.114 – 7.126 and 7.131 – 7.136.

479 See statements of China in the minutes of the DSB meetings of 27 March 2018 (WT/DSB/M/410), para. 11.1; 27 April 2018 (WT/DSB/M/412), para. 5.4; and 18 December 2018 (WT/DSB/M/413), para. 8.2.

480 Minutes of the DSB meeting of 27 March 2018 (WT/DSB/M/410), para. 11.3; see also the US statements in the minutes of the DSB meetings 27 April 2018 (WT/DSB/M/412), paras. 5.10 – 5.11; 18 December 2018 (WT/DSB/M/413), para. 8.5; and 28 January 2019 (WT/DSB/M/425), para. 5.3. Only with regard to one aspect of its Section 301 allegations the US considered that China had violated WTO law, and, indeed, brought a WTO case against China (DS542, request for consultations filed on 23 March 2018 [WT/DS542/1]). By contrast, former Appellate Body member Hillman (2018b), pp. 3 – 6, argues that, beyond this one WTO case filed by the US, many of the Chinese technology transfer policies addressed in the Section 301 investigation could be breaches of WTO law and should be challenged through WTO dispute settlement.

481 See Charnovitz (2018a) and (2018b), p. 235 – 237 (e.g., p. 236: *„To the author's knowledge, the Trump Administration has not offered any WTO law defence for its Section 301 actions."*).

riffs China itself had disregarded Art. 23 of the DSU.[482] Only in August 2019, more than a year after it had started to impose the tariffs, the US belatedly asserted that the Section 301 tariffs were justified by the public morals exception of Art. XX(a) of the GATT, stating that the Chinese policies offended US public morals.[483] If, though, disapproval of economic policies of another country, however well-founded, were enough to justify protectionist measures under Art. XX(a) of the GATT, then it is difficult to see where the limits of this exception are.[484] In sum, both the steel and aluminum tariffs and the tariffs against China seriously threaten the rule-based order of the multilateral trading system.

The blocking of all appointments to the Appellate Body can be seen as another way in which the Trump administration undermines the rule of law in international trade. In order to put this measure in the context of the overall trade policy of the Trump administration, it is helpful to take a closer look at the current United States Trade Representative (USTR), Robert A. Lighthizer, whom Trump appointed in January 2017, and who was confirmed by the Senate in May 2017. As mentioned earlier, Lighthizer had been Deputy USTR from 1983 to 1985 under President Reagan and had afterwards worked in private practice as a trade remedy lawyer representing US industries against foreign competitors.[485] He has long been known as a harsh critic of the WTO dispute settlement system and the Appellate Body.[486] For instance, in a tes-

482 See statements of the US at the DSB meetings of 18 December 2018 (WT/DSB/M/423), paras. 8.3 and 8.6 – 8.7; and 28 January 2019 (WT/DSB/M/425), para. 5.3.

483 First written submission of the US of 27 August 2018 in the dispute *US – Tariff Measures on Certain Goods from China* (DS543), paras. 11 – 13 and 63 – 91. In addition, the US claimed that by retaliating against the tariffs, China had forfeited its right to seek redress through WTO dispute settlement, relying for that purpose on various general DSU principles, such as the objective to achieve a prompt and satisfactory settlement of the dispute (idem, paras. 35 – 62). For a first assessment of these arguments, see Qin (2019).

484 See Babu (2018) for a discussion of the WTO case law on the public moral exception and the dangers inherent in its potentially broad scope (p. 351: „*WTO Panel/AB have shown considerable leeway to the Member's determination of what constitutes a public moral in their given setting. However, there is a danger that such lenient interpretation and broadening scope of the public moral defence would pave the way for invoking the exception as a defence for almost every government measure challenged at the WTO DSB.*").

485 Supra, fn. 416; on the biography and views of Lighthizer, see Peterson (2018); Hanke (2018); and Slobodian (2018).

486 Perhaps ironically, Lighthizer himself had once, in 2003, been nominated to the Appellate Body, together with Merit Janow (who was then chosen) (Office of the USTR, United States Nominates WTO Appellate Body Candidates, 5 September 2003 [https://ustr.gov/ar

timony before the US Senate in 2007 he stated: „*Clearly, one of the biggest threats to our trade laws is from the dispute settlement system at the WTO. The system has fundamentally lost its way, and the decisions being issued by the WTO are gutting our trade laws ... Rogue WTO panel and Appellate Body decisions have consistently undermined U.S. interests by inventing new legal requirements that were never agreed to by the United States.*“[487] And even earlier, in 2000, he proposed to replace binding dispute settlement with a pre-WTO, more diplomatic type of dispute resolution: „*I guess my prescription, really, is to move back to more of a negotiating kind of a settlement. Something where you have somebody make a decision but have it not be binding. Having moral suasion and negotiation and the like. The thought was that binding dispute resolution will eliminate problems and conflicts and controversies between countries. And in fact the opposite is the case. It's created more.*“[488] Once in office as USTR, he echoed these earlier thoughts when he remarked in September 2017: „*Back when [I was a Deputy USTR] there was a system, it was before 1995, before the WTO, under the GATT, and there was a system where you would bring panels and then you would have a negotiation. And, you know, trade grew and we resolved issues eventually. And, you know, it's a system that, you know, was successful for a long period of time. Now, under this binding dispute-settlement process, we have to figure out a way to have – from our point of view, to have it work.*“[489] In a similar vein, Lighter commented in January 2018 on a WTO dispute settlement case brought by Canada against the US.[490] He described the case as „*a massive attack on all of our trade laws*“ and added that „*[i]t also underscores why so many of us are concerned about binding dispute arbitration.*

chive/Document_Library/Press_Releases/2003/September/United_States_Nominates_WTO_Appellate_Body_Cidates.html]). Questioned at the time whether he had „*the kind of judicial and diplomatic temperament that is usually associated with members of the WTO's Appellate Body*“, given his fierce criticism of the WTO dispute settlement system, he answered: „*Your choices, in my view, are to do one of two things ... Do you criticize the system and hope to kill it, or do you think it is worthwhile to go to Geneva and apply a strict constructionist's perspective, and add a certain credibility?*“ (Rushford [2003]).

487 Lighthizer (2007), p. 6.

488 Lighthizer (2000).

489 Center for Strategic and International Studies, U.S. Trade Policy Priorities: Robert Lighthizer, United States Trade Representative, event in Washington on 18 September 2017, transcript, p. 9.

490 *US – Certain Systemic Trade Remedies Measures*, request for consultations filed by Canada on 10 January 2018 (WT/DS535/1).

What sovereign nation would trust to arbitrators or the flip of a coin their entire defense against unfair trade?"[491] In light of these statements, the open-ended blocking of all appointments to the Appellate Body seems a perfectly sensible strategy because it achieves, in effect, what Lighthizer had already proposed in 2000, namely the elimination of binding dispute settlement and a return to a pre-WTO diplomatic dispute resolution system. Lighthizer's preference of diplomatic power-play over binding legal decisions was also illustrated by an exchange with a US senator in March 2019. The senator pointed out that the US had just won an important case against China before a WTO panel,[492] and questioned what would happen if China appealed the decision, and the Appellate Body were unable to rule on the appeal, due to the blockage of appointments, thus preventing the decision from becoming legally binding. Lighthizer showed no concern, suggesting enforcement through negotiations instead: „*[I]n the context of our discussion with China we are trying to resolve this case in a way that we think achieves our goals and avoids the possibility of an Appellate Body decision ... So my hope with respect to that specific case that we can work it out in the context of this negotiation.*"[493]

A further indication that the current US administration is opposed to legally binding dispute settlement, and therefore not really interested in a resolution of the appointment crisis, is its reaction to specific proposals by other member states on how to address the stated concerns of the US. Most instructive in this respect is the US response to a communication of November 2018 by 16 members, including the EU and China, which proposes specific solutions for five of the six issues of procedure and interpretative approach complained about by the US, namely Rule 15, the 90-day deadline, appellate review of municipal law, advisory opinions, and precedential effect.[494] These proposals were discussed at the General Council meeting of 12 December 2018.[495] In that

491 Closing Statement of Lighthizer at the Sixth Round of NAFTA Negotiations, 29 January 2018 (https://ustr.gov/about-us/policy-offices/press-office/fact-sheets/2018/january/closing-statement-ustr-robert).

492 Panel report, *China – Agricultural Producers.*

493 And, indeed, that is what happened. Although China disagreed with the panel report, it did not appeal it, and the report was adopted at the DSB meeting of 26 April 2019 (minutes [WT/DSB/M/428], paras. 7.1 – 7.5).

494 See supra, fn. 93.

495 Minutes of the General Council meeting of 12 December 2018 (WT/GC/M/175), paras. 6.1 – 6.257.

meeting, the US did not comment in any way on the specifics of the proposals but rather rejected them wholesale, with just two sentences: „*[O]n a close reading, the proposals would not effectively address the concerns that Members have raised. … Rather than returning the WTO dispute settlement system to what was agreed to by Members in the Dispute Settlement Understanding, the proposals instead appear to endorse changing the rules to accommodate and authorize the very approaches that have given rise to Members' concerns.*“[496]

However, looking at the proposals,[497] the US claim that they „*endorse changing the rules to accommodate and authorize the very approaches that have given rise to Members' concerns*“ (i.e., primarily the concerns of the US) is patently wrong. Rather, the proposals go a long way toward changing current practices and meeting US demands. First, on the 90-day deadline of Art. 17.5 of the DSU, the November 2018 communication proposes to amend Art. 17.5 of the DSU to the effect that if the Appellate Body believes that it will not be able to submit its report within 90 days, it is obliged to seek the agreement of the parties to an extension, and in case the parties fail to agree, the Appellate Body must in consultation with parties propose measures that might enable it to meet the deadline, such as limit the scope of the appeal or the length of parties' submissions. This proposal would force the Appellate Body, as long demanded by the US, to return to its pre-2011 practice of seeking the consent of the parties for a delay, and offers a practical approach to how the Appellate Body might stay within the deadline despite the obvious workload problems.

Second, regarding advisory opinions, the communication proposes to amend Art. 17.12 of the DSU, pursuant to which the „*Appellate Body shall address each of the issues raised*“ by a party, by adding the phrase „*to the extent necessary for the resolution of the dispute.*“ As discussed in detail earlier, the US demands that the Appellate Body should address only issues which are necessary for the resolution of the dispute, which is contrary to the wording of Art. 17.12 of the DSU in its present form. The proposed amendment would allow and indeed require the Appellate Body to comply with this US demand.

Third, concerning appellate review of municipal law, the communication proposes to add to Art. 17.6 of the DSU, which limits appeals to issues of law, a

496 Minutes of the General Council meeting of 12 December 2018 (WT/GC/M/175), paras. 6.161 – 6.162.

497 In the communication (supra, fn. 93), all proposed DSU amendments are set out on p. 3, preceded by explanations on pp. 1 – 2.

clarifying footnote stating that these issues of law „*do not include the panel findings with regard to the meaning of the municipal measures of a party but do include the panel findings with regard to their legal characterisation under the covered agreements*". To recall, the question of the qualification of municipal law under Art. 17.6 of the DSU is currently not explicitly answered in the DSU, and the Appellate Body has, in effect, interpreted the DSU to allow the review of municipal law on appeal, while the US is of the opinion that the DSU prohibits such review. With the proposed clarifying footnote this interpretive question would now be answered explicitly in the DSU, and, importantly, in the direction demanded by the US (albeit not all the way).

Fourth, on precedential effect, it is proposed that the DSB meet once a year in the presence of the Appellate Body and that members at that meeting may express their views on the development of the jurisprudence of the Appellate Body, in addition to the discussion of specific Appellate Body reports at the time of their adoption in the DSB. Although this proposal would obviously fall quite short of the (unreasonable) US demand that Appellate Body reports should have no precedential effect whatsoever, at least it would potentially increase the influence of the membership on the Appellate Body, which is one of the overarching objectives of the US.

Fifth, and finally, with regard to Rule 15, the communication proposes to amend Art. 17.2 of the DSU on appointments to the Appellate Body by adding the following sentence: „*The outgoing person shall complete the disposition of an appeal in which the oral hearing has been held.*" This is the only one of the five proposals which, indeed, seems to „*endorse changing the rules to accommodate and authorize the very approaches that have given rise to Members' concerns*" because the proposed amendment would provide explicit authorization in the DSU of the transitional rule contained in Rule 15. However, whereas with regard to all other issues the US is opposed to the substance of the Appellate Body approaches, the US complaint concerning Rule 15 is only about the alleged lack of a legal basis in the DSU, but not the substance of the rule, which the US explicitly supports.[498] Therefore, the proposed amendment remedies the very problem the US perceives, namely it provides a sound DSU basis for a practice the US agrees with.

After having rejected all of these proposals, is there anything the US proposes instead? According to the US, the answer is simple, namely „*the WTO Appellate*

498 See supra, fn. 63 and accompanying text.

Body should follow the rules [WTO members] had agreed to in 1995. ... And so, the Appellate Body should circulate its reports within 90 days of an appeal. A person who had ceased to be an Appellate Body member could not continue deciding appeals as if his term had been extended by the Dispute Settlement Body. ... The Appellate Body could not make findings on issues of fact, including but not limited to those relating to domestic law. ... The Appellate Body could not give advisory opinions on issues that would not assist the DSB in making a recommendation to bring a WTO-inconsistent measure into compliance with WTO rules. ... The Appellate Body could not assert that its reports served as precedent or provide authoritative interpretations. ... And the Appellate Body could not change Members' substantive rights or obligations as set out in the text of the WTO agreements."[499] In other words, the US purports that the appointment crisis could be resolved if only the Appellate Body complied with its demands. However, even if one were to agree, contrary to the results of the present study, that such compliance with the US demands would mean a return to what had been agreed to in 1995, and, furthermore, the Appellate Body would be willing to give in to these demands, it would be almost impossible to fulfill them in the current situation created by the US blockage of appointments. This is most obvious in the case of the 90-day deadline. With a significant backlog of cases[500] and currently only three sitting Appellate Body members, there is just no way that the Appellate Body could submit its reports within anything near that deadline. And not allowing Appellate Body members whose terms have expired to complete the work on appeals they have been assigned to would, of course, make that situation even worse. On the other issues, i.e., appellate review of facts and municipal law, advisory opinions, precedential effect and various questions of substantive law, the Appellate Body can only make rulings if and when it gets a case in which such an issue arises. In addition, since the US is adamant that Appellate Body rulings have no precedential effect, it would be difficult for the Appellate Body to announce a change of practice with binding effect for the future that could satisfy the US, and the US has never said what specific actions or announcements on the part of the Appellate Body would cause it to end its blockage. Finally, and most importantly,

499 Minutes of the General Council meeting of 12 December 2018 (WT/GC/M/175), statement of the US, paras. 6.163 – 6.168. The US has since repeated this statement more or less verbatim several times, see minutes of the DSB meeting of 25 February 2019 (WT/DSB/M/426), para. 5.25; minutes of the General Council meeting of 7 May 2019 (WT/GC/M/177), paras. 4.151 – 4.152.

500 As of 30 August 2019, there were 13 appeals pending before the Appellate Body.

once the terms of two further Appellate Body members expire in December 2019, the Appellate Body will no longer have the necessary quorum to decide appeals, and for that reason alone can no longer do anything to please the US.

In light of the above review of the five proposals of the November 2018 communication and the proposed alternative of the US, it is difficult not to agree with the statement of China at the General Council meeting of 12 December 2018 that it *„felt disappointed and confused, but not surprised“* by the US reaction.[501] Disappointed because the US did not in any way engage with the proposals even though they meet many of its demands; confused because the reason stated by the US for refusing them and, equally, the proposed US alternative make little sense; and, nevertheless, not surprised because consenting to changes that would address some of its concerns would make it more difficult for the US to keep up the blockage and thereby to accomplish its presumed objective of further undermining legally binding dispute settlement.

501 Minutes of the General Council meeting of 12 December 2018 (WT/GC/M/175), para. 6.245.

VI. Conclusions

This concluding chapter will, first, briefly summarize the main results of the study, and, second, address the question as to what extent legal analyses like the present one could be relevant for the resolution of the appointment crisis or for other practical purposes.

Following Chapter I's introduction to the topic, Chapter II explained the legal rules governing the appointment of Appellate Body members, and then demonstrated that the US had already used the appointment process in the past as a means to influence the direction of the Appellate Body, starting with the refusal to reappoint US Appellate Body members whom the US judged as having not been sufficiently supportive of the US in appeals with US participation, and culminating 2016 in the vetoing of the reappointment of Appellate Body member Seung Wha Chang.

Chapter III traced the development of the current appointment crisis, which started in early 2017. At the beginning, the US only blocked the launch of one appointment process, for a position that became vacant in December 2017, stating that the launch would be premature. But then, in August 2017, it declared that it would not consent to the launch of any new appointment processes, invoking as reason the Appellate Body's practice of allowing outgoing Appellate Body members to complete appeals they had already been assigned to (the Rule 15 issue), which the US considered to be a breach of the DSU. However, the Rule 15 issue as sole reason for the blockage was a mere pretext, which was confirmed one year later, in August 2018, when the US cited a much broader set of concerns as justification for its continued blockage. It accused the Appellate Body of having violated the DSU and other WTO agreements not only with regard to Rule 15, but concerning various issues of, on the one hand, procedure and interpretative approach, and, on the other, substantive law, notably trade remedy law. While the US mentioned the alleged Appellate Body violations in the area of substantive law only in passing, without going into detail, it explained its concerns regarding the issues of procedure and interpretative approach at great length before the DSB. Since August 2018, the US has repeated these allegations whenever the appointments were tabled in the DSB or the General Council, and has stated that it would not unblock the appointment process unless its concerns were addressed, without though, making any specific proposals on how to address them.

Chapter IV, the core of the study, analyzed in detail the six issues of procedure and interpretative approach that were the main focus of the reasons stated by the US for its blockage, that is, Rule 15, the 90-day deadline of Art. 17.5 of the DSU, advisory opinions, appellate review of facts and of municipal law, and precedential effect of Appellate Body reports. The analysis showed that only concerning one of these six issues, namely appellate review of municipal law, there is a case to be made that the Appellate Body has disregarded the DSU, but that this one breach is neither clear nor serious enough to legally justify blocking all appointments to the Appellate Body, particularly since the blockage itself clearly violates the DSU, namely the requirement of Art. 17.2 of the DSU that vacancies on the Appellate Body have to be filled when they arise.

Chapter V put the central legal findings of the study in a broader context. It asked, first, whether the concerns of the US are genuine or were merely contrived for political reasons, and, second, whether the current appointment crisis, which started after the inauguration of President Trump, is a logical extension of earlier US policies or a break with the past.

The answer to the first question was that although some arguments indeed appear to be fabricated, overall there is genuine dissatisfaction and frustration of many on the US side with the Appellate Body. This is due in large part to the fact that the WTO dispute settlement system and the Appellate Body have developed differently than expected by the US at the close of the Uruguay Round in 1995. First, the Appellate Body has played a much more important role in the dispute settlement system than expected, both in quantitative and qualitative terms; second, the US has been sued more often and lost more often as defendant before the Appellate Body than anticipated; and, third, efforts to negotiate new or to amend existing agreements have largely failed, contrary to expectations, so that Appellate Body interpretations disliked by the US could not be overturned through negotiations.

On the second question, the Chapter revealed that even though many of the US complaints about the Appellate Body are long-standing, and have been voiced by various US administrations, the blockage of all appointments to the Appellate Body is still an expression of a major shift of US trade policy under the Trump administration. Whereas in the past the US had been a major proponent of a rule-based multilateral trading system grounded in the belief that free trade benefits all („win-win"), the Trump administration is driven by the mercantilist view that international trade is a zero-sum game, in which powerful countries like the US can gain most if they can exert their power unrestrained by law. In that view, legally binding dispute settlement is not in the interest of the US, and, consequently, debilitating the WTO dispute settlement system by blocking all appointments to the Appellate Bod makes sense for the US.

After this summary, we will close with a few thoughts on whether legal analyses like the present one, which seek a better understanding of the legal concerns raised by the US, can actually be helpful in resolving the appointment crisis, or have any other practical value. According to the US, the answer is yes. Given that many, if not most, members disagree with the US depiction of the Appellate Body as a rogue rule-breaker, the US has uttered amazement that other members can read the DSU differently than itself, and has called for gaining a deeper understanding of the issues as a prerequisite for any solution: *„[I]t was striking that a few Members ... would not acknowledge that the Appellate Body had been acting contrary to the unambiguous text of the DSU. The United States would like to understand how it was that Members could supposedly understand the same, clear words in such disparate ways. ... [I]t was vital that Members understand how it is that they had come to that point where the Appellate Body ... was disregarding the clear rules that had been set by those same Members. .... Equally important was the need to understand why the Membership itself had been so reluctant over the course of so many years to take corrective action in response to Appellate Body rule-breaking. ... Members should first have those understandings in order to determine how they could find appropriate and effective solutions to prevent this from happening in the future"*.[502]

So, is there a chance that the US and other members might reach common ground on the evaluation of the Appellate Body's record through the power of legal reasoning and discourse, and on that basis find a way out of the appointment crisis? We do not think that this is likely. As to the members opposing the US, after having heard at great length the arguments of the US on the alleged misconduct of the Appellate Body, they are apparently not convinced, and, as Chapter IV of the present study has demonstrated, with good

502 Minutes of the General Council meeting of 7 May 2019 (WT/GC/M/177), statement of the US, paras. 4.154 – 4.157; see also statements of the US at the General Council meeting of 23 July 2019, item 7 (https://geneva.usmission.gov/2019/07/23/statements-delivered-by-ambassador-dennis-shea-wto-general-council-meeting-july-23-2019), and at the General Council meeting of 24 July 2019, item 4 (https://geneva.usmission.gov/2019/07/24/statements-delivered-by-ambassador-dennis-shea-wto-general-council-meeting-geneva-july-24-2019).

reason. Indeed, since the US has begun to explain its concerns in more detail in the DSB, from August 2018 onwards, not only has the US remained entirely alone in blocking the appointment process, the number of members explicitly supporting an immediate launch of that process has actually increased.[503] As to the US itself, it seems even less likely that further legal arguments will make a difference and induce the US to change its position, regardless of the strength of these arguments. After having denigrated the Appellate Body in the harshest terms since the start of the crisis, it is difficult to see how the US could retreat now and admit mistake without losing face. Moreover, given that, as described in Section V.B, the current US administration is not in favor of legally binding dispute settlement, it has no incentive to give up the politically convenient argument that the Appellate Body has „*broken* [*the rules*] *with impunity*“,[504] no matter how far-fetched this claim may be. This pessimistic view about the prospects of bringing the parties closer through the exchange of legal arguments is shared by others, for example, by Alan Wolff, a former US trade diplomat and currently a Deputy Director-General of the WTO, who said in June 2018: „*It had been my belief that a greater understanding shown of respective legal interpretations would have assisted in resolving the current impasse over the continued existence of the Appellate Body. I have recently come to the conclusion that this may not be correct. ... This is a political decision that is highly unlikely to turn on legal merits.*“[505]

Does it follow that analyses of whether the Appellate Body has complied with the DSU and other WTO agreements are only of academic interest, and have no practical value? The answer is no, for at least two reasons, one focusing on the short term and the other on the long term.

In the short term, it is important to provide a clear counterweight to the constantly repeated and morally charged US accusation that the Appellate Body is a shameless rule-breaker, not in order to try to convince the US that its accusations are wrong, let alone to get it to publicly acknowledge any such thing, but to create a level playing field for a candid discussion of the underlying political differences. It has to be established in the public forum that the disputed legal issues are, as a rule, difficult questions of legal interpretation, which the Appellate Body has answered in good faith (whether one

503 See supra, fn. 90 – 91 and accompanying text.

504 Minutes of the General Council meeting of 7 May 2019 (WT/GC/M/177), statement of the US, para. 4.154.

505 Wulff (2018).

agrees with these answers or not), rather than easy questions answered by unambiguous texts, which the Appellate Body has willfully distorted.[506] Otherwise, there is the danger that the US might gain the moral high ground, albeit without justification, in the mind of the public, and maybe even in that of some negotiators, which might unfairly tilt any negotiations aimed at finding a way forward. Apart from rejecting the partisan US allegations of Appellate Body rule-breaking and moral misconduct, though, there is every reason to engage constructively with the US on how to reform the dispute settlement system (and the WTO more generally), even if one should firmly believe that all Appellate Body interpretations are legally correct. If a WTO member as important as the US is obviously no longer satisfied with the way the dispute settlement system works, it is in the interest of the organization and the membership as a whole to somehow accommodate that member and find a new equilibrium.[507]

Looking at the long term, with December 2019, when the Appellate Body will cease to be functional, fast approaching, it is quite uncertain what the future of the Appellate Body will be, whether it will be able to continue in anything similar to its present shape, whether it will be substantially overhauled, and if so how, or whether it will wither and die. Whatever its future, there is much to be learned from the unprecedented experience of more than 20 years of appellate decision-making at the WTO. That experience can continue to provide valuable input for international trade law, international law more generally, and the design and development of international courts and other international dispute settlement systems. An important part of that experience is how the Appellate Body has dealt with the perennial and difficult challenge of

506 See, for instance, the US-appointed Appellate Body member Graham (2016), p. 115: „*We work with the words on paper. But that is rarely as simple as it might sound. The Dispute Settlement Understanding ... states that findings of the dispute settlement system ‚cannot add to or diminish the rights and obligations provided in the covered agreements'. But, in almost every appeal that comes before the Appellate Body, the very heart of the question at issue is whether an interpretation advocated by one of the participants would correctly reflect the balance struck in the treaty provisions, or would add to or detract from the rights and obligations of a WTO Member. Whether we have struck the balance correctly is often in the eye of the beholder. ... We try hard to discern and give meaning to that balance as reflected in the treaty text and to get our interpretations right. We can't expect all Members always to agree with us. We don't always agree even among ourselves. But we do bring to these discussions respect for one another and our honest best efforts, by our own lights.*"

507 For a proponent of such an approach and proposals on how it could be accomplished, see McDougall (2018).

judicial bodies which, on the one hand, are expected not to make political decisions but simply to apply the law as written, and, on the other, unavoidably have to engage to some degree in (potentially controversial) value judgments when they interpret legal texts.[508] The contested interpretations of the DSU at issue in the present appointment crisis are a perfect illustration of this challenge.

508 On the indeterminacy of law and the unavoidability of value judgements in legal interpretation, see, for instance, Lehne (2004), pp. 85 – 100.

Bibliography

Alvarez-Jimenez, Alberto (2009), The WTO Appellate Body's Exercise of Judicial Economy, Journal of International Economic Law 12, pp. 393 – 415.

Anderson, Scott/Friedbacher, Todd/Lau, Christian/Lockhart, Nicolas/Remy, Jan Yves/Sandford, Iain (2017), Using arbitration under article 25 of the DSU to ensure the availability of appeals, CTEI Working Paper 2017 – 17.

Ansong, Alex (2019), The WTO Appellate Body: Are There Any Viable Solutions?, Global Trade and Customs Journal 14, pp. 169 – 178.

Anuradha, R.V. (2018), Petrificus Totalus: The Spell of National Security!, Asian Journal of WTO & International Health Law and Policy 13, pp. 311 – 332.

Appleton, Arthur E. (2016), Judging the Judges or Judging the Members? Pathways and Pitfalls in the Appellate Body Appointment Process, in: Leila Choukrone (ed.), Judging the State in International Trade and Investment Law, Springer, pp. 11 – 32.

Babu, R. Rajesh (2016), Decision making in the WTO: From Negotiated Law-making to Judicial Law-making, in: Julien Chaisse/Tsai-Yu Lin (eds.), International Economic Law and Governance. Essays in Honour of Mitsuo Matsushita, Oxford University Press, pp. 487 – 514.

Babu, R. Rajesh (2018), WTO and the Protection of Public Morals, Asian Journal of WTO & International Health Law and Policy 13, pp. 333 – 354.

Bacchus, James (2005), Appellators: the quest for the meaning of and/or, World Trade Review 4, pp. 499 – 523.

Bacchus, James (2015), Not in Clinical Isolation, in: Gabrielle Marceau (ed.), A History of Law and Lawyers in the GATT/WTO. The Development of the Rule of Law in the Multilateral Trading System, Cambridge University Press, pp. 507 – 516.

Bacchus, James (2018), Might Unmakes Right. The American Assault on the Rule of Law in World Trade, CIGI Papers No. 173, May 2018.

Bacchus, James/Lester, Simon (2019), Of Precedent and Persuasion. The Crucial Role of an Appeal Court in WTO Disputes, Cato Institute, Free Trade Bulletin, No. 74, 12 September 2019 (https://www.cato.org/sites/cato.org/files/2019-09/FTB_74.pdf)

Bahri, Amrita (2019), 'Appellate Body Held Hostage': Is Judicial Activism at Fair Trial?, Journal of World Trade 53, pp. 293 – 316.

Bederman, David J. (2016), International Law Frameworks, 4th ed., Foundation Press.

Bentes, Pablo (2017), transcript of remarks at the GBD Colloquium „Disputed Court: A Look at the Challenges To (And From) The WTO Dispute Settlement System" on 20 December 2017 (http://www.gbdinc.org/wp-content/uploads/2018/01/TRANSCRIPT_BENTES_DISPUTE-SETTLEMENT_12-20-2017.pdf).

Beshkar, Mostafa/Chilton, Adam S. (2016), Revisiting Procedure and Precedent in the WTO: An Analysis of *US – Countervailing and Anti-Dumping Measures* (*China*), World Trade Review 15, pp. 375 – 395.

Bhardwaj, Prakhar (2019), Towards a Coherent Theory of Panel Recommendations for Expired Measures, forthcoming in Journal of International Economic Law 22, issue 3, advance access publication of 27 September 2019.

Bhala, Raj (1999a), The Myth about Stare Decisis and International Trade Law (Part One of a Trilogy), American University International Law Review 14, pp. 845 – 956.

Bhala, Raj (1999b), The Precedent Setters: De Facto Stare Decisis in WTO Adjudication (Part Two of a Trilogy), Journal of Transnational Law and Policy 9, pp. 1 – 152.

Bhala, Raj (2001), The Power of the Past: Towards De Jure Stare Decisis in WTO Adjudication (Part Three of a Trilogy), George Washington International Law Review 33, pp. 873 – 978.

Bhala, Raj/Gantz, David A. (2006), WTO Case Review 2005, Arizona Journal of International & Comparative Law 23, pp. 107 – 345.

Bhala, Raj/Gantz, David A./Keating, Shannon B./Simoes, Bruno Germain (2014), WTO Case Review 2013, Arizona Journal of International & Comparative Law 31, pp. 475 – 510.

Bhala, Raj/Gantz, David A./Keating, Shannon B./Witmer, Eric (2019), WTO Case Review 2017, Arizona Journal of International & Comparative Law 36, pp. 253 – 366.

Bhatia, Ujal Singh (2018), The Legitimacy of the WTO Appellate Body, address at the Brandeis Institute for International Judges 2018, 30 May to 2 June 2018, in: WTO Appellate Body, Annual Report for 2018, March 2019 (WT/AB/29), pp. 124 – 129.

Blumstein, Paul (2017), China Inc. in the WTO Dock, CIGI Papers No. 158, December 2017.

Bohanes, Jan/Lockhart, Nicolas (2009), Standard of Review in WTO Law, in: Daniel Bethlehem et al. (eds.), The Oxford Handbook of International Trade Law, Oxford University Press, pp. 378 – 436.

Bond, Eric W./Trachtman, Joel (2016), *China–Rare Earths:* Export Restrictions and the Limits of Textual Interpretation, World Trade Review 15, pp. 189 – 209.

Bown, Chad P. (2019), The 2018 US-China Trade Conflict After 40 Years of Special Protection, Peterson Institute for International Economics Working Paper 19 – 7, April 2019.

Bown, Chad P./Kolb, Melanie (2019), Trump's Trade War Timline: An Up-to-Date Guide, updated 23 August 2019, Peterson Institute for International Economics (https://www.piie.com/sites/default/files/documents/trump-trade-war-timeline.pdf).

Bown, Chad P./Prusa, Thomas J. (2011), U.S. Anti-Dumping: Much Ado about Zeroing, in: Will Martin/Aaditya Mattoo (eds.), Unfinished Business? The WTO's Doha Agenda, World Bank/London Publishing Partnership, pp. 355 – 392.

Bradley, Kieran (2014), Vertical Precedent at the Court of Justice of the European Union: When Push Comes to Shove, in: Kieran Bradley/Noes Travers/Anthony Whelan (eds.), Of Courts and Constitutions. Liber Amicorum in Honour of Nial Fennelly, Hart Publishing, pp. 47 – 65.

Brewster, Rachel (2011), The System of Precedent (or the Lack Thereof) at the WTO, in: Carl Baudenbacher/Simon Pflanzer (eds.), International Dispute Resolution, Vol. 3, German Law Publishers, pp. 191 – 197.

Brownlie, Ian (1998), Principles of Public International Law, 5th ed., Oxford 1998.

Camarena González, Rodrigo (2016), From jurisprudence constante to stare decisis: the migration of the doctrine of precedent to civil law constitutionalism, Transnational Legal Theory 7, pp. 257 – 286.

Charnovitz, Steve (2018a), Comments regarding the Proposed Determination of Action Pursu-ant to Section 301, International Economic Law and Policy Blog, 24 July 2018 (https://ielp.worldtradelaw.net/2018/07/the-section-301-action-against-china-fed-reg-filing-by-steve-charnovitz.html).

Charnovitz, Steve (2018b), How American Rejectionism Undermines International Economic Law, Trade, Law and Development 10, pp. 226 – 269.

Chua, Adrian T. (1998), Precedent and Principle of WTO Panel Jurisprudence, Berkeley Journal of International Law 16, pp. 171 – 196.

Claussen, Kathleen (2018), The Other Trade War, Minnesota Law Review Headnotes 103, pp. 1 – 19.

Claussen, Kathleen (2019), Can International Trade Law Recover? Forgotten Statutes: Trade Law's Domestic (Re)turn, American Journal of International Law Unbound 113, pp. 40 – 44.

Clemons, H. Vern (1996), The Ethos of the International Court of Justice Is Dependent Upon the Statutory Authority Attributed to Its Rhetoric: A Metadiscourse, Fordham International Law Journal 20 (1996), pp. 1470 – 1510.

Cohen, Harlan Grant (2015), Theorizing Precedent in International Law, in: Andrea Bian-chi/Daniel Peat/Matthew Windsor (eds.), Interpretation in International Law, Oxford University Press, pp. 268 – 289.

Colares, Juscelinio F. (2009), A Theory of WTO Adjudication: From Empirical Analysis to Biased Rule Development, Vanderbilt Journal of Transnational Law 42, pp. 383 – 439.

Cossy, Mireille (2015), From theory to practice. Drafting and applying the Dispute Settlement Understanding, in: Gabrielle Marceau (ed.), A History of Law and Lawyers in the GATT/WTO. The Development of the Rule of Law in the Multilateral Trading System, Cambridge University Press, pp. 300 – 310.

Creamer, Cosette D. (2019), Can International Trade Law Recover? From the WTO's Crown Jewel to its Crown of Thorns, American Journal of International Law Unbound 113, pp. 51 – 55.

Daku, Mark/Pelc, Krzysztof J. (2017), Who Holds Influence over WTO Jurisprudence?, Journal of International Economic Law 20, pp. 233 – 255.

Davies, Arwel (2015), The GATT Article III:8(a) Procurement Derogation and *Canada – Renewable Energy*, Journal of International Economic Law 18, pp. 543 – 554.

Diamond, Richard (2008), Privatization and the Definition of Subsidy: A Critical Study of Appellate Body Textualism, Journal of International Economic Law 11, pp. 649 – 678.

Dunoff, Jeffrey L. /Pollack, Mark A. (2017), The Judicial Trilemma, American Journal of International Law 111, pp. 225 – 268.

Ehlermann, Claus-Dieter (2002), Six Years on the Bench of the „World Trade Court“. Some Personal Experiences as Member of the Appellate Body of the World Trade Organization, Journal of World Trade 36, pp. 605 – 639.

Ehlermann, Claus-Dieter (2015), Revisiting the Appellate Body, in: Gabrielle Marceau (ed.), A History of Law and Lawyers in the GATT/WTO. The Development of the Rule of Law in the Multilateral Trading System, Cambridge University Press, pp. 489 – 491.

Elsig, Manfred/Eckhardt, Jappe (2015), The Creation of the Multilateral Trade Court: Design and Experimental Learning, World Trade Review 14 (2015), Special Issue: Judicial Politics in International Trade Relations, pp. s13-s32.

Elsig, Manfred/Pollack, Mark A. (2014), Agents, trustees, and international courts: The politics of judicial appointment at the World Trade Organization, European Journal of International Relations 20, pp. 391 – 415.

Erixon, Fredrik (2014), After the Bali Agreement: Lessons from the Doha Round for the WTO's Post-Bali Agenda, ECIPE Policy Briefs, No. 2/2014.

Evenett, Simon J. (2011), Saving the WTO from the Doha Round, 17 April 2011, unpaginated (https://voxeu.org/article/saving-wto-doha-round).

Fabry, Elvire/Tate, Erik (2018), Saving the WTO Appellate Body or Returning to the Wild West of Trade? Jacques Delors Institute, Policy Paper No. 225, 7 June 2018.

Fidler, David P. (2017), President Trump, Trade Policy, and American Grand Strategy: From Common Advantage to Collective Carnage, Asian Journal of WTO & International Health Law and Policy 12, pp. 1 – 31.

Frederike Roessler (2017), Dispute Settlement in the WTO. From a Deliberately Designed to a Spontaneously Grown Order, in: Manfred Elsig/Bernard Hoekman/Joost Pauwelyn (eds.), Assessing the World Trade Organization. Fit for Purpose?, Cambridge University Press, pp. 99 – 119.

Froman, Michael (2015), We are at the end of the line on the Doha Round of trade talks, op-ed in the Financial Times of 13 December 2015.

Ganesan, A.V. (2015), The Appellate Body in its formative years – A Personal Perspective, in: Gabrielle Marceau (ed.), A History of Law and Lawyers in the GATT/WTO. The Development of the Rule of Law in the Multilateral Trading System, Cambridge University Press, pp. 517 – 546.

Gao, Henry (2018), Dictum on Dicta: Obiter Dicta in WTO Disputes, World Trade Review 17, pp. 509 – 533.

Gardener, Richard K. (2008), Treaty Interpretation, Oxford University Press.

Gathii, James Thuo (2004), Process and Substance in WTO Reform, Rutgers Law Review 56, pp. 885 – 925.

Gathii, James Thuo (2006), International Justice and the Trading Regime, Emory International Law Review, 19, pp. 1407 – 1430.

Graham, Thomas R. (2014), Present at the Creation, Journal of International Business and Law 12, pp. 317 – 325 (manuscript of a speech held on 6 February 2013).

Graham, Thomas R. (2016), Speaking up: The state of the Appellate Body, speech on 22 November 2016, in: Appellate Body, Annual Report for 2016, March 2017 (WT/AB/27), pp. 112 – 117.

Guillaume, Gilbert (2011), The Use of Precedent by International Judges and Arbitrators, Journal of International Dispute Settlement 2, pp. 5 – 23.

Hanke, Jakob (2018), Charge of the Lighthizer brigade, Politico, 2 October 2018 (https://www.politico.eu/article/the-charge-of-the-robert-lighthizer-brigade-trade-war-us-donald-trump).

Hassan, Mena (2014), A WTO Agreement on Trade Facilitation: Can it really facilitate trade?, dissertation of the University of St. Gallen.

Haynes, Jason (2014), The Emergence of a Doctrine of *de jure horizontal stare decisis* at the Caribbean Court of Justice: Fragmentation of Pluralism of International Law?, Journal of International Dispute Settlement 5, pp. 498 – 530.

Helmersen, Sondre Torp (2016), The Use of Scholarship by the WTO Appellate Body, Goettingen Journal of International Law 7, pp. 309 – 351.

Hillebrand Pohl, Jens (2017), How to break the impasse over appellate body nominations, 29 September 2017 (https://www.maastrichtuniversity.nl/blog/2017/09/how-break-impasse-over-appellate-body-nominations).

Hillebrand Pohl, Jens (2019), Blueprint for a Plurilateral WTO Arbitration Agreement under Article 25 of the Dispute Settlement Understanding, in: Denise Prévost/Iveta Alexovicová/Jens Hillebrand Pohl (eds.), Restoring Trust in Trade. Liber Amicorum in Honour of Peter Van den Bossche, Hart, pp. 139 – 156.

Hillman, Jennifer (2017), Independence at the top of the triangle: Best resolution of the Judicial Trilemma?, American Journal of International Law 111, pp. 364 – 368.

Hillman, Jennifer (2017), Remarks at the GBD Colloquium „Disputed Court: A Look at the Challenges To (And From) The WTO Dispute Settlement System" on 20 December 2017 in Washington, DC (http://www.gbdinc.org/wp-content/uploads/2018/01/C245-Transcript-HILLMAN-12-20-2017.pdf).

Hillman, Jennifer (2018a), Three Approaches to Fixing the World Trade Organization's Appellate Body: The Good, the Bad, and the Ugly?, working paper, Institute of International Economic Law, Georgetown University Law Center (https://www.law.georgetown.edu/wp-content/uploads/2018/12/Hillman-Good-Bad-Ugly-Fix-to-WTO-AB.pdf).

Hillman, Jennifer (2018b), Testimony before the U.S.-China Economic and Review Security Commission, Hearing on U.S. tools to address Chinese market distortions, Washington, DC, 8 June 2018 (https://www.uscc.gov/sites/default/files/Hillman%20Testimony%20US%20China%20Comm%20w%20Appendix%20A.pdf.).

Hoekman, Bernard M./Mavroidis, Petros C. (2019), Burning Down the House? The Appellate Body in the Centre of the WTO Crisis, EUI Working Papers RSCAS 2019/56, July 2019.

Horn, Henrik /Weiler, Joseph H.H. (2005), European Communities – Trade Description of Sardines: Textualism and Its Discontents, in: Horn, Henrik/Mavroidis, Petros C. (eds.), The WTO Case Law of 2002. The American Law Institute Reporters' Studies, pp. 248 – 275.

Howse, Robert (2003), The Most Dangerous Branch? WTO Appellate Body Jurisprudence on the Nature and Limits of the Judicial Power, in: Thomas Cottier/Petros C. Mavroidis (eds.), The Role of the Judge in International Trade Regulation. Experience and Lessons for the WTO, University of Michigan Press, pp. 11 – 41.

Howse, Robert (2014), The World Trade Organization 20 Years On: Global Governance by the Judiciary, European Journal of International Law 27 (2014), pp. 9 – 77.

Hsiang, Jerome/Nyarko, Julian (2015), Precedent Citation at the WTO. Shifting the Empirical Focus to Panelists, 15 January 2015, unpublished manuscript.

Hudec, Robert E. (1993), Enforcing international trade law. The Evolution of the modern GATT legal system, Butterworth Legal Publishers.

Hufbauer, Gary Clyde (2011), WTO Judicial Appointments: Bad Omen for the Trading System, 13 June 2011 (https://piie.com/blogs/realtime-economic-issues-watch/wto-judicial-appointments-bad-omen-trading-system).

Irvin, Douglas A. (2017), Clashing over Commerce: A History of US Trade Policy, University of Chicago Press.

Irwin, Douglas A./Weiler, Joseph (2008), Measures Affecting the Cross-Border Supply of Gambling and Betting Services (DS 285), World Trade Review 7, pp. 71 – 113

Jackson, John (1998), The World Trade Organization. Constitution and Jurisprudence, The Royal Institute of International Affairs, Chatham House Papers.

Jenks, C. Wilfred (1964), The Prospects of International Adjudication, Oceana Publications.

Kerr, William A. (2015), Food Security, Strategic Stockholding and Trade-Distorting Subsidies: Is There a Permanent Solution?, Estey Journal of International Law and Trade Policy 16, pp. 1 – 13.

Kerr, William A. (2018), Eliminating the Constraints on Trade Policy – The Strategy that Underpins US Negotiations in the Trump Administration, Estey Journal of International Law and Trade Policy 19, pp. 75 – 84.

Kho, Stephen/Petersen, Thor (2019), The United States, China, and the WTO National Security Exception, 16 August 2019, unpaginated (https://www.chinabusinessreview.com/turning-the-tables-the-united-states-china-and-the-wto-national-security-exception)

Kleinmann, David/Guinan, Joe (2011), The Doha Round: An Obituary, Global Governance Programme, Policy Brief, Issue 2011/1, June 2011.

Kohona, Palitha T.B. (1994), Dispute Resolution under the World Trade Organization. An Overview, Journal of World Trade 28, pp. 23 – 47.

Kong, Qingjiang/Guo, Shuai (2019), Towards a Mega-Plurilateral Dispute Settlement Mechanism for the WTO?, Journal of World Trade 53, pp. 273 – 292.

Kucik, Jeffrey/Pelc, Krzysztof J. (2016), Do International Rulings Have Spillover Effects? The View from Financial Markets, World Politics 68, pp. 713 – 751.

Kuijper, Peter Jan (2018), From the Board: The US attack on the WTO Appellate Body, Legal Issues of Economic Integration 45, pp. 1 – 12.

Lacarte-Muró, Julio (2015), Launching the Appellate Body, in: Gabrielle Marceau (ed.), A History of Law and Lawyers in the GATT/WTO, Cambridge University Press, pp. 476 – 481.

Lacarte-Muró, Julio/Castro, Fernando Piérola (2004), Comparing the WTO and GATT dispute settlement mechanisms: What was accomplished in the Uruguay Round, in: Julio Lacarte-Muró/J. Granados (eds.), Inter-governmental Trade Dispute Settlement: Multilateral and Regional Approaches, Cameron May, pp. 31 – 60

Lee, Jaemin (2018), Commericalizing national security? National security exceptions' outer parameter under GATT Article XXI, Journal of International Economic Law 13, pp. 277 – 310.

Lee, Yong-Shik (2019), Three Wrongs Do Not Make a Right: The Conundrum of the US Steel and Aluminum Tariffs, World Trade Review 18, pp. 481 – 501.

Lehne, Jens (2004), Constitutional Compliance. A Game-Theoretic Analysis, Staempfli Pub-lishers/Bruylant/Sakkoulas Publishers.

Lester, Simon (2007), Appellate Body Appointments Blocked, International Economic Law and Policy Blog, 19 November 2007 (http://worldtradelaw.typepad.com/ielpblog/2007/11/appellate-body.html).

Lester, Simon (2012), The Development of Standards of Appellate Review for Factual, Legal and Law Application Questions in WTO Dispute Settlement, Trade Law and Develop-ment 4, pp. 125 – 149.

Lester, Simon (2018), The Origins of the „Cogent Reasons" Approach to the Precedential Value of Appellate Body Reports, International Economic Law and Policy Blog, 24 June 2019 (https://worldtradelaw.typepad.com/ielpblog/2018/03/appellate-body-factual-questions.html).

Lester, Simon (2019), The Appellate Body's Review of the Meaning of Domestic Law, International Economic Law and Policy Blog, 4 March 2018 (https://ielp.worldtradelaw.

net/2019/06/the-origins-of-the-cogent-reasons-approach-to-the-precedential-value-of-appellate-body-reports.html).

Lester, Simon/Zhu, Huan (2019), A proposal for „rebalancing" to deal with „national security" trade restrictions, Fordham International Law Journal 42, pp. 1451 – 1474.

Lighthizer, Robert E. (2000), Remarks at the conference „America's trade agenda after the Battle in Seattle: A forum on WTO and U.S. trade law reform" on 20 July 2000, unpaginated (http://libertyparkusafd.org/Hamilton/conferences/Remarks%20by%20the%20Honorable%20Robert%20Lighthizer.htm).

Lighthizer, Robert E. (2007), Testimony the U.S. Senate Finance Committee on Finance, Hearing on Trade Enforcement for a 21st Century Economy, 12 June 2007.

Lim, C.L. (2005), The Amicus Brief Issue at the WTO, Chinese Journal of International Law 4, pp. 85 – 120.

Luanratana, Woraboon/Romano, Allesandro (2014), Stare Decisis in the WTO: Myth, Dream, or a Siren's Song?, Journal of World Trade 48, pp. 773 – 794.

Lundmark, Thomas (2017), The methodology of using precedent, in: Nis Jul Clausen et al. (eds.), Festskrift til Hans Viggo Godsk Pedersen, Djøf Forlag, pp. 335 – 353.

MacCormick, D. Neil/Summers, Robert S. (eds.) (1997), Interpreting Precedent: A Comparative Study, Routledge.

Magnus, John (2017), Remarks at the GBD Colloquium „Disputed Court: A Look at the Challenges To (And From) The WTO Dispute Settlement System" on 20 December 2017 in Washington, DC (http://www.gbdinc.org/wp-content/uploads/2018/02/C245-Dispute-Settlement-Transcript-of-Remarks-by-John-Magnus-12-20-2017.pdf).

Magnuson, William (2010), WTO Jurisprudence & Its Critiques: The Appellate Body's Anti-Constitutional Resistance, Harvard International Law Journal Online 51, pp. 121 – 154.

Matsushita, Mitsuo (2012), The Dispute Settlement Mechanism at the WTO: The Appellate Body – Assessment and Problems, in: Narlikar, Amrita/Daunton, Martin/Stern, Robert M. (eds.), The Oxford Handbook on the World Trade Organization, Oxford University Press, pp. 507 – 534.

Matsushita, Mitsuo (2015), Reflections on the functioning of the Appellate Body, in: Gabrielle Marceau (ed.), A History of Law and Lawyers in the GATT/WTO. The Development of the Rule of Law in the Multilateral Trading System, Cambridge University Press, pp. 547 – 558.

Mavroidis, Petros C./Messerlin, Patrick A./Wauters Jasper M. (2008), The Law and Economics of Contingent Protection in the WTO, Edward Elgar.

Mavroidis, Petros C./Prusa, Thomas J. (2018), Die Another Day: Zeroing in on Targeted Dumping – Did the AB Hit the Mark in *US–Washing Machines?*, World Trade Review 17, pp. 239 – 264.

McDougall, Robert (2018), Standoff on WTO tribunal is more about the scope of intergovernmental adjudication than Trump unilateralism, 12 January 2018, unpaginated (https://www.ictsd.org/opinion/standoff-on-wto-tribunal-is-more-about-the-scope-of-intergovernmental-adjudication).

McDougall, Robert (2018), The Crisis in WTO Dispute Settlement: Fixing Birth Defects to Restore Balance, Journal of World Trade 52, pp. 867 – 896.

McRea, Donald (2006), Treaty interpretation and the development of international trade law by the WTO Appellate Body, in: Giorgio Sacerdoti/Alan Yanovich/Jan Bohanes (eds.), The WTO at Ten. The Contribution of the Dispute Settlement System, Cambridge University Press, pp. 360 – 371.

Murrill, Brandon J. (2018), Congressional Research Services, The Supreme Court's Overruling of Constitutional Precedent, 24 September 2018.

Nedumpara, James J. (2012), Antidumping Proceedings and 'Zeroing' Practices: Have we entered the Endgame?, Global Trade and Customs Journal 7, pp. 15 – 26.

Oesch, Matthias (2003), Standards of Review in WTO Dispute Resolution, Oxford University Press.

Pauwelyn, Joost (2016), Minority rules: precedent and participation before the WTO Appellate Body, in: Joanna Jemielniak/Laura Nielsen/Henrik Palmer Olsen (eds.), Establishing Judicial Authority in International Economic Law, Cambridge University Press, pp. 141 – 172.

Pauwelyn, Joost (2019), WTO Dispute Settlement Post 2019: What to Expect? What Choice to Make?, working paper, Graduate Institute and Georgetown Law, 7 July 2019 (https://papers.ssrn.com/sol3/papers.cfm?abstract_id=3415964)

Pauwelyn, Joost/Elsig, Manfred (2013), The Politics of Treaty Interpretation: Variations and Explanations across International Tribunals, in: Dunoff, Jeffrey L./Pollack, Mark A. (eds.), Interdisciplinary Perspectives on International Law and International Relations. The State of the Art, Cambridge University Press, pp. 445 – 473.

Payosova, Tetyana/Hufbauer, Gary Clyde/Schott, Jeffrey J. (2018), The Dispute Settlement Crisis in the World Trade Organization: Causes and Cures, Peterson Institute for International Economics, Policy Brief 18 – 5, March 2018.

Pelc, Krzysztof J. (2014), The Politics of Precedent in International Law: A Social Network Application, American Political Science Review 108, pp. 547 – 564.

Pelc, Krzysztof J. (2016), The welfare implications of precedent in international law, in: Joanna Jemielniak/Laura Nielsen/Henrik Palmer Olsen (eds.), Establishing judicial authority in international economic law, Cambridge University Press, pp. 173 – 187.

Petersmann, Ernst-Ulrich (2018), Between 'Member-Driven' WTO Governance and 'Constitutional Justice': Judicial Dilemmas in GATT/WTO Dispute Settlement, Journal of International Economic Law 21, pp. 103 – 122.

Petersmann, Ernst-Ulrich (2019), How Should WTO Members React to Their WTO Crises?, World Trade Review 18, pp. 503 – 525.

Peterson, Matt (2018), The Making of a Trade Warrior, The Atlantic, 29 December 2018 (https://www.theatlantic.com/politics/archive/2018/12/robert-lighthizers-bid-cut-chinas-trade-influence/578611).

Picciotto, Sol (2005), The WTO's Appellate Body: Legal Formalism as a Legitimation of Global Governance, Governance: An International Journal of Policy, Administration, and Institutions 18, pp. 477 – 503.

Piérola, Fernando (2014), General Thoughts on the Standard of 'Cogent Reasons' in the Treatment of WTO Jurisprudence, Global Trade and Customs Journal 9, pp. 427 – 429.

Qin, Julia (2019), US-China Tariff War: A Lesson about WTO Law, International Economic Law and Policy Blog, 11 September 2019 (https://ielp.worldtradelaw.net/2019/09/us-china-tariff-war-a-lesson-about-wto-law.html).

Raghu Ram, Jayant (2018), Cracks in the 'Crown Jewel' – Whither 'Prompt Settlement' of WTO Disputes?, Trade, Law and Development 10, pp. 302 – 376.

Raina, Akhil (2018), Meditations in an Emergency: The Appellate Body Deadlock – What It Is, Why It Is a Problem, and What to Do About It, Global Trade and Customs Journal 13, pp. 376 – 386.

Ramírez Hernández, Ricardo (2019), Farewell Speech, 28 May 2018, in: Appellate Body, Annual Report for 2018, March 2019 (WT/AB/29), pp. 118 – 121.

Roessler, Frieder (2015), Changes in the jurisprudence of the WTO Appellate Body during the past twenty years, Journal of International Trade Law 14, pp. 129 – 146.

Rubini, Luca (2017), The Age of Innocence. The Evolution of the Case Law of the WTO Dispute Settlement: Subsidy as a Case Study, in: Elsig, Manfred/Hoekman, Bernard/Pauwelyn, Joost (eds.), Assessing the World Trade Organization. Fit for Purpose?, Cambridge University Press, pp. 276 – 317.

Ruggiero, Renato (1997), The Future Path of the Multilateral Trading System, address to the Korean Business Association, Seoul, Korea, 17 April 1997 (https://www.wto.org/english/news_e/sprr_e/seoul_e.htm).

Rushford, Greg (2003), Bob Lighthizer, WTO jurist?, Rushford Report, October 2003, unpaginated (http://www.rushfordreport.com/2003/10_2003_Publius.htm).

Sacerdoti, Giorgio (2015), Introduction, in: Giorgio Sacerdoti et al. (eds.), WTO case law in 2014, 27 March 2015, Bocconi Legal Studies Research Paper No. 2587648, pp. 1 – 6.

Sacerdoti, Giorgio (2016), Introduction, in: Giorgio Sacerdoti (ed.), The WTO in 2015: Systemic issues of the dispute settlement system and the Appellate Body's case law, Bocconi Legal Studies Research Paper No. 27803652016, 16 May 2016, pp. 1 – 6

Sacerdoti, Giorgio (2017), Introduction, in: Giorgio Sacerdoti et al. (eds.), WTO case law in 2016, 1 March 2017, Bocconi Legal Studies Research Paper No. 2940107, pp. 1 – 10

Sacerdoti, Giorgio (2017), The WTO Dispute Settlement System. Consolidating Success and Confronting New Challenges, in: Manfred Elsig/Bernard Hoekman/Joost Pauwelyn (eds.), Assessing the World Trade Organization. Fit for Purpose?, Cambridge University Press, pp. 147 – 174.

Sacerdoti, Giorgio (2018), A Comment on Henry Goa, 'Dictum on Dicta: Obiter Dicta in WTO Disputes', World Trade Review 17, pp. 535 – 540.

Sadurski, Wojciech (2015), Supranational public reason: On legitimac of supranational normproducing authorities, Global Constitutionalism 4, pp. 396 – 427.

Schott, Jeffrey J./Hufbauer, Gary Clyde (2014), Putting the Trade Facilitation Agreement back on Track after India's Obstruction, 5 August 2014 (https://blogs.piie.com/realtime/?p=4441).

Schwab, Susan S. (2011), After Doha: Why the Negotiations Are Doomed and What We Should Do About It, Foreign Affairs 90 (2011), No. 3, pp. 104 – 117.

Shaffer, Gregory (2019), A Tragedy in the Making? The Decline of Law and the Return of Power in International Trade Relations, The Yale Journal of International Law Online (https://cpb-us-w2.wpmucdn.com/campuspress.yale.edu/dist/8/1581/files/2018/12/Shaffer_YJIL-Symposium_A-Tragedy-in-the-Making_12.08.18 – 1zx9zvv.pdf).

Shaffer, Gregory/Elsig, Manfred/Puig, Sergio (2016), The extensive (but fragile) authority of the WTO Appellate Body, Law and Contemporary Politics 79, pp. 237 – 273.

Shahabuddeen, Mohammed (1996), Precedent in the World Court, Cambridge University Press.

Silverman, Jared R. (1996), Multilateral Resolution over Unilateral Retaliation: Adjudicating the Use of Section 301 before the WTO, University of Pennsylvania Journal of International Economic Law 17, pp. 233 – 294.

Slobodian, Quinn (2018), You Live in Robert Lighthizer's World Now, Foreign Policy, 6 August 2018 (https://foreignpolicy.com/2018/08/06/you-live-in-robert-lighthizers-world-now-trump-trade).

Steger, Debra P. Steger (2015), The founding of the Appellate Body, in: Gabrielle Marceau (ed.), A History of Law and Lawyers in the GATT/WTO. The Development of the Rule of Law in the Multilateral Trading System, Cambridge University Press, pp. 447 – 465.

Steinberg, Richard (2004), Judicial Lawmaking at the WTO: Discursive, Constitutional, and Political Constraints, American Journal of International Law 98, pp. 247 – 275.

Steinberg, Richard H. (2018), The Impending Dejudicialization of the WTO Dispute Settlement System?, American Journal of International Law Proceedings 112, pp. 316 – 321.

Stewart, Terence P. (1993), Dispute Settlement Mechanisms, in: Stewart, Terence P. (ed.), The GATT Uruguay Round. A Negotiating History (1986 – 1992), Volume II: Commentary, Kluwer Law and Taxation Publishers, pp. 2663 – 2881.

Stewart, Terence P. (2018), Can the WTO be Saved From Itself? Not without a major crisis, and probably not even then, manuscript of a speech held on 13 April 2018 before the Washington International Trade Association (http://www.stewartlaw.com/Content/Documents/Terence%20Stewart%20-%20WITA%20paper%20(April%2013 %202018).pdf).

Stewart, Terence P./McDonough, Patrick J./Smith, Jennifer M./ Jorgensen, Sandra K. (2013), The Increasing Recognition of Problems with WTO Appellate Body Decision-Making: Will the Message Be Heard?, Global Trade and Customs Journal 8, pp. 390 – 412.

Sutherland, Peter/Bhagwati, Jagdish/Botchwey, Kwesi/FitzGerald, Niall/Hamada, Koichi/Jackson, John H./Lafer, Celso/de Montbrial, Thierry (2004), The Future of the WTO. Addressing institutional challenges in the new millenium, Report by the Consultative Board to the Director-General Supachi Panitchpakdi, published by the WTO.

Tarullo, Daniel K. (2003), Paved with good intentions: the dynamic effects of WTO review of antidumping action, World Trade Review 2, pp. 373 – 393.

Terris, Daniel/Romano, Cesare P.R./ Swigart, Leigh (2007), The International Judge: An Introduction to the Men and Women who Decide the World's Cases, Brandeis University Press.

Unterhalter, David (2015), The Appellate Body under Review, in: Gabrielle Marceau (ed.), A History of Law and Lawyers in the GATT/WTO. The Development of the Rule of Law in the Multilateral Trading System, Cambridge University Press, pp. 466 – 475.

Van Damme, Isabelle (2009), Treaty Interpretation by the WTO Appellate Body, Oxford University Press, 2009.

Van den Bossche, Peter (2006), From afterthought to centrepiece: the WTO Appellate Body and its rise to prominence in the world trading system, in: Giorgio Sacerdoti/Alan

Yanovich/Jan Bohanes (eds.), The WTO at Ten: The contribution of the Dispute Settlement System, Cambridge University Press, 2006, pp. 289 – 325.

Van den Bossche, Peter/Zdouc, Werner (2017), The Law and Policy of the World Trade Organization, 4th ed., Cambridge University Press.

VanGrasstek, Craig (2013), The History and Future of the World Trade Organization, published by the WTO.

VanGrasstek, Craig (2017), Back to the Future: US Trade Policy under the Trump Administration, in: Carlos A. Primo Braga/Bernard Hoekman (eds.), Future of the Global Trade Order, 2nd ed., European University Institute, pp. 49 – 79.

Vidigal, Geraldo (2018), Living Without the Appellate Body: Hegemonic, Fragmented and Network Authority in International Trade, Amsterdam Center for International Law No. 2019 – 04, 4 March 2019 (http://dx.doi.org/10.2139/ssrn.3343327).

Vidigal, Geraldo (2018), Westphalia Strikes Back: The 2018 Trade Wars and the Threat to the WTO Regime, Amsterdam Center for International Law No. 2018 – 13, 2 October 2018 (http://dx.doi.org/10.2139/ssrn.3259127).

Voon, Tania (2019), Can International Trade Law Recover? The Security Exception in WTO Law: Entering a New Era, American Journal of International Law Unbound 113, pp. 45 – 50.

Voon, Tania/Yanovich, Alan (2006), The Facts Aside: The Limitation of WTO Appeals to Issues of Law, Journal of World Trade 40, pp. 239 – 258.

Weiler, Joseph H.H. (2001), The Rule of Lawyers and the Ethos of Diplomats. Reflections on the Internal and External Legitimacy of WTO Dispute Settlement, Journal of World Trade 35, pp. 191 – 207.

Williams, Brock R./Hammond, Keigh E. (2019a), Escalating U.S. Tariffs: Timeline, Congressional Research Services, updated 6 September 2019 (https://fas.org/sgp/crs/row/IN10943.pdf).

Williams, Brock R./Hammond, Keigh E. (2019b), Escalating U.S. Tariffs: Affected Trade, Congressional Research Services, updated 6 September 2019 (https://fas.org/sgp/crs/row/IN10971.pdf).

Williams, Nancy (2019), The Resilience of Protectionism in U.S. Trade Policy, Boston University Law Review 99, pp. 683 – 718.

Wolfe, Robert (2013), First diagnose, then treat: what ails the Doha Round?, EUI Working Pa-pers RSCAS 2013/85, November 2013.

WTO (2007), World Trade Report 2007. Six decades of multilateral trade cooperation: What have we learnt?, published by the WTO.

WTO (2017), A Handbook on the WTO Dispute Settlement System. Prepared by the Legal Affairs Division and the Rules Division of the WTO Secretariat, and the Appellate Body Secretariat, 2nd ed., Cambridge University Press.

WTO (2018a), GATT disputes: 1948 – 1995. Volume 1: Overview and one-page case summaries, published by the WTO.

WTO (2018b), GATT disputes: 1948 – 1995. Volume 2: Dispute settlement procedures, published by the WTO.

Wulff, Alan Wm. (2018), The Rule of Law in the Age of Conflict, keynote address at the closing ceremony of the World Trade Institute master programs, University of Bern, 29

June 2018, unpaginated (https://www.wto.org/english/news_e/news18_e/ddgra_02jul18_e.htm).

Zimmermann, Thomas A. (2006), Negotiating the Review of the WTO Dispute Settlement Understanding, Cameron May.

Table of WTO reports

Argentina – Financial Services: Argentina – Measures Relating to Trade in Goods and Services; Appellate Body report (WT/DS453/AB/R), circulated on 14 April 2016, adopted on 9 May 2016.

Australia – Salmon: Australia – Measures Affecting Importation of Salmon; Appellate Body report (WT/DS18/AB/R), circulated on 20 October 1998, adopted on 6 November 1998.

Brazil – Aircraft (Article 21.5 – Canada): Brazil – Export Financing Programme for Aircraft – Recourse by Canada to Article 21.5 of the DSU; Appellate Body report (WT/DS46/AB/RW), circulated on 21 July 2000, adopted on 4 August 2000.

Brazil – Taxation (Japan): Brazil – Certain Measures Concerning Taxation and Charges; Appellate Body report (WT/DS472/R, WT/DS497/R), circulated on 30 August 2017, adopted on 11 January 2019.

Canada – Aircraft (Article 21.5 – Brazil): Canada – Measures Affecting the Export of Civilian Aircraft – Recourse by Brazil to Article 21.5 of the DSU; Appellate Body report (WT/DS70/AB/RW), circulated on 21 July 2000, adopted on 4 August 2000.

Canada – Dairy: Canada – Measures Affecting the Importation of Milk and the Exportation of Dairy Products; Appellate Body report (WT/DS103/AB/R, WT/DS113/AB/R), circulated on 13 October 1999, adopted on 27 October 1999.

Canada – Renewable Energy: Canada – Certain Measures Affecting the Renewable Energy Generation Sector / Canada – Measures Relating to the Feed-in Tariff Program; Appellate Body report (WT/DS412/AB/R, WT/DS426/AB/R), circulated on 6 May 2013, adopted on 24 May 2013.

Canada – Welded Pipe: Canada – Anti-Dumping Measures on Imports of Certain Carbon Steel Welded Pipe from the Separate Customs Territory of Taiwan, Penghu, Kinmen and Matsu; panel report (WT/DS482/R), circulated on 21 December 2016, adopted on 25 January 2017.

Canada – Wheat Exports and Grain Imports: Canada – Measures Relating to Exports of Wheat and Treatment of Imported Grain; Appellate Body report (WT/DS276/AB/R), circulated on 30 August 2004, adopted on 27 September 2004.

Chile – Price Band System: Chile – Price Band System and Safeguard Measures Relating to Certain Agricultural Products; Appellate Body report (WT/DS207/AB/R), circulated on 23 September 2002, adopted on 23 October 2002.

China – Agricultural Producers: China – Domestic Support for Agricultural Producers; panel report (WT/DS511/R), circulated on 28 February 2019, adopted on 26 April 2019.

China – Auto Parts: China – Measures Affecting Imports of Automobile Parts; Appellate Body report (WT/DS339/AB/R, WT/DS340/AB/R, WT/DS342/AB/R), circulated on 15 December 2008, adopted on 12 January 2009.

China – GOES: China – Countervailing and Anti-Dumping Duties on Grain Oriented Flat-Rolled Electrical Steel from the United States; Appellate Body report (WT/DS414/AB/R), circulated on 18 October 2012, adopted on 16 November 2012.

China – Publications and Audiovisual Products: China – Measures Affecting Trading Rights and Distribution Services for Certain Publications and Audiovisual Entertainment Products; Appellate Body report (WT/DS363/AB/R), circulated on 21 December 2009, adopted on 19 January 2010.

China – Rare Earths: China – Measures Related to the Exportation of Rare Earths, Tungsten, and Molybdenum; panel report (WT/DS431/R, WT/DS432/R, WT/DS433/R), circulated on 26 March 2014, adopted on 29 August 2014; Appellate Body report (WT/DS431/AB/R, WT/DS432/AB/R, WT/DS433/AB/R), circulated on 7 August 2014, adopted on 29 August 2014.

China – Raw Materials: China – Measures Related to the Exportation of Various Raw Materials; Appellate Body report (WT/DS394/AB/R, WT/DS395/AB/R, WT/DS398/AB/R), circulated on 30 January 2012, adopted on 22 February 2012.

Colombia – Textiles: Colombia – Measures Relating to the Importation of Textiles, Apparel and Footwear; Appellate Body report (WT/DS461/AB/R), circulated on 7 June 2016, adopted on 22 June 2016.

EC – Asbestos: European Communities – Measures Affecting Asbestos and Asbestos-Containing Products; Appellate Body report (WT/DS135/AB/R), circulated on 12 March 2001, adopted on 5 April 2001.

EC – Bananas III: European Communities – Regime for the Importation, Sale and Distribution of Bananas; Appellate Body report (WT/DS27/AB/R), circulated on 9 September 1997, adopted on 25 September 1997.

EC – Bananas III: (Article 21.5 – Ecuador II) / EC – Bananas III (Article 21.5 – US): European Communities – Regime for the Importation, Sale and Distribution of Bananas – Second Recourse to Article 21.5 of the DSU by Ecuador (WT/DS27/AB/RW2/ECU); Appellate Body report, circulated on 26 November 2008, adopted on 11 December 2008 / European Communities – Regime for the Importation, Sale and Distribution of Bananas – Recourse to Article 21.5 of the DSU by the United States (WT/DS27/AB/RW/USA), circulated on 26 November 2008, adopted on 22 December 2008.

EC – Export Subsidies on Sugar: European Communities – Export Subsidies on Sugar; Appellate Body report (WT/DS265/AB/R, WT/DS266/AB/R, WT/DS283/AB/R), circulated on 28 April 2005, adopted on 19 May 2005.

EC – Fasteners (China): European Communities – Definitive Anti-Dumping Measures on Certain Iron or Steel Fasteners from China; Appellate Body report (WT/DS397/AB/R), circulated on 15 July 2011, adopted on 28 July 2011.

EC – Hormones: European Communities – Measures Concerning Meat and Meat Products (Hormones); Appellate Body report (WT/DS26/AB/R, WT/DS48/AB/R), circulated on 16 January 1998, adopted on 13 February 1998.

EC and certain member States – Large Civil Aircraft (Article 21.5 – US): European Communities and Certain Member States – Measures Affecting Trade in Large Civil Aircraft – Recourse to Article 21.5 of the DSU by the United States; panel report (WT/DS316/RW), circulated on 22 September 2016, adopted on 28 May 2018; Appellate Body report (WT/DS316/AB/RW), circulated on 15 May 2018, adopted on 28 May 2018.

EC and certain member States – Large Civil Aircraft: European Communities and Certain Member States – Measures Affecting Trade in Large Civil Aircraft; Appellate Body report (WT/DS316/AB/R), circulated on 18 May 2011, adopted on 1 June 2011.

EU – Biodiesel (Argentina): European Union – Anti-Dumping Measures on Biodiesel from Argentina; panel report (WT/DS473/R), circulated on 29 March 2016, adopted on 26 October 2016; Appellate Body report (WT/DS473/AB/R), circulated on 6 October 2016, adopted on 26 October 2016.

EU – Biodiesel (Indonesia): European Union – Anti-Dumping Measures on Biodiesel from Indonesia; panel report (WT/DS480/R), circulated on 25 January 2018, adopted on 28 February 2018.

EU – Energy Package: European Union and its member States – Certain Measures Relating to the Energy Sector; panel report (WT/DS476/R), circulated on 10 August 2018 (appealed by the EU on 21 September 2018).

EU – Fatty Alcohols (Indonesia): European Union – Anti-Dumping Measures on Imports of Certain Fatty Alcohols from Indonesia; Appellate Body report (WT/DS442/AB/R), circulated on 5 September 2017, adopted on 29 September 2017.

EU – PET (Pakistan): European Union – Countervailing Measures on Certain Polyethylene Terephthalate from Pakistan; Appellate Body report (WT/DS486/AB/R), circulated on 16 May 2018, adopted on 28 May 2018.

India – Patents (US): India – Patent Protection for Pharmaceutical and Agricultural Chemical Products; Appellate Body report (WT/DS50/AB/R), circulated on 19 December 1997, adopted on 16 January 1998.

India – Solar Cells: India – Certain Measures Relating to Solar Cells and Solar Modules; Appellate Body report (WT/DS456/AB/R), circulated on 16 September 2016, adopted on 14 October 2016.

Indonesia – Import Licensing Regimes: Indonesia – Importation of Horticultural Products, Animals and Animal Products; Appellate Body report (WT/DS477/AB/R, WT/DS478/AB/R), circulated on 9 November 2017, adopted on 22 November 2017.

Indonesia – Iron or Steel Products: Indonesia – Safeguard on Certain Iron or Steel Products; Appellate Body report (WT/DS490/AB/R, WT/DS496/AB/R), circulated on 15 August 2018, adopted on 27 August 2018.

Japan – Agricultural Products II: Japan – Measures Affecting Agricultural Products; Appellate Body report (WT/DS76/AB/R), circulated on 22 February 1999, adopted on 19 March 1999.

Japan – Alcoholic Beverages II: Japan – Taxes on Alcoholic Beverages; panel report (WT/DS8/R, WT/DS10/R, WT/DS11/R), circulated on 11 July 1996, adopted on 1 November 1996, DSR 1996:I, p. 125; Appellate Body report (WT/DS8/AB/R, WT/DS10/AB/R, WT/DS11/AB/R), circulated on 4 October 1996, adopted on 1 November 1996, DSR 1996:I, p. 97.

Mexico – Anti-Dumping Measures on Rice: Mexico – Definitive Anti-Dumping Measures on Beef and Rice, Complaint with Respect to Rice; Appellate Body report (WT/DS295/AB/R), circulated on 29 November 2005, adopted on 20 December 2005.

Philippines – Distilled Spirits: Philippines – Taxes on Distilled Spirits; Appellate Body report (WT/DS396/AB/R, WT/DS403/AB/R), circulated on 21 December 2011, adopted on 20 January 2012.

Russia – Traffic in Transit: Russia – Measures Concerning Traffic in Transit; panel report (WT/DS512/R), circulated on 5 April 2019, adopted on 26 April 2019.

Thailand – H-Beams: Thailand – Anti-Dumping Duties on Angles, Shapes and Sections of Iron or Non-Alloy Steel and H-Beams from Poland; Appellate Body report (WT/DS122/AB/R), circulated on 12 March 2001, adopted on 5 April 2001.

US – Anti-Dumping and Countervailing Duties (China): United States – Definitive Anti-Dumping and Countervailing Duties on Certain Products from China; Appellate Body report (WT/DS379/AB/R), circulated on 11 March 2011, adopted on 25 March 2011.

US – Carbon Steel (India): United States – Countervailing Measures on Certain Hot-Rolled Carbon Steel Flat Products from India; Appellate Body report (WT/DS436/AB/R), circulated on 8 December 2014, adopted on 19 December 2014.

US – Carbon Steel: United States – Countervailing Duties on Certain Corrosion-Resistant Carbon Steel Flat Products from Germany; Appellate Body report (WT/DS213/AB/R), circulated on 28 November 2002, adopted on 19 December 2002.

US – Certain EC Products: United States – Import Measures on Certain Products from the European Communities (WT/DS165/AB/R), circulated on 11 December 2000, adopted on 10 January 2001.

US – Clove Cigarettes: United States – Measures Affecting the Production and Sale of Clove Cigarettes; Appellate Body report (WT/DS406/AB/R), circulated on 4 April 2012, adopted on 24 April 2012.

US – Continued Suspension / Canada – Continued Suspension: United States – Continued Suspension of Obligations in the EC – Hormones Dispute / Canada – Continued Suspension of Obligations in the EC – Hormones Dispute; Appellate Body reports (WT/DS320/AB/R, WT/DS321/AB/R), circulated on 16 October 2008, adopted on 14 November 2008.

US – Continued Zeroing: United States – Continued Existence and Application of Zeroing Methodology; panel report (WT/DS350/R), circulated on 1 October 2008, adopted on 19 February 2009; Appellate Body report (WT/DS350/AB/R), circulated on 4 February 2009, adopted on 19 February 2009.

US – COOL (Article 21.5 – Canada and Mexico): United States – Certain Country of Origin Labelling (COOL) Requirements – Recourse to Article 21.5 of the DSU by Canada and Mexico; Appellate Body report (WT/DS384/AB/RW, WT/DS386/AB/RW), circulated on 18 May 2015, adopted on 29 May 2015.

US – COOL: United States – Certain Country of Origin Labelling (COOL) Requirements – Recourse to Article 21.5 of the DSU by Canada and Mexico; Appellate Body report (WT/DS384/AB/RW, WT/DS386/AB/RW), circulated on 29 June 2012, adopted on 29 May 2015.

US – Corrosion-Resistant Steel Sunset Review: United States – Sunset Review of Anti-Dumping Duties on Corrosion-Resistant Carbon Steel Flat Products from Japan; Appellate Body report (WT/DS244/AB/R), circulated on 15 December 2003, adopted on 9 January 2004.

US – Countervailing and Anti-Dumping Measures (China): United States – Countervailing and Anti-Dumping Measures on Certain Products from China; panel report (WT/DS449/R), circulated on 27 March 2014, adopted on 22 July 2014; Appellate Body report (WT/DS449/AB/R), circulated on 7 July 2014, adopted on 22 July 2014.

US – Countervailing Duty Investigation on DRAMS: United States – Countervailing Duty Investigation on Dynamic Random Access Memory Semiconductors (DRAMS) from Korea; Appellate Body report (WT/DS296/AB/R), circulated on 27 June 2005, adopted on 20 July 2005.

US – Countervailing Measures (China) (Article 21.5 – China): United States – Countervailing Duty Measures on Certain Products from China – Recourse to Article 21.5 of the DSU by

China; Appellate Body report (WT/DS437/AB/RW), circulated on 16 July 2019, adopted on 15 August 2019.

US – Differential Pricing Methodology: United States – Anti-Dumping Measures Applying Differential Pricing Methodology to Softwood Lumber from Canada; panel report (WT/DS534/R), circulated on 9 April 2019 (appealed by Canada on 4 June 2019).

US – FSC (Article 21.5 – EC): United States – Tax Treatment for „Foreign Sales Corporations" – Recourse to Article 21.5 of the DSU by the European Communities; Appellate Body report (WT/DS108/AB/RW), circulated on 14 January 2002, adopted on 29 January 2002

US – FSC: United States – Tax Treatment for „Foreign Sales Corporations"; Appellate Body report (WT/DS108/AB/R), circulated on 24 February 2000, adopted on 20 March 2000.

US – Gambling: United States – Measures Affecting the Cross-Border Supply of Gambling and Betting Services; Appellate Body report (WT/DS285/AB/R), circulated on 7 April 2005, adopted on 20 April 2005.

US – Gasoline: United States – Standards for Reformulated and Conventional Gasoline; Appellate Body report (WT/DS2/AB/R), circulated on 29 April 1996, adopted on 20 May 1996, DSR 1996:I, p. 3.

US – Hot-Rolled Steel: United States – Anti-Dumping Measures on Certain Hot-Rolled Steel Products from Japan; Appellate Body report (WT/DS184/AB/R), circulated on 24 July 2001, adopted on 23 August 2001.

US – Lamb: United States – Safeguard Measures on Imports of Fresh, Chilled or Frozen Lamb Meat from New Zealand and Australia; Appellate Body report (WT/DS177/AB/R, WT/DS178/AB/R), circulated on 1 May 2001, adopted on 16 May 2001.

US – Large Civil Aircraft (2nd complaint) (Article 21.5 – EU): United States – Measures Affecting Trade in Large Civil Aircraft (Second Complaint) – Recourse to Article 21.5 of the DSU by the European Union; Appellate Body report (WT/DS353/RW) circulated on 28 March 2019, adopted on 11 April 2019.

US – Large Civil Aircraft (2nd complaint): United States – Measures Affecting Trade in Large Civil Aircraft (Second Complaint); Appellate Body report (WT/DS353/AB/R), circulated on 12 March 2012, adopted on 23 March 2012.

US – Lead and Bismuth II: United States – Imposition of Countervailing Duties on Certain Hot-Rolled Lead and Bismuth Carbon Steel Products Originating in the United Kingdom; Appellate Body report (WT/DS138/AB/R), circulated on 10 May 2000, adopted on 7 June 2000.

US – Line Pipe: United States – Definitive Safeguard Measures on Imports of Circular Welded Carbon Quality Line Pipe from Korea; Appellate Body report (WT/DS202/AB/R), circulated on 15 February 2002, adopted on 8 March 2002.

US – Offset Act (Byrd Amendment): United States – Continued Dumping and Subsidy Offset Act of 2000; Appellate Body report (WT/DS217/AB/R, WT/DS234/AB/R), circulated on 16 January 2003, adopted on 27 January 2003.

US – Oil Country Tubular Goods Sunset Reviews: United States – Sunset Reviews of Anti-Dumping Measures on Oil Country Tubular Goods from Argentina; Appellate Body report (WT/DS268/AB/R), circulated on 29 November 2004, adopted on 17 December 2004.

US – Pipe and Tube Products (Turkey): United States – Countervailing Measures on Certain Pipe and Tube Products (Turkey); panel report (WT/DS523/R), circulated on 18

December 2018 (appealed by the US on 25 January 2019 and by Turkey on 30 January 2019).

US – Section 211 Appropriations Act: United States – Section 211 Omnibus Appropriations Act of 1998; Appellate Body report (WT/DS176/AB/R), circulated on 2 January 2002, adopted on 1 February 2002.

US – Section 301 Trade Act: United States – Sections 301 – 310 of the Trade Act 1974; panel report (WT/DS152/R), circulated on 22 December 1999, adopted on 27 January 2000.

US – Shrimp (Article 21.5 – Malaysia): United States – Import Prohibition of Certain Shrimp and Shrimp Products – Recourse to Article 21.5 of the DSU by Malaysia; panel report (WT/DS58/RW), circulated on 15 June 2001, adopted on 21 November 2001; Appellate Body report (WT/DS58/RW/AB), circulated on 22 October 2001, adopted on 21 November 2001.

US – Shrimp (Thailand) / US – Customs Bond Directive: United States – Measures Relating to Shrimp from Thailand / United States – Customs Bond Directive for Merchandise Subject to Anti-Dumping/Countervailing Duties; Appellate Body report (WT/DS343/AB/R, WT/DS345/AB/R), circulated on 16 July 2008, adopted on 1 August 2008.

US – Shrimp II (Viet Nam): United States – Anti-Dumping Measures on Certain Shrimp from Viet Nam; Appellate Body report (WT/DS429/AB/R), circulated on 7 April 2015, adopted on 22 April 2015.

US – Shrimp: United States – Import Prohibition of Certain Shrimp and Shrimp Products; Appellate Body report (WT/DS58/AB/R), circulated on 12 October 1998, adopted on 6 November 1998.

US – Softwood Lumber IV: United States – Final Countervailing Duty Determination with Respect to Certain Softwood Lumber from Canada; Appellate Body report (WT/DS257/AB/R), circulated on 19 January 2004, adopted on 17 February 2004.

US – Stainless Steel (Mexico): United States – Final Anti-Dumping Measures on Stainless Steel from Mexico; panel report (WT/DS344/R), circulated on 20 December 2007, adopted on 20 May 2008; Appellate Body report (WT/DS344/AB/R), circulated on 30 April 2008, adopted on 20 May 2008.

US – Steel Safeguards: United States – Definitive Safeguard Measures on Imports of Certain Steel Products; Appellate Body report (WT/DS248/AB/R, WT/DS249/AB/R, WT/DS251/AB/R, WT/DS252/AB/R, WT/DS253/AB/R, WT/DS254/AB/R, WT/DS258/AB/R, WT/DS259/AB/R), circulated on 10 November 2003, adopted on 10 December 2003.

US – Supercalendered Paper: United States – Countervailing Measures on Supercalendered Paper from Canada; panel report (WT/DS505/R), circulated on 5 July 2018 (appealed by the US on 27 August 2018).

US – Tuna II (Mexico) (Article 21.5 – US) / US – Tuna II (Mexico) (Article 21.5 – Mexico II): United States – Measures Concerning the Importation, Marketing and Sale of Tuna and Tuna Products – Recourse to Article 21.5 of the DSU by the United States / United States – Measures Concerning the Importation, Marketing and Sale of Tuna and Tuna Products – Second Recourse to Article 21.5 of the DSU by Mexico; Appellate Body report (WT/DS381/AB/RW/USA, WT/DS381/AB/RW2), circulated on 14 December 2018, adopted 11 January 2019.

US – Tuna II (Mexico): United States – Measures Concerning the Importation, Marketing and Sale of Tuna and Tuna Products; Appellate Body report (WT/DS381/AB/R), circulated on 16 May 2012, adopted on 13 June 2012.

US – Upland Cotton (Article 21.5 – Brazil): United States – Subsidies on Upland Cotton – Recourse to Article 21.5 of the DSU by Brazil; Appellate Body report (WT/DS267/AB/RW), circulated on 2 June 2008, adopted on 20 June 2008.

US – Upland Cotton: United States – Subsidies on Upland Cotton; Appellate Body report (WT/DS267/AB/R), circulated on 3 March 2005, adopted on 21 March 2005.

US – Wheat Gluten: United States – Definitive Safeguard Measures on Imports of Wheat Gluten from the European Communities; Appellate Body report (WT/DS166/AB/R), circulated on 22 December 2000, adopted on 19 January 2001.

US – Wool Shirts and Blouses: United States – Measure Affecting Imports of Woven Wool Shirts and Blouses from India; Appellate Body report (WT/DS33/AB/R), circulated on 25 April 1997, adopted on 23 May 1997, DSR 1997:I, p. 323.

US – Zeroing (EC): United States – Laws, Regulations and Methodology for Calculating Dumping Margins („Zeroing"); Appellate Body report (WT/DS294/AB/R), circulated on 18 April 2006, adopted on 9 May 2006.

US – Zeroing (Japan): United States – Measures Relating to Zeroing and Sunset Reviews; panel report (WT/DS322/R), circulated on 20 September 2006, adopted on 23 January 2007; Appellate Body report (WT/DS322/AB/R), circulated on 9 January 2007, adopted on 23 January 2007.

www.ingramcontent.com/pod-product-compliance
Lightning Source LLC
LaVergne TN
LVHW082339200926
848481LV00012B/3392